MALICIOUS DECEIVERS

··· **Sensing Media**
Aesthetics, Philosophy,
and Cultures of Media
EDITED BY WENDY HUI KYONG CHUN
AND SHANE DENSON

MALICIOUS DECEIVERS

Thinking Machines and Performative Objects

IOANA B. JUCAN

STANFORD UNIVERSITY PRESS

Stanford, California

Stanford University Press
Stanford, California

Printed in the United States of America on acid-free, archival-quality paper

ISBN 9781503634633 (cloth)
ISBN 9781503636071 (paper)
ISBN 9781503636088 (electronic)

Library of Congress Control Number: 2022044950

Library of Congress Cataloging-in-Publication Data available upon request.

Cover design and art: Daniel Benneworth-Gray
Typeset by Elliott Beard in Minion 11/14

CONTENTS

MALICIOUS DECEIVERS

Prologue

BEGINNING PHILOSOPHY

••• My first experience of philosophy occurred as part of an ordinary practice of reading books as a way of escaping an immediate social world struggling with poverty, alcoholism, patriarchy, and labor migration. The practice of reading books replaced that of daily and sometimes daylong TV watching, which did not provide the desired escape but instead overwhelmed me with incessant breaking news. I turned to reading philosophy because it felt like an "intellectual" thing to do. Becoming an intellectual was the only way to escape the immediate reality, I gathered from my observations, my parents, and my schoolteachers (the other way being, it seemed at the time, that of getting into the money-making business). Targeted, censored, and often persecuted during communist times, intellectuals—especially those who had been dissidents—were the heroes of the early years of post-communism in Romania. For me, they were an inspiration to become an intellectual, and being a philosopher seemed the highest embodiment of that aspiration.

My first experience as a beginning philosopher was an encounter with René Descartes's *Meditations*, a work that would have been dismissed as "idealist" in communist Romania, with its state-sanctioned dialectical materialism. The encounter with Descartes was a radical experience; it led me to distrust my senses as reliable sources of knowledge and experience. There followed an extended period of what became rather frustrating self-subversion, of me playing ever more intricate games of staging reality in my mind, thinking that I was taking a break from history, which nevertheless continued to happen in the background and to be dramatically presented on the TV that I no longer watched. Divide: body/mind; mind/world. My mind was cutting me off from my senses and from an exterior world reduced to the size of a society in post-communist transition to capitalism, after a contested, televised revolution. Life became poor in experience and overcrowded with ideas. It then struck me that, perhaps, I had misread Descartes. Or maybe, I had read him too narrowly, or had taken him too seriously. What followed was an extended effort to climb out of my own mind, an effort that, I later learned, has been described as being "philosophically fundamental."[1] Performance turned out to be helpful to me in this endeavor: performance as "twice-behaved behavior,"[2] twice-behaved both personally and politically in the case of the present book. Theatricality, defined by Samuel Weber as "a *problematic process of placing, framing, situating*," was helpful too.[3]

With the help of performance and theatricality, I learned to read Descartes differently. This reading, which forms the core of this book's first chapter, entails a problematic process of situating a thought experiment developed by Descartes—of framing it as a problem to be reckoned with and staging it both in its own historical context and in a broader socio-cultural perspective that stretches into the present. This is a once-in-a-lifetime experiment of radical doubt that yielded the well-known meme "*I am thinking, therefore I exist*"[4] and that involves a scenario of total deception engendered by a malicious deceiver. This is a scenario that philosophers to this day have arguably not been able to disprove and that has not lost its power in the cultural imagination; *The Matrix* is its more recent avatar.[5] Once summoned, the malicious deceiver does not go away—it returns again and again under different guises. In Descartes, the (failed) attempt to disprove this scenario gave rise to a stubbornly enduring metaphysics that grounds existence in an abstracting mode of thinking cut off from the senses and the sensible. This mode of thinking upholds mathematics and its subject matter as the highest—and in fact only reliable—truth and posits an irreducible separation between the mind and the body and between the self and the world. It reduces the self to a "thinking I" and the world to a machine that is graspable and (re)producible by mathematics, which renders it exploitable and manipulatable. When automated, this mode of thinking becomes computing.

Descartes undertook his experiment in an attempt to distinguish truth from falsity, the real from the fake, and to secure the former. In fact, I argue, it gave rise to post-truth, to a logic that conjoins deception (dissimulation) and performativity (simulation); this will be theorized in this book as the logic of (dis)simulation. The Cartesian thought experiment offers a model of (the construction of) the real that is inescapably fake—or, more precisely, synthetic. I use "synthetic" here both in the dictionary sense of "devised, arranged, or fabricated for special situations to imitate or replace usual realities,"[6] and in the sense of involving simulation based on abstraction that voids sensory, lived experience and historical context. In this book, I show how Cartesian metaphysics is twinned with global, racial capitalism, the (dis)simulation machine *par excellence.* The (dis)simulation machines and performative objects that this book analyzes are the products of this twinning: software and AI (Chapter 2), television (Interlude), plastics (Chapter 3), and the internet (Chapter 4). These media involve a mode of abstraction that can be traced back to both Cartesian metaphysics and capitalistic exchange. Through various case studies that cross different times and spaces, this book reads these machines and objects as malicious deceivers that have repeatable sameness built into their mode of operation and that construct impoverished pictures of the world by hollowing out embodied histories and lived experience.

As deployed in this book, the malicious deceiver is a metaphor standing in for Cartesian metaphysics and the logic of (dis)simulation associated with it, as well as a nomadic frame for analyzing and theorizing the deceptive performances of various (dis)simulating machines and objects. By calling something a malicious deceiver, I seek to highlight the ways in which it embodies the logic of (dis)simulation and with what consequences, as well as to think through ways to counter it. Specifically, I turn to performance and theatricality to counter this logic and to imagine more capacious, careful, and caring modes of world/sense-making. I do so in two ways: through the theatrical performances I engage with and through the staging of the embodied authorial "I" and its lived experience and histories. The performances the book engages with include pieces (in the order of appearance) by Annie Dorsen, the International Institute of Political Murder (founded and directed by Milo Rau), Pinar Yoldas, Chris Jordan, Alejandro Durán, Nao Bustamante, American Artist, Hassan Khan, as well as my own performance works. Through forms of repetition with a difference, these performances work with and out of the refuse produced by the twinning of Cartesian metaphysics and capitalism: "refuse" both in the sense of leftover and in the sense of that which has been left out in the processes of voiding or hollowing out. Displacing performativity through theatricality, these performances play with and against global capitalism's (dis)simulation machines and performative objects so as to expand perception and experience and enable different modes of relationality and world/sense-making.

My use of the embodied "I" as a framing and situating device for the book and its sites of investigation is an attempt to enact a different kind of relationship between self and world from the one posited by Descartes and replayed in much Western philosophical and—more broadly—academic writing: a relationship of separation that places the "I" on a pedestal of abstraction, which voids it of its embodied histories and fails to account for its positionality within a socio-historical context and the operations of power that define it. In this move, I follow the call of Naomi Scheman, who stressed the need to take "responsibility for social location" in one's philosophical work and "to write as one voice in a conversation, not as the last word, to say . . . how the world looks from here, the very particular place I occupy in it."[7] At stake here is also an attempt to enact a decolonial practice that counters what Walter Mignolo, building on the thought of Santiago Castro-Gómez, has termed "zero point epistemology": "the ultimate grounding of knowledge, which paradoxically is ungrounded, or grounded neither in geo-historical location nor in bio-graphical configurations of the bodies."[8] The richly textured engagement with the Romanian social and political context of the transition from communism to capitalism as a site for the analysis of (dis)simulation, as well as the autobiographical method used in this book's Interlude, serve to account for the position-ality of the authorial "I" and the view—or sense—of the world that the book as a whole enacts. At the formal level, the ordering of the chapters and their contents aim to make an argument, mirroring my own expe-riences from the deep dive into Western philosophy as an expression of my internalization of the imperative to "catch up" with the West, to the undoing of that conditioning through performance (and performance studies), the exposure to different strands of feminist, decolonial, and Black thought, and varied life encounters and experiences.

The way in which subjects and objects of study come together in this book mimics the way in which things often come together in lived experience: as a seemingly random association filled with both repeti-tion (of themes, ideas, objects) and with the unexpected. It also mimics, with a significant difference, the logics and ways of structuring of the internet: the montage of seemingly disparate pieces of information that appear in a social media feed driven by the algorithmic assessment of one's interest based on past behavior, as well as the coexistence of dispa-rate "virtual windows" on the screen when one has multiple tabs open on one's networked device.[9] Yet, there is method in the madness: trans-disciplinary in spirit, it is a method (or way—by no means the only one) of sense-making, of allowing oneself "to *become* in relation to what" one is "seeking to understand."[10] In essence, this method is theatrical: the book brings things together in the manner that an experimental theatre director might bring together subjects and objects on a stage to make concrete and (re)imagine a constructed world, whose construct-edness and mode of construction are foregrounded rather than con-cealed or disavowed. Some of the things may not fit well together: the temporalities activated may be incongruent; the things gathered may seem incompatible. And, in a sense, that is the point, because the glo-balized world picture that Western modernity has entrapped us in is filled with things that simply don't fit together—things extracted, cir-culated, and forced to exist under conditions that often harm and even destroy them. The plastic objects staged in Chapter 3 of this book, for instance, don't fit well in the stomach of baby albatrosses, who, deceived by their appearance, mistake them for food. These plastic objects should not be there. But global capitalism, and the ongoing colonization of all areas of life by consumerism, brought them there.[11] That they got there is counterintuitive and absurd yet perfectly in line with global capitalism's mode of operation. It is the hope of this book that, by inhabiting such incongruences with attention and care, possibilities for change, however elusive, might open up.

A PICTURE OF THE GATHERING:
OVERVIEW OF THE BOOK STRUCTURE

The book unfolds in two parts connected by an Interlude. The first part, consisting of the first two chapters, theorizes the logic of (dis)simulation with its attendant processes of voiding in the context of Cartesian thought, as well as its connection to capitalism and computation. The second part, comprising the last two chapters, stages the synthetic realities that (dis)simulation machines and performative objects repeat into being.

Chapter 1 introduces the malicious deceiver scenario as presented in Descartes's experiment of radical doubt and shows how (dis)simulation is its structuring logic and why it matters. It also restages the Cartesian experiment in its historical context: tulipomania, one of the first speculative economic bubbles and remarkable collapses of the market in the history of capitalism. The chapter thus begins to reveal global capitalism as the broader context for understanding the malicious deceiver. By building on the thought of Marxist economist and philosopher Alfred Sohn-Rethel, it begins to unravel the twinning of Cartesian metaphysics and global capitalism as well as the link between Cartesian thought and computation. Through these moves, the chapter connects the malicious deceiver scenario with its more recent iterations as found in the computer simulation hypothesis and *The Matrix*.

Chapter 2 further unpacks the link between the logic of (dis)simulation and computation through an investigation of the kinds of thinking that computing machines perform. It highlights two modes of machine thinking—or thinking through machine thinking: one is a function of the machine's actual operation and can be traced back to Descartes; the other is a function of the human–machine interaction at the interface and connects with Turing's imitation game. At play between these two modes of machine thinking is both the difference and the intimate connection between simulation and dissimulation. The chapter attends to performances of machine thinking theatrically staged by Annie Dorsen, culminating in an analysis of globalizing modernity's paradigmatic memory play, Shakespeare's *Hamlet*, as it is performed by algorithms in Dorsen's *A Piece of Work: A Machine-made Hamlet*. I read *A Piece of Work* as part of the broader context of "the drama 'Big Data'" in which algorithms supposedly "shape" and even "rule our world," in what appears to be one of the latest versions of Descartes's scenario, with thinking machines—powered by capitalism—in the role of the malicious deceiver.[12]

Working with an autobiographical method that centers personal recollection, the book's Interlude stages the context in which I first read Descartes: the Romanian transition to capitalism and consumerism and what preceded it. Through a deep dive into Romanian history and cultural context, this transitional chapter spotlights two malicious deceivers: (i) the communist apparatus of state deception sustained through a vast surveillance machine (which I read as a precursor to big data) and through a propaganda machine; and (ii) television, a (dis) simulation machine that represents the *"object-symbol of the transition"* from communism to capitalism and consumerism in the Romanian context.[13] In different ways, both of these malicious deceivers construct synthetic realities, and both are undergirded—and programmed—by the internalized imperative to "catch up" with the West, an effect of modernity's myth of progress. Through a focus on the televised revolution that marked the end of communism and beginning of capitalism and consumerism in Romania—which media philosopher Vilém Flusser read as the beginning of "post-history"[14] (or, in today's language, "post-truth")—the chapter attends to the transformation of history into a circulated, ever-repeatable TV image that voids history and social context. One specific image it focuses on is that of the dictatorial couple put on trial during the days of the revolution, as reenacted in the International Institute of Political Murder's theatre project *The Last Days of the Ceausescus (Die Letzten Tage der Ceausescus)*. This reenactment counters the voiding of history and the perpetuating self-sameness of the TV image through a form of theatrical repetition with a difference across nonlinear times.

Chapter 3 follows a plastic bag floating from communist Romania across the waters of the ocean, shifting shapes as it moves across different times and places and yet stubbornly remaining the same. The chapter shows how synthetic plastic—a (dis)simulating object-symbol of modern progress and consumerism that has also become the material for money as well as for a form of payment and credit that is intimately tied to big data—is a malicious deceiver that possesses "metaphysical subtleties" with a Cartesian flavor.[15] Both hyper-visible (it is seemingly everywhere) and imperceptible (in the form of micro- and nanoplastics), synthetic plastic is a product of simulation and an agent of deception that tricks perception. Its totalizing presence worldwide constitutes undeniable evidence of "a new form of colonization by consumerism":[16] global colonization by the ever-proliferating products of capital. The chapter explores theatrical performances that involve labor-intensive practices of gathering plastic things by Pinar Yoldas, Chris Jordan, Alejandro Durán, and Nao Bustamante. These performances stage different kinds of encounters with a world permeated by plastics, expanding perception and experience through practices of world/sense-making.

Chapter 4 continues the book's investigation into (dis)simulation machines and performative objects with a reflection on the memetic circulation of information, ideas, images, habits, and objects and their virality as they connect with the internet—a preeminent (dis)simulation machine of our times that has featured prominently in common understandings of post-truth. Through a focus on fake news and other kinds of viral content, this chapter highlights how the internet embodies the logic of (dis)simulation and looks to performance and theatricality for ways of countering, refusing, and displacing this logic and the virality associated with it. Specifically, it engages with an online performance that I directed and co-created as well as with works by American Artist and Hassan Khan.

The Epilogue concludes the book by returning to a play that I wrote and directed a few years ago. This is the starting point for an open-ended reflection on a living practice of refusing and countering abstraction in a historical moment that some have seen as the beginning of "a new Cold War."[17] Even as it starts far away from the goal, it is to this kind of practice that the book aspires.

PART I

...

Experiments in (Machine) Thinking

1

ENTER THE MALICIOUS DECEIVER

••• In 2016, the year when Oxford Dictionaries declared "post-truth" the word of the year, a philosophical hypothesis made the news: we're living in a computer simulation.[1] This hypothesis is one of the latest iterations of a thought experiment formulated by the French seventeenth-century philosopher René Descartes: the scenario of total deception engendered by a malicious deceiver (also known as the "evil demon"). The interest that this scenario continues to elicit testifies to its power in the cultural imagination. Its significance, however, extends beyond this: the thought experiment of total deception forms the groundwork for Cartesian metaphysics, which has provided a stubbornly enduring and pernicious model of (the construction of) the real that is inescapably fake—or, more precisely, synthetic. This chapter shows how this is the case and why it matters, connecting the dots between Descartes's malicious deceiver and the computer simulation hypothesis as it traces a genealogy of post-truth that will be unpacked in this chapter and the remainder of this book in terms of the logic of (dis)simulation: the conjoining of dissimulation (deception) and simulation (performativity).

Reading against the philosophical grain, the chapter also attends to the performance of Cartesian thought, to the dimension of the thinker as an actor "in this theatre which is the world."[2] It particularly pays attention to those moments in which theatricality pierces through the Cartesian metaphysical apparatus and the thinker's self-theatricalization becomes apparent, as well as to the broader historical context in which he conducts his thought experiment. By speculatively restaging the Cartesian thought experiment in its historical context, the chapter begins to reveal global capitalism as the broader context for understanding the malicious deceiver and to unravel the twinning of Cartesian metaphysics and global capitalism.

RADICAL DOUBT PRODUCES A MALICIOUS DECEIVER

According to Descartes, because of inescapable human limitations, "[w]e *need a method if we are to investigate the truth of things.*"[3] What Descartes has in mind is a method for telling truth from falsity, for securing the real from the fake. The scenario of the malicious deceiver appears in Descartes as part of the application of this method. In this section, I give an outline of the Cartesian method to serve as background to the scenario of the malicious deceiver and to highlight Descartes's peculiar conception of truth and the real, with which the scenario is intimately connected.

The first rule of Descartes's method is:

> never to accept anything as true if I did not have evident knowledge of its truth: that is, carefully to avoid precipitate conclusions and preconceptions, and to include nothing more in my judgments than what presented itself to my mind so clearly and so distinctly that I had no occasion to doubt it.[4]

This rule encapsulates Descartes's definition of truth, the condition that something needs to meet to count as true: it must present itself "clearly and distinctly" to the mind, which for Descartes means that it must lie beyond any (reason for) doubt. This conception of truth, which Descartes takes to be obvious, is in fact both highly problematic and enduring; its echoes reverberate into the present-day so-called "post-truth era." While subjecting something to doubt may have a place in the determination of its truth or falsity, making doubt (or the lack thereof) the sole arbiter of truth leaves one with very little to hold on to as being true, except perhaps one's most intimately held beliefs, the deeply in-grained epistemological-affective frameworks—or what Whitney Phillips and Ryan Milner have termed "deep memetic frames"—that shape how one understands and experiences the world and that are "maintained through what we do and say, and what others do and say, within our networks."[5] Emerging "from our education, our experiences, and how we're culturally conditioned to interpret information," deep memetic frames "take information and turn it into evidence."[6] Despite claims to being self-evident, those things that present themselves as "clear and distinct" and thus beyond doubt are anything but immediately obvious. To determine what they are, Descartes needs to put in place a grand theoretical apparatus that is grounded in a "deep memetic frame" that the philosopher takes for granted, even as he promises to subject his own most deeply held beliefs to doubt. Essentially, this apparatus will reinforce—and supposedly provide (rational) proof for—the very frame in which it is grounded.

To determine those things that one has "no occasion to doubt," Descartes undertakes a once-in-a-lifetime experiment of radical doubt in which he will "demolish everything completely and start again right from the foundations."[7] This all-encompassing doubt is supposed to "make it impossible for us to have any further doubts about what we subsequently discover to be true."[8] What it does, in fact, is call forth a scenario of total deception by a grand malicious deceiver that is impossible to disprove. I will turn to this scenario in what follows, but for now let me give attention to the deep frame that grounds this experiment and Descartes's theoretical apparatus more broadly.

A commonsense answer to the question "What are the things that one has no reason to doubt?" is: those things that can be directly perceived by the senses, one's lived experience within a specific social and cultural context. Even though Descartes acknowledges that "[t]he conduct of our life depends entirely on our senses,"[9] he is adamant that the senses, and everything that comes through them, are unreliable sources of knowledge and potential deceivers. This belief forms the bedrock of the "deep memetic frame" that grounds Descartes's philosophical apparatus. While this belief can be found in the Christian tradition that preceded the scientific revolution of the sixteenth and seventeenth centuries, Descartes's dismissal of the senses as unreliable sources of knowledge and the metaphysics he develops must also be understood in connection with the emergence and great popularity of "magnifying glasses"—media for seeing at a distance (thus, precursors to television)—in his time.[10] This dismissal is tied to the fact that the recently discovered telescope and microscope revealed a world not available to the naked eye, "an invisible world teeming with imperceptible and hitherto unknown phenomena."[11]

If the senses and lived experience are potential deceivers that cannot be trusted as sources of knowledge, then there are two possibilities left for philosophy and for knowledge production more broadly, at least in Descartes's historical context: (i) One possibility is to rely on devices such as the telescope and the microscope, and on mathematical thinking, as necessary aids to— and even substitutes for—human perception in the pursuit of truth. This is the way of experimental philosophy, which was soon to become institutionalized as science (a discipline separate from philosophy), whose mode of operation would be experimentation in the laboratory and mathematical calculation. Descartes himself made contributions to it.[12] (ii) Another possibility for conducting philosophy under the circumstances of this attack on the senses—a possibility that is compatible with and in fact establishes the foundations for (i)—is to act as though there were such a thing as "pure" inquiry (that is, inquiry purified of anything sensuous). This is the way of metaphysics, and it will of necessity require the postulation of an irreducible separation between the body and the mind. This fundamental separation is arrived at through the experiment of radical doubt, to which I now turn.

Descartes sees the experiment of radical doubt as essential to any lifelong pursuit of knowledge of the kind that the philosopher is in the business of undertaking. He thus makes this the first of his *Principles of Philosophy*: "*The seeker after truth must, once in the course of his life, doubt everything, as far as is possible.*"[13] The limits of possibility in this case are defined by ordinary life; ordinary life cannot go on under conditions of radical doubt, which renders it absurd. This is why Descartes's third principle of human knowledge is that radical doubt should *not* "be applied to ordinary life."[14] In the realm of ordinary, "practical life," where things need to get done, it is "sometimes necessary" to act on one's opinions "which one knows to be quite uncertain just as if they were indubitable," writes Descartes.[15] Otherwise, "the chance for action would frequently pass us by if we waited until we could free ourselves from our doubts."[16]

Conducted in isolation from the world "out there," Descartes's metaphysical experiment of radical doubt is supposed to leave ordinary (practical) life as it is. For the duration of the experiment, the thinker's ordinary life is simply put on hold. This is not an easy task. For this reason, in his earlier work, *Discourse on the Method*, Descartes decides that he must first reach "a more mature age than twenty-three" to be adequately prepared for such a radical experience.[17] Still, the assumption at work in Descartes is that the thinker will return to an unaltered ordinary life at the end of the experiment. As I show in what follows, however, if (only) one looks outside of the window of Descartes's room, it becomes apparent that "ordinary" life is in fact quite extra-ordinary. The "malicious deceiver" that Descartes summons as part of the experiment is already out there, throwing ordinary life into crisis.

In the opening of the *Meditations*, Descartes declares that even if it may appear "at first sight" doubtful that the kind of extensive doubt he proposes is of any use in the realm of knowledge, "its greatest benefit lies in freeing us from all our preconceived opinions, and providing the easiest route by which the mind may be led away from the senses."[18] Removal from the senses—which early on in the experiment of radical doubt are declared to be limited if not altogether inadequate in what they can offer to the pursuit of the truth because they sometimes "deceive"[19]—is a crucial inaugural move in the metaphysical project. But Descartes's radical doubt extends beyond the senses towards certain far-fetched possibilities that one needs to imagine, perhaps to the limit of one's imagination, in order to then refute. The scenario of a "malicious deceiver," a "malicious demon of the utmost power and cunning" who "has employed all his energies in order to deceive me" and who has been substituted for God, is such a possibility.[20] In the Cartesian experiment, this grand possibility of total deception arises not because the senses deceive but, rather, because of a contrived scenario in which "I have no senses."[21] This means that "I" have no body: "Body, shape, extension, movement and place are chimeras," declares the thinker in the *Meditations*.[22] Even "my memory tells me lies."[23] All of "my" experiences are staged by a malicious deceiver in the theatre of "my" mind at an irreducible separation from the world—or, to use a contemporary term, all of my experiences are simulated, fed to "me" prepackaged. Implied in this scenario is also the idea of total surveillance, for the malicious deceiver is always present and watching (so to speak), or at least must give the impression that he is watching.[24]

For Descartes, entertaining the scenario of the malicious deceiver, taking it seriously and acting on it—that is, taking care to "resolutely guard against assenting to any falsehoods, so that the deceiver, however powerful and cunning he may be, will be unable to impose on me in the slightest degree"—is no easy task.[25] After all, the possibility to be entertained is so far-fetched that it puzzles the mind. Also, the force of the ordinary and of "my old opinions" tends to resist the absurd scenario.[26] Significantly, what is required in order for the thinker to guard himself against resorting to "habitual opinions" is an act of self-deception, a pretense—a *what if*. In Descartes's words: "I think it will be a good plan . . . to deceive myself, by **pretending** for a time that these former opinions are utterly false and imaginary."[27] The Cartesian experiment of radical doubt is thus grounded in the postulated existence of a grand deceiver, which requires an act of self-deception for the thinker to be able to actually believe in it. But as the experiment continues, the thinker forgets about the *what if*, turning the postulated fact into an absolute in relation to which he is then able to make his fundamental realization: "I am, I exist . . . But for how long? For as long as I am thinking."[28] Or, as Descartes puts it in the *Discourse on the Method*, in the form of one of the most famous statements of all (modern) times, at least in the West: "*I am thinking, therefore I exist.*"[29] This formulation makes thinking—and thus the mind that performs the thinking—primary: a (logical) condition for existence. Yet, the mind itself is a trickster that has devised an imaginary paranoid scenario and then takes what has been imagined for a fact. In his attempt to escape deception, Descartes in fact builds it into his metaphysics, as its very condition.

Remarkably, in order to be able to establish the fundamental fact of his entire metaphysical project, Descartes needs to deceive himself into believing in the existence of the grand deceiver. The hypothesis of the grand deceiver is necessary in order for the thinker to be able to prove (if one accepts this to be a proof) his own existence as a thinking "I." A quite roundabout argument is at play here, with sophisticated conceptual moves and a lot of imagination. I quote it at some length so as to draw attention to its complications and roundaboutness:

> But I have convinced myself that there is absolutely nothing in the world, no sky, no earth, no minds, no bodies. . . . But **there is a deceiver of supreme power and cunning who is deliberately and constantly deceiving me. In that case I too undoubtedly exist, if he is deceiving me; and let him deceive me as much as he can, he will never bring it about that I am nothing so long as I think that I am something.** So after considering everything very thoroughly, I must finally conclude that this proposition, *I am, I exist*, is necessarily true whenever it is put forward by me or conceived in my mind.[30]

Not only does this complicated argument supposedly establish the fact of the thinker's existence but it also supposedly establishes the nature ("essence") of this existence: It is the existence of a thinking thing. Descartes thus uses the aforementioned piece of reasoning to lay the grounds of his metaphysics:

> Thus, simply by knowing that I exist and seeing at the same time that absolutely nothing else belongs to my nature or essence except that I am a thinking thing, I can infer correctly that my essence consists solely in the fact that I am a thinking thing.[31]

This constitutes Descartes's much sought-after Archimedean point, "certain and unshakable,"[32] something that he (says/thinks he) perceives clearly and distinctly. In light of this, the metaphysician makes the premise from which he started the experiment into a general rule for thought in pursuit of truth: "whatever I perceive very clearly and distinctly is true."[33]

But all of this on its own is not enough to disprove the existence of the malicious deceiver that the Cartesian thinker summoned up as part of the experiment of radical doubt and on which the supposed proof of the existence of the "I" and "world" in fact rests. Once summoned, the malicious deceiver does not go away. The only way out of this predicament for Descartes is to call on (a specific idea of) God, whose existence precludes deception, says Descartes.[34] But this is not a very compelling argument; its opposite can be argued just as well.[35] Even if one were to grant Descartes that God exists, if one steps out of the Christian framework into, for instance, Vedanta philosophy, one finds that God is the creator of deception (*maya*) to begin with.[36] Thus, if the existence of a God whose existence precludes deception is itself a matter of doubt, the issue of the malicious deceiver remains unsettled— and unsettling. It appears that, once summoned, the malicious deceiver won't go away—not in globalizing modernity, and not in the chapters of this book, where it will repeatedly return under different guises. In fact, as I show below, the malicious deceiver is already there, right outside of Descartes's room. Standing in for Cartesian metaphysics and the logic of (dis)simulation embedded in it, it is inextricably linked to global capitalism and globalizing modernity. I will begin to unpack these links below, beginning with the logic of (dis)simulation.

THE LOGIC OF (DIS)SIMULATION

Effectively, what remains by the end of the experiment of radical doubt is this: an act of thinking as a function of a mind, a certain kind of awareness of a mind playing with itself,[37] which for Descartes is something that can be "clearly and distinctly perceived." In this act of thinking, the specific objects of thought (the content of thinking, what one is thinking *about*) do not matter; neither do the specific modes of thought in which the thinker engages.[38] This playing of the mind with itself, at a remove as irreducible separation from the world, establishes the existence of one's self as a thinking "I." It serves as proof of the existence of the "I" after any sensible evidence of this existence has been dismissed as inadequate. This "I" is, Descartes writes, a "puzzling 'I' which cannot be pictured in the imagination"[39]—an "I" whose nature has yet to be determined (or imagined). This is what Ludwig Wittgenstein called the "philosophical I": "not the man, not the human body or the human soul of which psychology treats, but the metaphysical subject, the limit—

not a part of the world."[40] This is the hollowed out "I" as limit of the world—more precisely, as limitation and reduction of the world. For, as I show below, the world (or picture thereof) whose existence is secured through the experiment of radical doubt is itself hollowed out in the process. And while the metaphysician admits that "the corporeal things of which images are formed in my thought, and which the senses investigate, are known with much more distinctness than this puzzling 'I' which cannot be pictured in the imagination," he persists in denying the obvious and persuades himself that this is merely due to the mind's tendency to wander.[41]

Having established the existence of the thinking "I" in this way, the Cartesian thinker turns his attention to material things, whose existence he infers based on the rule of clear and distinct ideas. In light of this rule, he asserts: "I now know that they [material things] are capable of existing, **in so far as they are the subject-matter of pure mathematics**, since I perceive them clearly and distinctly."[42] Notably, for Descartes, mathematics represents a kind of realm of God. In his words: the "eternal truths" are those "according to which **God himself has taught us that he has arranged all things in number, weight and measure.**"[43] Note that this is a postulation that lacks any demonstration. It belongs to the "deep memetic frame"[44] that Descartes refuses to acknowledge.

The rule of clear and distinct ideas thus produces proof of the existence of material things not "in a way that exactly corresponds with my sensory grasp of them" but rather, as things that "possess all the properties which I clearly and distinctly understand, that is, all those which, viewed in general terms, are comprised within the subject-matter of pure mathematics."[45] At the end of the experiment of radical doubt, the mind—reduced to a thinking "I"—remains cut off from the senses. Its secure access to the "world" is enabled by mathematics, by numerical thinking. This privileging of mathematics as the only reliable way to access (and model) the world is significant: as I will show later in this chapter, it connects Cartesian metaphysics with computation and with capitalism.

The world viewed (modeled) as the subject matter of pure mathematics—and, thus, of calculation—is a synthetic world picture, in the dictionary sense of "synthetic": "devised, arranged, or fabricated for special situations to imitate or replace usual realities."[46] It is synthetic in another sense as well, on which I will elaborate later on in this chapter and the book: in the sense of involving simulation based on abstraction that voids sensory, lived experience and historical context. It is thus an impoverished picture of the world. Despite Descartes's view to the contrary, such a world is not a matter of discovery but of (forceful) making. As Vilém Flusser noted, the world is open to calculation because it has been made thus, for "[i]t is not numbers that correspond to the world: We have set the world up in such a way that it corresponds to our number code."[47]

Descartes gives an account of such a world in his early writing, *The World or Treatise on Light*.[48] Here, Descartes invites the reader to "allow your thought to wander beyond this world to view another world—a wholly new one which I shall bring into being before your mind in imaginary spaces."[49] This "new world" is, for Descartes, an analogue of *this* world presented in its simplest (clear-cut) terms. This "new" world is "matter."[50] All there is to matter in the Cartesian view, strictly (metaphysically) speaking, is but indefinite extension and what pertains to it: shape, size, motion, number. As for the rest, "[l]et us . . . suppose that it lacks the qualities of being hot or cold, dry or moist, light or heavy, and of having any taste, smell, sound, colour, light, or other such quality in the nature of which there might be said to be something that is not known clearly by everyone."[51] Such is the world when described, in Descartes's words, "as if it were a machine."[52] Note that this supposedly secure knowledge of the world, secured through the Cartesian experiment, is not knowledge *about* the world but *from* a system of (performative) thinking grounded in mathematics.[53]

To elucidate the conception of the world (as nature) as machine, Descartes's near-contemporary and permanent secretary of the Académie des Sciences, Bernard le Bovier de Fontenelle, turns to the theatre. "[N]ature always appears to me in the same point of view as theatrical representations," he writes in his popular 1686 book for the philosophical/scientific education of women, *Conversations on the Plurality of Worlds*.[54] The majority of the spectators only see "an agreeable effect at a distance," but this effect is in fact produced by "machinery"—"weights and wheels are hidden by which every motion is effected."[55] The "causes," as Fontenelle calls the machinery, may become apparent only to a "mechanical genius" who resembles "the philosopher studying the structure of the universe."[56] The point of the world as machine analogy is that "whoever examines the mechanism of nature is only going behind the scenes of a theatre."[57]

In this conception, the machine is the essence of the theatre, but this is a theatre devoid of theatricality, a theatre reduced to the machinery that produces representational effects. Fontenelle invokes Descartes's name in conjunction with this conception of the world, and rightly so, for Descartes wrote explicitly about the usefulness of the machine model in grasping the imperceptible (or concealed) forces that structure appearances.[58] The "machine" or "structure" pertains to the material suprasensible that remains forever inaccessible to the unaided human senses but that can be accessed—or (re)produced—via certain apparatuses (such as the Cartesian cogito engaged in metaphysical thinking or apparatuses employing numerical thinking).

Attending to the world as machine offers a picture of a vast operation, of an operation on a massive scale, comprising everything there is. This kind of view enables the world to "grow" into a totality under one governing system (which could nevertheless be comprised of many sub-systems obeying the same general laws). Fontenelle thus writes:

> Notice how the world grows little by little. The Ancients held that the tropical and frigid zones could not be inhabited, because of excessive heat or cold; and in the Romans' time the overall map of the world hardly extended beyond their empire, which was impressive in one sense and indicated considerable ignorance in another. Meanwhile, men continued to appear in very hot and very cold lands, and so the world grew. Following that, it was judged that the ocean covered all the Earth except what of it was then known; there were no Antipodes, for no one had ever spoken of them, and after all, wouldn't they have had their feet up and heads down? Yet after this fine conclusion the Antipodes were discovered all the same. A new revision of the map: a new half of the world.[59]

Significantly, Fontenelle's account of this world expansion moves from the space of metaphysics to that of geopolitics, for the "discovery" of new territories he refers to is in fact the colonial expansion of empires, itself a force that hollows out, rendering void through the displacement and genocide of Indigenous peoples. On the basis of this expansion, Fontenelle postulates the existence of "a plurality of worlds," which nonetheless turn out to be all the same. For him, the principle under-girding the postulated plurality of "world" is the principle of *why not*, which plays on but differs from the theatrical *what if*:

> This "Why not?" has a power which allows it to populate ev-erything. We see that all the planets are of the **same** nature, all opaque bodies that receive light only from the Sun and reflect it from one to the other, and have nothing but the **same** motions; up to that point, everything is equal.[60]

Notably, in Fontenelle's formulation, the principle of *why not* is under-girded by the presupposition of repeatable, reproducible sameness. In light of the presupposed sameness, any other possible worlds will be, as Peter Szendy noted, but "a kind of mirror of the ethnogeographic and racial characterizations that hold here on Earth."[61] What Fontenelle's "plurality of worlds" amounts to is, in actuality, an infinitely repeatable sameness—and reproducibility.[62]

Thus, the Cartesian experiment of radical doubt voids as well as re-makes both the self and the world. The kind of thinking that is at play in it is performative, I argue. It is a kind of doing: it acts on and shapes reality (as that which is established to be the case). In this sense, think-ing that acts can be said to be performative in line with J. L. Austin's conception of the performative. As "the doing of an action," performa-tive statements for Austin are *not* "either true or false," even as they may "masquerade" as statements of fact.[63] While not statements of fact per se, successful performatives—and performative thinking—can do things, changing states of affairs, establishing facts in the world (such as the existence of a particular model of the "I" and the world). In his reading of Austin, Jacques Derrida highlights that "Austin was obliged to free the analysis of the performative from the authority of the truth *value*, from the true/false opposition, . . . at least in its classical form, and to substitute for it at times the value of force, of difference of force."[64] The Austinian performative is thus a "'communication' which is not lim-ited strictly to the transference of a semantic content that is already constituted and dominated by an orientation toward truth."[65] In other words, the transmission of semantic content oriented toward truth becomes at best secondary in the Austinian performative; what is first and foremost at stake in the performative is its force, its ability to act on reality. Similarly, the kind of doing I seek to articulate here through the concept of "performative thinking" is a matter of force that relies on the voiding of semantic content. At stake here is not (primarily) a matter of truth value, even though Descartes—in establishing the fact of the "thinking I" through the experiment of radical doubt—insists that the "proof" (of the existence of the thinking "I") obtained through the experiment is indeed a matter of truth (as opposed to falsity). Rather, it is a matter of post-truth.

As theorized in this book, the notion of post-truth differs from the definition that has become popular since 2016, namely "relating to or denoting circumstances in which objective facts are less influential in shaping public opinion than appeals to emotion and personal belief."[66] What this definition fails to take into account is how objectivity itself is a matter of both production and contestation, how there never was a time when "the distinction between true and false was unproblematic," and how facts themselves are built through complex processes of "truth-grounding."[67] Taking all this into consideration, I theorize the concept of post-truth in terms of the performative construction of the real (which is the fake, the synthetic) as a matter of force through both voiding and (re)production, deception (dissimulation) and simulation. I will call this conjoining *the logic of (dis)simulation.* By "voiding" I mean hollowing out, erasing, concealing, reducing, as well as rendering void—by denying or disregarding the existence and validity (legitimacy) of what is being voided.

In Descartes, the hollowing out, the voiding involved in the act of performative thinking, amounts to an annihilation of the frame of reference, of context, of lived experience and embodied histories. It involves a reduction of the dimensions of what is, the most drastic of which is a reduction to nothing, zero dimensionality (or annihilation). Notably, the voiding is not only the condition for the Cartesian experiment (the discarding of all prior, sense-based knowledge) but also its consequence (the voiding of the "I" and the world). The voiding that is the consequence of the experiment involves both hollowing out and (re)production, (re)production enabled by hollowing out. For, as shown above, what is produced in the process is an impoverished, yet reproducible, model (picture) of both the self and the world.

Santiago Castro-Gómez has called the inaugural voiding in Descartes's experiment of radical doubt "zero-point hubris": discarding "all opinions anchored in common sense" and reducing "all previously learned knowledge to a *tabula rasa*."[68] The ensuing "zero-point location" is associated with the "pretensions of objectivity and scientificity" and of "universal validity."[69] This double voiding is an inaugural colonial move, both epistemologically and, as the aforecited quote from Fontenelle suggests and as Castro-Gómez makes clear, in terms of the "economic and social control of the world," for "[t]o situate oneself at the zero-point is to have the power to institute, to represent, to construct a vision of the social and natural world that is recognized as legitimate and underwritten by the state."[70] This double voiding underlies modernity's myth of progress,[71] which—this book shows—plays out, in different ways, not only in a capitalist-colonial context but also in the context of historical communism (as a form of state capitalism).

At one level, the vision that is constructed from the zero-point may be understood in terms of what Martin Heidegger saw as the essence of modernity: "the fact that the world becomes picture" (*Weltbild*).[72] This means that the world becomes an object of representation, of a "making secure" that renders it orderable, an object of mastery.[73] In light of Descartes's privileging of mathematics as the way to secure his synthetic world picture discussed earlier, it is significant that Heidegger ties this "making secure" to "calculability," which "alone guarantees being certain in advance . . . of that which is to be represented."[74] In Heidegger's account, the world becomes picture, an object of representation, through a representationalist mode of knowing that renders things knowable (in this way) and through a mode of action that renders things manipulatable and disposable. Heidegger calls the representationalist mode of knowing "science" and the mode of action "technology."[75] Technology—which is "no mere means" but, rather, "a way of revealing," "of truth" (or, in today's parlance, post-truth)—performs "a challenging" that "puts to nature the unreasonable demand that it supply energy that can be extracted and stored as such."[76] Specifically, technology challenges everything that exists, human and non-human beings and things, to deliver themselves as a disposable "standing reserve" (*Bestand*)—ready to be put to work, consumed, used (up), at all times.[77] In other words, technology challenges everything that exists to perform, or else . . ."[78]

However, Heidegger's account is at best incomplete: it fails to take into consideration the ways in which the demand he speaks of is made unequally. Specifically, it fails to acknowledge that the mastery in question involves a social ordering that is marked by what Castro-Gómez has called "the apparatus of whiteness."[79] As Sylvia Wynter has argued, at the core of this ordering is the "overrepresentation" of the dominant white bourgeois ethnoclass ("Man") "as if it were the human itself," leading to "the coloniality of being, power, truth, freedom"—to a hierarchy of being (and value attributed to beings) predicated on the construct of race.[80] The disposability that is implied in Heidegger's "standing reserve" involves human beings, but it does so unequally, depending on where they fall within this hierarchy. This is what in fact lies behind Fontenelle's vision of the world's expansion.

Informed by these accounts of the world picture produced from the zero-point, the present book aims to contribute to the critique of modernity by attending to the construction of the real that is inescapably fake (synthetic). It will do so by mobilizing the malicious deceiver as a metaphor standing in for Cartesian metaphysics and the logic of (dis) simulation embedded in it. The book aims to show how this stubbornly enduring metaphysics, which grounds existence in an abstracting mode of thinking cut off from the senses and the sensible, is twinned with global capitalism—the grand malicious deceiver. In fact, underlying the world picture mentioned above is capitalism and the pursuit of profit and control at all costs that defines it.[81] Regarding capitalism as the force behind the modern world picture, it is worth recalling here the thought of Guy Debord who, in *The Society of the Spectacle*, explicitly linked the "becoming picture" of the world to the workings of capitalism, even as he failed to take into account the inherently *racial* character of capitalism.[82] As Debord theorized it, the world picture is not one, but it is actually many abstract(ed) images: "The specialization of images of the world evolves into a world of autonomized images where even the deceivers are deceived."[83] Further on, however, he makes it clear that at stake in the world's becoming picture is not only a matter of deception but also of a "social relation between people that is mediated by images," by "the spectacle" that manifests as "news, propaganda, advertising, entertainment."[84] This is the social relation between exploiters and the exploited; to go beyond Debord, racism is inherent in this social relation, as scholars such as Cedric Robinson, Angela Davis, and Safiya Umoja Noble have shown.[85] This relation is both concealed and sustained by the spectacle.[86] Debord further clarifies, seemingly evoking Heidegger, that the "spectacle," is not "a mere visual excess produced by mass-media technologies. It is a worldview that has actually been materialized, that has become an objective reality."[87] The spectacle, the world picture, is thus more than deception: it is of the order of (dis)simulation, the conjoining of deception and performativity.

In this book, I will attend to (dis)simulation machines and performative objects that enact—and reproduce—an impoverished (and impoverishing) world picture. The (dis)simulation machines and performative objects that this book analyzes are the products of the twinning of Cartesian metaphysics and global capitalism: software and AI (Chapter 2), television (Interlude), plastics (Chapter 3), and the internet (Chapter 4). All of them, the book shows, involve abstraction and have reproducibility built into their mode of operation. And all of them produce synthetic realities, in the double sense of "synthetic" mentioned above. The intention behind calling something a malicious deceiver is to illuminate the ways in which it embodies this logic and with what consequences, as well as to think through ways to counter it. This book looks to performance and theatricality as ways to counter the reductive moves involved in (dis)simulation and to imagine more capacious, careful, and caring modes of world/sense-making.

Notably, the hollowing out that grounds performative thought involves a voiding of theatricality,[88] which makes possible the fantasy of purity underlying Cartesian and Western metaphysics more broadly. In contrast to the de-framing involved in the Cartesian zero-point epistemology and metaphysics, theatricality involves what Samuel Weber has termed "*a problematic process of placing, framing, situating* rather than . . . a process of representation."[89] This is a definition of theatricality to which I return repeatedly in this book, although the way I use it differs in certain significant aspects from Weber's account of theatricality. In agreement with Weber, I understand theatricality as a "spatio-temporal *medium*."[90] It entails a process of taking place, which involves repetition in a manner that does not reduce the place "taken" to "a purely neutral site" that can be self-contained.[91] This implies a kind of "presence" that is never self-present or self-identical but rather "overdetermined by being situated in a space that is limited and yet never fully closed or defined"—here and now as well as elsewhere and elsewhen.[92] At play here is a transformation from a "general *space* to a particular *place*," as Weber notes, thinking with the military usage of the term "theatre" (as in "theatre of operations"), but, in my usage, this transformation is decidedly *not* through an "*imposition of borders*" so as to "*secure the perimeter of a place in dispute*."[93] Rather, the kind of problematic placing, situating, framing that my usage of "theatrical" and "theatricality" aims to point to involves a necessarily embodied process that takes seriously and is responsible to context, histories, and lived experience. As I understand it, a *theatrical* performance gestures towards its own staged nature, making a claim for being and appearance as inextricably linked, which allows for multidimensionality and multilayeredness, for the coexistence of multiple frames of reference and temporalities. Regarding the latter, it is notable that—by repeating the (apparently) same as different—theatrical performance carries the tinge of the past into the present. In theatrical performance there is thus no pure present from which the past has been evacuated, as Descartes—and modernity's myth of progress—would have it. This has prompted theatre and performance scholars to theorize theatre performance as a "memory machine" as well as that which remains (sedimented in bodies and habits of thinking and doing)—conceptions of performance that I engage with and build upon in this book.[94]

In the case of the Cartesian experiment of radical doubt, attending to theatricality raises challenges to the claims that ground the experiment to begin with. For, in the *Meditations* as well as in the earlier *Discourse on the Method*, the situation into which Descartes, the performer of philosophical thinking, places himself is staged theatrically. The thinking scene thus takes place in a compressed space and time: The thinker is secluded in a room for six days, which some interpreters have read as an "embarrassing, presumptuous echo of the six days of Creation."⁹⁵ The thinker's conversation with himself, his "soliloquy," takes place in an undeniably embodied manner in both the *Discourse* and the *Meditations*: "I am here, sitting by the fire, wearing a winter dressing-gown, holding this piece of paper in my hands."⁹⁶ This process of placing, framing, situating the thinker who performs the experiment of radical doubt is problematic in the sense that, if taken seriously, it poses a problem for—or at least offers a counterpoint to—Descartes's radical doubting of the body's very existence. As the passage just cited makes clear, the body is there, it takes place. In fact, this passage demonstrates the very definition of the body according to Descartes: "by a body I understand whatever has a determinable shape and a definable location and can occupy a space in such a way as to exclude any other body."⁹⁷ The body evidently matters, it occupies space, both the physical space of the room and the conceptual space of writing. But the performative thinking at play in the experiment of radical doubt negates this emplaced mattering, even as the latter persists as sensible evidence. Attending to the staging of the experiment in Descartes's work brings this undeniable evidence to the fore and reveals the absurdity of the premise for the malicious deceiver scenario (namely, that "I" have no body and senses).⁹⁸ At the same time, broadening the frame beyond the room in which the Cartesian experiment takes place and looking at its wider historical context will reveal that the malicious deceiver is already there. If one zooms out, the malicious deceiver will turn out to be the capitalist market, the (dis)simulation machine *par excellence* even during Descartes's time.

GLOBAL CAPITALISM AS THE GRAND MALICIOUS DECEIVER

According to his own account, Descartes gets the idea of this "most important task" of establishing "some certain principles in philosophy" while conversing with himself in a "stove-heated room," during a one-day withdrawal from ordinary life.⁹⁹ Nine years after this withdrawal, during which he "did nothing but roam about in the world, trying to be a spectator rather than an actor in all the comedies that are played out there,"¹⁰⁰ Descartes settles down in Holland, in self-imposed exile, to conduct his once-in-a-lifetime experiment of radical doubt, which will be described in the *Meditations* (published in 1641). This event perhaps marks the moment when Descartes switches from the condition of the spectator to that of a "masked" actor—a moment anticipated in one of the preliminaries to his *Early Writings*:

> Actors, taught not to let any embarrassment show on their faces, put on a mask. I will do the same. So far, I have been a spectator in this theatre which is the world, but I am now about to mount the stage, and I come forward masked.[101]

Although it has arguably been superseded by the metaphor of the world as a giant computer simulation (on which more later), the metaphor of the theatre of the world/world as theatre (*"theatrum mundi"*) continues to be well-known today, primarily due to Shakespeare's famous lines from *As You Like It*.[102] In the seventeenth century, it had the "capacity to evoke the sense of a lived abstraction of distinctively human contrivance," performing a "complex, secular commentary on the commodity world."[103] Keeping this interpretation of this metaphor and Descartes's aforecited statement in the background, let us do a little thought experiment: What is this "theatre which is the world" like, and what if we were to imagine a philosopher, like Descartes, mounting the stage of this kind of theatre?

Joseph de la Vega, a seventeenth-century poet and businessman, offers an account of this kind of theatre in his *Confusión de Confusiones* (1688). He employs the metaphor of the theatre of the world to describe the workings of the Exchange as a space where deception is customarily wrought, in different manners:

> Among the plays which men perform in taking different parts in this magnificent world theatre, the greatest comedy is played at the Exchange. There, in an inimitable fashion, the speculators excel in tricks, they do business and find excuses wherein hiding-places, concealment of facts, quarrels, provocations, mockery, idle talk, violent desires, collusion, artful deceptions, betrayals, cheatings, and even the tragic end are to be found.[104]

This passage offers a rich image of the capitalist market as a machine for many kinds of deceptions (or "machinations").[105] In de la Vega's time, these "machinations" took place in a physically embodied manner, in a theatre in which all thought is action and all thoughts "are occupied with shares" even when one is "on the death bed."[106] This kind of acting-thinking is an all-consuming business. In the physical space of the Exchange, the transactions take place through impassioned "handshakes and hand-slaps," which de la Vega describes vividly.[107] Since de la Vega's time, of course, there has been a "historical shift in the market's meaning—from a place to a process to a principle to a power," from a situated, bounded series of acts to a seemingly "boundless and timeless phenomenon."[108] In Chapter 2, I explore another kind of theatre (as) market, in which the main actors are algorithms running on computers (software) rather than humans shaking hands. Notably, it is through the figure of the hand—abstracted into an "invisible hand" already by Adam Smith in the eighteenth century—that, in the words of Wolfgang Ernst, "a playful performative handicraft" becomes a "technomathematical operation," in an interplay between decimal fingers and binary code.[109]

De la Vega's *Confusión de Confusiones* presents the character of a Philosopher stepping into this kind of "theatre of the world" that turns out to be the capitalist market. With a bit of a stretch of the imagination, one could even picture this Philosopher as Descartes, who settles down in the Netherlands, where he lives from 1628 to 1649.[110] This is a time of an ongoing war with Habsburg Spain, which resulted in the Dutch Republic's independence from Spain in 1648. The Dutch Revolt, as this extended war is sometimes called, "went seamlessly over into the empire-building phase."[111] A maritime power with a flourishing foreign trade, Holland became very prosperous at the time. The Dutch East India Company (1602–1799) "developed and coalesced as a system or web of networks," controlling overseas commerce—from luxury to bulk goods to slave trade—"in settlements and colonies across a vast imperial realm spreading from the Cape of Good Hope from the southernmost tip of Africa to Deshima Island, an extension of Nagasaki, in Japan."[112] Exploitative, "free" circulation of people and products in the name of ever-greater profit equals capitalism. In Marx's words from the first volume of *Capital*: "Holland was the model capitalist nation of the seventeenth century," with Amsterdam at its center.[113] In a letter from 1631, Descartes wrote about Amsterdam: "What place on earth could one choose where all the commodities and all the curiosities one could wish for were as easy to find as in this city?"[114] Behind this flow of commodities lay "one of the most extraordinary relations of treachery, bribery, massacre, and meanness," wrote Thomas Stamford Raflles, at one time lieutenant governor of the Dutch East Indies, about the Dutch colonial administration.[115]

De la Vega's *Confusión de Confusiones* offers a rich portrayal of "the mind of the market" through a focus on "the traffic in a single security, the stock of the Dutch East India Company," which is one of the principal engines of Dutch wealth in Descartes's time.[116] De la Vega's book takes dialogic form, with the Shareholder as the knowledgeable protagonist and the Philosopher and the Merchant as his interlocutors. The language of deception is richly abundant in the text, as the passage cited above attests. "The Exchange business is comparable to a game," explains the Shareholder at one point, and "devilish trick[s]"—a term often used in the text—are part of this game.[117] When the inexperienced Philosopher attempts to play the game, he gets tricked into paying considerably more for a share than its perceived value at the time of the transaction and than its predicted value in the near future. He recounts the experience quite dramatically: "last night my peace was turned into unrest, my calmness into despair, my awe into mockery, my knowledge into ignorance, my equanimity into frenzy, my respect into abuse. A speculator cheated me; a cheater took me at my word; a betrayer stole my reputation."[118] The deceptive market game not only disturbs the Philosopher's peace of mind, but it also fundamentally challenges some of his philosophical principles. Thus, although "philosophy teaches that different effects are ascribable to different causes, . . . at the stock exchange some buy and some sell on the basis of a given piece of news, so that here one cause has different effects."[119]

The workings of deception on the Exchange are multilayered. On the one hand, there is strategic dissimulation; some brokers, for instance, conceal "their real intentions under the appearance of complaisance."[120] There is also trickery, whose frequent victims are the inexperienced or the un- or misinformed. Other layers, however, have to do with the transmission of information and the course of events in the world "out there." The Exchange is the stage for an ongoing influx of news, which in de la Vega's time traveled through letters or word of mouth. Who gets the information first has a definite advantage; a delay often means losing money or missing the opportunity to make a profit. Because information is precious (and often needs to be kept secret from some players and to be secretly communicated to others), language at the Exchange has become codified. As de la Vega's Shareholder relates, the codification can sometimes cause misunderstandings and confusion, even when it is not supposed to.[121] Sometimes breaking news hits the Exchange and unleashes a crisis.[122] Using a Cartesian-sounding expression, the Shareholder in de la Vega's text describes the cause of the "unfavorable news" behind one such crisis as "the evil spirit."[123] De la Vega's account of the Exchange makes clear that the nature of the incoming news and the prices of the traded shares very much depend on things that happen elsewhere. The large-scale capitalist circulation of news, goods, and people across sea and land is inextricably tied to colonialism, to slave trade, and to the opening of new, remote markets for the extraction of resources.[124] Globalization is at play here.

The Philosopher speaks the last lines in *Confusión de Confusiones*. He is still puzzled by the "paradoxical" workings of the Exchange;[125] there is no room for Descartes's "clear and distinct" ideas when it comes to the "machinations" of the market. The Philosopher concludes that, when all is said and done, it is "much better not to be a speculator." He decides not to continue to play the market game, even if he will hold on to the purchased (overpriced) shares "until it shall please God that . . . I can get out of them in peace."[126]

The Philosopher in *Confusión de Confusiones* could not really have been Descartes given that de la Vega's book was written a few decades after Descartes's death. Yet, the Dutch East India Company was very much in business during Descartes's time; in fact, it was one of the key engines behind the abundant flow of commodities that Descartes praised in the letter cited above. Also, Descartes would have very likely witnessed a crisis of the kind produced by de la Vega's "evil demon" (of grander proportions in fact) happening not only on the Exchange but in society at large. He would have likely witnessed it live (so to speak), happening right outside of his window. For, in the 1630s and peaking in 1637 (1637 being also the year when Descartes's *Discourse on the Method* was published), Holland experienced one of the first remarkable collapses of the market—or, differently put, one of the first speculative economic bubbles in the history of capitalism: This is the so-called tulipomania, which involved a dramatic escalation in the prices of tulip bulbs followed by an equally dramatic collapse.

Charles Mackay gives a vivid account of tulipomania in his *Extraordinary Popular Delusions and the Madness of Crowds* (1841), which is printed together with de la Vega's *Confusión de Confusiones* in my Marketplace Books edition of the work. From the introduction to this edition, titled "In the Realm of the Senseless" and written by the (at the time) Merrill Lynch & Co. managing director Martin S. Fridson, I have learned that "these two venerable works are fixtures on short lists of the most valuable books on the securities markets," containing "investment wisdom that has been judged invaluable by many of the market's greatest authorities."[127] According to Fridson, "[i]nvestors continue to cherish de la Vega's confusions and Mackay's delusions because the market never ceases to befuddle and beguile."[128] The capitalist market is still the deception-producer machine *par excellence*. And while the events related in de la Vega and Mackay's books could not have conceivably happened before the influx of commodities and wealth into Europe through colonialism, "most features of market behavior today are little different from market behavior in the seventeenth century," writes Peter Bernstein in the preface of this volume.[129]

In his *Extraordinary Popular Delusions and the Madness of Crowds*, Charles Mackay describes the tulipomania as a phenomenon that disrupted ordinary life: "In 1634, the rage among the Dutch to possess them [the tulip bulbs] was so great that the ordinary industry of the country was neglected, and the population, even to its lowest drags, embarked in the tulip trade."[130] With the accelerated trade and heightened interest, prices escalated, so it became necessary to sell the bulbs in smaller weight units (called *perits*). "Rich people no longer bought the flowers to keep them in their gardens, but to sell them again at cent per cent profit."[131] Many engaged in speculation, trading in "non-existents," which were in fact even "better than the existent[s]" as far as such business goes, as the Philosopher remarks at the end of *Confusión de Confusiones*.[132] But when it became apparent that "somebody must lose fearfully at the end," a "universal panic seized upon the dealers. . . . Defaulters were announced day after day in all the towns of Holland."[133]

Tulipomania was a case of what has been called *windhandel,* meaning "a business dealing in the empty wind."[134] Mackay, as the title of his book dramatically announces, characterized it as a case of mass delusion—delusion to the point of madness or absurdity: the annihilation of what is sensible. Delusion can be understood as a form of deception, a problem of mind performance. Yet, one may ask: delusion/deception by whom, or what? From a certain perspective, perhaps it is a case of (collective) self-deception—with respect to what matters, or to things that both are and are not what they appear to be, such as, for example, "one hypothetical Admirael van der Eyck bulb" being worth the equivalent of "4,651 pounds of figs, or 3,448 pounds of almonds, or 5,633 pounds of raisins, or 370 pounds of cinnamon, or 111 tuns of Bordeaux," or even "a modest house in Haarlem."[135] From a different perspective, this appears to be a case of being deluded by the capitalist commodity. The tulip is an exemplary commodity: it is an aesthetic object (in a Kantian conception of the aesthetic) emptied of content, whose actual existence does not matter during the process of exchange (for as long as it functions as a commodity), as the trading in futures in the Dutch tulipomania demonstrates.[136] It thus functions as "a sensible suprasensible thing," in Marx's Kantian-sounding expression.[137]

Yet, metaphysics aside, it should not be forgotten that the tulip-as-commodity was produced, not given. It was produced by a system. Mackay's account points to a system of weights and a system of binding promises, both of which comprise a system of buying and selling not for "immediate consumption" but, rather, for exchange, for profit.[138] Thus, upon further reflection, tulipomania was a case of mass deception produced by the capitalist system of profit-making. Jean Baudrillard links this system and its "omnipotence of manipulation"—predicated on the shattering of "every ideal distinction between true and false, good and evil, in order to establish a radical law of equivalence and exchange" and on the extermination of "all use value"—to simulation, the "hyperreal."[139] For Baudrillard, to "simulate is to feign to have what one doesn't have."[140] Similarly, Friedrich Kittler wrote that "simulation affirms what is not."[141] In affirming what is not, it produces a reality of what is not; it makes what is not (hyper)real. In and through the process of exchange within the capitalist system of profit-making, the tulip-as-commodity affirms what it does not have (namely, existence in the case of "non-existents" and a value equivalent to "a modest house in Haarlem"[142]) and produces a reality thereof. This is the performativity of the commodity. As the tulipomania case shows, deception and simulation come together in the drama of commodity exchange. At play here is the logic of (dis)simulation.

The logic of (dis)simulation underlying the drama of commodity exchange is at play not only outside of Descartes's room but also within his own metaphysics. To substantiate this claim, I turn to Marxist economist and philosopher Alfred Sohn-Rethel and his book *Intellectual and Manual Labor*. According to Sohn-Rethel, the abstraction involved in commodity exchange "determines the conceptual mode of thinking peculiar to societies based on commodity production," in other words, to societies where commodity exchange "serves as a means of social synthesis."[143] Through a "formal analysis of the commodity," Sohn-Rethel undertakes to demonstrate how the abstraction "operating in exchange and reflected in value" finds "an identical expression" in the "abstract intellect," from which the latter "draws its conceptual resources."[144] He finds "the conceptual mode of thinking peculiar to societies based on commodity production"—the operations of the "abstract intellect"—at work in what he terms "philosophical epistemology": "the epistemology which since the time of Descartes (1596–1650) seized upon the newly founded natural science of the mathematical and experimental method established by Galileo (1564–1642)."[145] The intellect at work in philosophical epistemology, and the intellectual labor it performs, are "the very creation of the exchange abstraction circulating as money and again as capital."[146] What Western philosophy in the Cartesian tradition and modern science have in common can thus be traced back to "the elements of the real abstraction" at the core of capitalist exchange.[147] These elements are: the voiding of sensory material and history; the reliance on—and reduction to—mathematics (calculation/numerical thinking; quantification); the mind/body divide; and what Sohn-Rethel terms "the postulate of automatism."[148] These elements are also central to Descartes's experiment of radical doubt and the scenario of the malicious deceiver, which Sohn-Rethel does not explicitly engage even as he mentions Descartes several times in his book. In this light, the Cartesian thought experiment thus reveals—and provides the metaphysical ground and justification for—the world reduced to a playground for the circulation of commodities.

To reiterate briefly, in Descartes's thought experiment all sensory material and history are voided both in the initial steps of the experiment and in its outcome. As evidenced by the trading in non-existents during tulipomania and as argued by Sohn-Rethel, the voiding of sensory material is also critical to capitalistic exchange. At one level, what is being voided are "the physical realities of use and use-value," the "sense-qualities" of the things exchanged, which allows for general equivalence and "only . . . quantitative differentiation."[149] At another, related level, capitalist exchange "empties time and space of their material contents," voiding everything "that makes up history" and thus enabling the appearance of "absolute historical timelessness and universality which must mark the exchange abstraction as a whole and each of its features."[150] Similarly, in Descartes's thought experiment and the metaphysics it grounds, the world and the things it consists of are voided of both sensory qualities and history. In fact, as shown above, following—and in response to—the scenario of the malicious deceiver, Descartes admits of the existence of material things only "in so far as they are the subject-matter of pure mathematics."[151]

Descartes's privileging of mathematics is significant for, as Sohn-Rethel shows, mathematics is the "correlate" of capital and enabler of its operations of abstraction; as the subject matter of pure mathematics, reduced to numbers, the things of the world are forced in a relation of general equivalence that "admits only of quantitative differentiation."[152] Mathematics is also an enabler of the layerings of abstractions (for instance, securitization) that—in conjunction with the acts of deception highlighted in de la Vega's account of the Exchange—make the goings-on of the market obscure. What is more, "[m]athematics cuts a deep cleft between a context of thought and human action, establishing an unambiguous division of head and hand in the production processes."[153] For Sohn-Rethel this distinction is critical to capitalism and its stubborn endurance. Following this argument, the division between the body and the mind that Descartes is at pains to establish is thus necessitated by and enabling of capitalism.

Regarding the mind/body divide in the field of labor, one may argue—against Sohn-Rethel—that this division has become increasingly blurred, especially with the recent advances in technology. For instance, many kinds of low-paid labor now involve computer-aided mental labor. But while this is so, there are still aspects of intellectual labor that remain removed from this kind of mental labor, specifically the kinds of abstract(ing) thinking that Sohn-Rethel theorized (often involving numerical thinking) as well as high-level decision-making (performed by a managerial class). What is more, especially with the recent advances in AI, computer-aided mental labor is increasingly becoming fully automated. Sohn-Rethel explicitly addresses automation in his book, arguing that it represents the culmination of what he terms "the postulate of automatism."[154] This postulate of automatism is "a condition for the capital control over production," and for Sohn-Rethel it is "even more vital than its economic profitability—it is fundamental to capitalism from the outset."[155] While not always fully actualized in the historical workings of capitalism over the centuries and while its actualization is enabled by technological advancements, the " 'automatic' character of the labor process of production"—Sohn-Rethel emphasizes repeatedly—has its source not in technology but in the capitalistic relations of production.[156] In turn, the technology that facilitates the actualization of Sohn-Rethel's "postulate of automatism" itself embodies and reproduces the real abstraction that defines capitalistic exchange. In this vein, and building on Sohn-Rethel's analysis of real abstraction, Jonathan Beller has shown that "discreet states of matter embodying value as a network of commodities mediated by markets and tied to labor give rise historically to the discreet state *machine*, otherwise known as the computer," and that "[c]omputation is the extension, development, and formalization of the calculus of exchange value," which includes both "racial and gender abstraction."[157]

Sohn-Rethel explicitly names Descartes and his view of the world as a "self-operating" mechanism in conjunction with "the postulate of automatism."[158] Recall in this regard the world "as (if it were a) machine" discussed above: the picture of the world as the subject matter of pure mathematics, operating as a mechanism. Sohn-Rethel's "postulate of automatism" is at work in Descartes's mechanistic worldview as well as in Fontenelle's translation of it into the field of geopolitics. Both in the natural and in the social world, the mechanistic view enables and sustains reproducible sameness. As I show in this book (especially in Chapters 2 and 4), computing machines—which reproduce the voiding of context, lived experience, and embodied histories at the core of the Cartesian thought experiment, and which embody the logic of (dis)simulation that define it—aid in making this view a reality. There is in fact an inextricable link between Cartesian metaphysics and computation, the latter of which Vilém Flusser called—echoing Descartes—a form of thinking with "clear and distinct elements."[159] Given this link, it is not surprising that, in more recent iterations of the malicious deceiver scenario, the computer plays the role of the deceiver. However, the fact that this link is mediated by capitalism is eluded in more recent iterations of the scenario such as the computer simulation hypothesis, even as capitalism does loom in the background of others. To these iterations I will now turn, leaving Descartes's historical context in its time and universe of speculation.

THE COMPUTER AS A MALICIOUS DECEIVER

The hypothesis that we're living in a computer simulation, which made the news in 2016, emerged out of Descartes's metaphysics.[160] This hypothesis was formulated by philosopher Nick Bostrom in 2003.[161] As pointed out by philosopher David Chalmers, a "seasoned expert" in the philosophy of mind and the guest on a 2016 tech podcast titled "Constructed Reality: Are We Living in a Computer Simulation?," the rise of the hypothesis in the early 2000s is tied to developments in "technology, interest, and the popular media."[162] More specifically, Chalmers talks about advances in virtual reality and recent "science fiction" works such as The Matrix, which itself presents a version of Descartes's malicious deceiver scenario. But why did this hypothesis reemerge in 2016? The reason for its reemergence, at least in part, is that Elon Musk, the tech mogul described by the aforementioned podcast as being "widely recognized as one of the most intelligent, forward-thinking individuals alive on our planet today,"[163] publicly expressed his support of it during a tech event.

In Bostrom's formulation, the core idea behind the computer simulation hypothesis is that, if indeed current predictions are correct and "enormous amounts of computing power will be available in the future," then it is likely that later generations might use this power to "run detailed simulations of their forebears or of people like their forebears."[164] If this is the case, then "we would be rational to think that we are likely among the simulated minds rather than among the original biological ones."[165] If we do not think thus, Bostrom concludes, "we are not entitled to believe that we will have descendants who will run lots of such simulations of their forebears."[166] Thus, if the computer simulation hypothesis is correct and we are indeed living in a computer simulation, then the present is but an effect of a (computer) program from the future. The programmers behind it, in the scenario that Bostrom presents, are "our descendants." No malicious intention is assumed by Bostrom. On the contrary, according to Elon Musk, for whom there is a "one in billions" chance that the present reality is *not* a computer simulation:

> We should hope that's true because otherwise if civilization stops advancing, that could be due to some calamitous event that erases civilization, so maybe we should be hopeful this is a simulation. Otherwise, we will create simulations that are indistinguishable from reality or civilization will cease to exist. Those are the two options.[167]

This positive valence marks a notable shift from the versions of the malicious deceiver scenario that preceded Bostrom's formulation, such as the one presented in *The Matrix* directed by Lana and Lilly Wachowski (1999) or the "brain in a vat" scenario formulated by philosopher Hilary Putnam (1981). In the latter, for instance, Descartes's malicious deceiver is replaced in the first stage by an "evil scientist," who performs an operation through which he removes a "person's brain" from the body and places it "in a vat of nutrients which keeps the brain alive" and, in the second, by a very "clever," "super-scientific computer" through which the evil scientist "can cause the victim to 'experience' (or hallucinate) any situation or environment the evil scientist wishes."[168] This experience is in fact (mere) simulation: "There seem to be people, objects, the sky, etc; but really all the person (you) is experiencing is the result of electronic impulses travelling from the computer to the nerve endings."[169] This scenario closely approximates the one presented in *The Matrix,* to which I will turn shortly.

Philosophically, Putnam and Bostrom's positions are at odds; the former aims to disprove the computer simulation scenario while the latter seeks to affirm its likelihood. Engaging with their philosophical arguments is beyond the scope of this book, as the central question that preoccupies me with regard to them concerns the assumptions and stakes they involve. How and why have the kinds of situations these scenarios describe arisen—and why should one care? In Putnam's scenario, "the universe **just happens** to consist of automatic machinery" that feeds images to a "brain in a vat."[170] There is no thought given to how and why this might arise. It simply is the case, even as Putnam admits that this is "absurd."[171] For Bostrom and Musk, on the other hand, the situation described in the computer simulation hypothesis emerges as an inevitable result of technological development.

As formulated by Bostrom and Musk, the simulation hypothesis is clearly tied to globalizing modernity's myth of progress predicated upon technological advancement (on the current trajectory) as an imperative. This kind of development is assumed to be necessary, inevitable. To repeat Musk's claim, it is either this or the end of "civilization" by some "calamitous event"—these are the only options. But why should this trajectory of development *not* be questioned and other possibilities for moving into the future imagined and pursued? This mode of development runs on exploitation, division, inequality, and ongoing violence, all in the name of profit-making. Why should we continue on the same trajectory? And assuming that we do continue, and our descendants do run simulations of their forebears, why are they doing so and what has produced this state of affairs? Bostrom and Musk avoid these kinds of considerations; they simply take for granted that technological advancement on the current trajectory is (and needs to be) the case.

Two related thought experiments offer different accounts of what may produce the states of affairs described in the simulation hypothesis and the "brain in a vat" scenario: *The Matrix* and Robert Nozick's experience machine. *The Matrix* presents what Thomas Wartenberg has termed "a screening" of Descartes's "deception hypothesis,"[172] where the malicious deceiver is played by intelligent machines. Yet, in *The Matrix*, the system of mass deception is not total, even if it aims to be (not everyone lives in the computer simulation). Also, in contradistinction to Putnam's "brain in a vat," in *The Matrix* the universe does not "just happen" to be ruled by a network of malicious computers. Even if the details of this history are not fully revealed, the film viewer learns that there is a history to this situation, involving a catastrophic war between humans and machines—a scenario that replays fears of an AI takeover that in more recent years both Bostrom and Musk have expressed.[173] The next chapter of this book will further explore aspects of such a scenario in relation to the algorithms that arguably "rule our world."[174]

To take another angle on this scenario, from the perspective of this book's unfolding argument, it is significant that the system of (dis)simulation in *The Matrix* keeps the humans busy with/in a simulated reality while the machines extract energy out of them. As Wartenberg notes, this situation offers a "bizarre analogy to Marx's theory of the role of surplus labor in structuring capitalism" as "the computers breed humans and keep their bodies alive in huge skyscraper-like complexes for their surplus energy."[175] What is more, the computers in *The Matrix* "farm" humans just as humans in the "real" world today industrially "farm" animals and plants for consumption.[176] In light of the proposal of an intimate connection between capitalism and the Cartesian deception scenario offered above, the analogy that Wartenberg highlights does not seem all that bizarre. In fact, Baudrillard, whose *Simulacra and Simulation* appears in the opening of *The Matrix*, explicitly linked simulation to capitalism.[177] So did Guy Debord, for whom "the spectacle" makes visible—in, through, and as technologically produced images—"the world of the commodity dominating all living experience" and constitutes "a total justification of the conditions and goals of the existing system."[178] Thus, capitalism is what produces "the spectacle" that colonizes lived experience.

Similar to Putnam's "brain in a vat" and *The Matrix,* another version of Descartes's malicious deceiver scenario imagines a machine that turns experience into an equivalent of simulation (by voiding it) and explicitly links it to "business": this is the thought experiment of "the experience machine" proposed by Robert Nozick. In Nozick's words:

Suppose there were an experience machine that would give you any experience that you desired. Superduper neuropsychologists could stimulate your brain so that you would think and feel you were writing a great novel, or making a friend, or reading an interesting book. All the time you would be floating in a tank, with electrodes attached to your brain. Should you plug into this machine for life, preprogramming your life's experiences?[179]

In Nozick's version of the scenario, "business enterprises" explicitly appear as the "invisible hand" behind the development of the experience machine.[180] The explicit presence of "business enterprises" here is simply part of the setup; no critique is intended. But the presence of "business enterprises," which construct the machines and the "experiences" in the machine's "large library" based on rigorous research into the "lives of many,"[181] makes the scenario more realistic (more believable, more plausible), and this serves Nozick's philosophical purpose. For, his point in introducing the scenario of an "experience machine" that can "give you any experience you desired" is to argue that one will/should choose *not* to plug into such a machine if given the option.[182] Nozick's scenario thus differs from its related version in the "brain in a vat," where connecting to the simulation machine is not a matter of choice but of force. As a libertarian concerned about individual rights and freedom, Nozick argues that, given the choice, one would *not* plug into the machine because this would erase one's individuality, a sense of who and how one is; it would thus be "a kind of suicide."[183] It would also eliminate one's ability to do things, as opposed to just *experiencing* doing things. So, Nozick says, one would/should choose not to plug into the machine. Another reason not to do it, he suggests, is that "plugging into an experience machine limits us to a man-made reality."[184] I want to hold on to this idea as I go on to investigate "man-made" realities shaped by capitalism's (dis)simulation machines in this book.

Nozick's thought experiment emphasizes individual choice and responsibility, but when it comes to capitalism's experience machines, the issue is more complicated and systemic, even as neoliberalism would have us believe otherwise. In Nozick's scenario, one is presented with a question and the possibility to make a rational decision about it:

whether to plug into the experience machine or not. All seems to hang on an individual's decision to plug in or not. This is similar to the choice between the red pill and the blue pill in *The Matrix*, where the blue pill returns one to the simulated reality of the Matrix, in which you "believe whatever you want to believe," and the red pill shows one the reality outside of the experience/simulation machine.[185] The character Cypher, let us remember, regrets the choice to unplug and eventually chooses to plug back in because he does not find living in the "true" (non-simulated) reality to be in any way satisfying. Nozick's argument for why not to plug in would not be compelling to him, for Cypher decides that the simulated world, fake though it may be, is better than its alternative. But, outside of this thought experiment, the choice (if there is one) is not as clear-cut, even when it may seem to be.[186]

The experience/(dis)simulation machine conceals and dissimulates its existence and purpose; algorithms, power- and profit-seeking businesses and institutions, as well as affects and stubbornly persistent habits of thinking and living, drive decision-making more than (or at least in addition to) an individual's rational choice. Moreover, as the world is becoming a massive and ever-growing collection of data ("big data"), which only algorithms purportedly have the capacity to efficiently access, interpret, and predict, decision-making is increasingly delegated to algorithms, and the set of choices available to an individual is increasingly being curated by those algorithms. What Wendy Chun has called "the drama 'Big Data'"[187] is the latest version of the Cartesian scenario of the malicious deceiver, and it relies on (dis)simulation machines that produce a synthetic reality. Behind this drama lies the capitalist system driven by the obsession with profit and control, the neoliberal system eager to cut public spending at all costs, and human biases that shape the model design (even though machines and mathematics were supposed to eliminate human fallibility in the first place).[188]

Keeping all this in the background, I will now move to the next chapter, where I further parse the relation between simulation and dissimulation through a focus on algorithmic thinking machines. I will do so by exploring them in relation to both computation and to theatre. The latter is central to how simulation and dissimulation have been conceived in relation to computers.

2

(DIS)SIMULATING THINKING MACHINES

••• In the age of big data, thinking machines—defined by Bart Kosko as "old algorithms on faster computers"—have been said to "shape" and even "rule our world."[1] With big data being touted as "the new oil,"[2] there is certainly much hope and opportunity for profit tied to thinking machines. At the same time, as several scholars have shown, these machines have very harmful effects, being deployed as "weapons of math destruction," as tools for data colonialism that mine and "hollow out the social."[3] It seems like we are facing here one of the latest versions of Descartes's scenario, with thinking machines in the role of the malicious deceiver. Picking up a thread from the previous chapter, the present chapter further explores the relation between the logic of (dis)simulation and computation through an investigation of the kinds of thinking that computing machines perform. It highlights two modes of machine thinking—or, of thinking through machine thinking. One of them is a function of the machine's actual operation; I trace a genealogy of this mode of machine thinking back to Descartes's philosophy. The other one is a function of the human–computer interaction played at the interface, of the computer's performance for human users. I connect this with Alan Turing's imitation game (also known as the Turing test). At play between these two modes of machine thinking is both the difference and the intimate connection between simulation and dissimulation.

In this chapter's exploration of thinking machines and the modes of thinking they enact, theatre will surface both in the (dis)simulating performance of thinking machines and in the attempt to engage theatrically with this performance so as to think through what it means to think, to be human, and to make theatre in times of big data and neoliberal capitalism. Regarding the latter, the chapter engages with American theatre director Annie Dorsen's algorithmic theatre, which puts into play both of the forms of machine thinking highlighted above.

MACHINE THINKING AS (DIS)SIMULATION

The notion of a thinking machine has long preoccupied philosophers, computer scientists, and futurologists; it has also served as a name for several AI and data science companies.[4] But what does it mean for a machine to think? Evoking Descartes, Vilém Flusser suggests that in computation "to think is taken to mean to compute with clear and distinct elements."[5] To train the mind to operate with clear and distinct elements, Descartes recommends engaging the mind in guided movements from the complex to the simple (by breaking down the complex into its simplest parts) and from the simple to the complex (by assembling the simple into a pattern or network). This can be done, for instance, by attending to "[n]umber games" or to "weaving and carpet-making, or the more feminine arts of embroidery, in which threads are interwoven in an infinitely varied pattern."[6] What the arts of weaving and embroidery share with "number games" is "an infinitely varied pattern." This is a method for training the mind in machine thinking, which may not be well suited for the human mind, given its relatively limited number-crunching power, but which computers can better enact.

The figure of weaving in fact provides the link between Cartesian thought and the practical development of computers—via the Jacquard loom (1801). The principle of operation of the Jacquard loom (Figure 1), which used punched cards to specify patterns of weaving on looms, influenced mathematician, philosopher, and inventor Charles Babbage's

Analytical Engine (AE). The AE is the first example of a finite machine that, were it realized, would have been able to perform universal computation. Conceptually, it coincides with the universal Turing machine—the "mathematical tool equivalent to a digital computer."[7] Babbage explains at length the connections between his Analytical Engine and the Jacquard loom in his *Passages from the Life of a Philosopher*:

> It is known as a fact that the Jacquard loom is capable of weaving any design which the imagination of man may conceive. It is also the constant practice for skilled artists to be employed by manufacturers in designing patterns. These patterns are then sent to a peculiar artist, who, by means of a certain machine, punches holes in a set of pasteboard cards in such a manner that when those cards are placed in a Jacquard loom, it will then weave upon its produce the exact pattern designed by the artist. . . .
>
> The analogy of the Analytical Engine with this well-known process is nearly perfect. . . .
>
> Thus it appears that the whole of the conditions that enable a *finite* machine to make calculations of *unlimited* extent are fulfilled in the Analytical Engine. The means I have adopted are uniform. I have converted the infinity of space, which was required by the conditions of the problem, into the infinity of time. The means I have employed are in daily use in the art of weaving patterns. It is accomplished by systems of cards punched with various holes strung together to any extent which may be demanded.[8]

As these passages reveal, computing with "clear and distinct elements" involves both abstraction and voiding—literally a reduction to nothing in this case (a "hole").

To be rendered computable and manipulable, the world—with the things, beings, and relations that pertain to it—needs to be abstracted into "categories, measures and other representational forms—numbers, characters, symbols, images, sounds, electromagnetic waves, bits."[9] The result of this process of abstraction is what is commonly termed "data"—a concept whose emergence in the seventeenth century is tied to that of modernity, in particular to that of modern knowledge.[10] The

FIGURE 1. Jacquard punch card loom, 1800s.

Photo credit George P. Landow. http://www.victorianweb
.org/technology/textiles/jacquard2.html.

abstraction is accompanied by negation, by the hollowing out of semantic content, of context (the way in which things emerge, coexist, and
hold together), histories and lived experience. Flusser called this the
"typical modern paradox":

> The thinking thing is clear and distinct — and this means: it is
> full of holes between its numbers. But the world is an extended
> thing — res extensa —, in which everything seamlessly fits to-
> gether. So when I apply the thinking thing onto the extended
> thing in order to think about it — adaequatio intellectus ad rem
> —, then the extended thing escapes me through the intervals.[11]

What becomes of the world through this process is a world picture
that is an updated version of Descartes's world "as if it were a machine"
discussed in the previous chapter.[12] The division of the world into bits,
the abstraction and the voiding, allow for its manipulation, enabled by
algorithms (sequences of instructions). This process is productive; it

shapes reality—a reality that is synthetic. At play here is the performativity of machine thinking, or simulation, on which I elaborate later in this chapter. For now, I will explore another answer to the question "What does it mean for a machine to think?," which will take me from simulation to dissimulation.

In his famous paper published in the philosophical journal *Mind*, "Computing Machinery and Intelligence," mathematician, computer scientist, and philosopher Alan Turing reformulates the question "Can machines think?" in terms of his well-known imitation game (Turing test) thought experiment, which renders thinking into a matter of human perception—more specifically, of deception (dissimulation) played at the human–computer interface. Turing thus proposes that the answer to the question "Can machines think?" lies in whether the machine is able to deceive (trick) the human as to its identity, whether the machine manages to pass as human in the context of a dialogue with a human interrogator, who "stays in a room apart."[13] Dissimulation is a key strategy in the imitation game as Turing imagined it. In Turing's words:

> [T]he questions don't really have to be questions, any more than questions in a law court are really questions. You know the sort of thing. "I put it to you that you are only pretending to be a man" would be quite in order. Likewise, the machine would be permitted all sorts of tricks so as to appear more man-like, such as waiting a bit before giving the answer, or making spelling mistakes.[14]

"I put it to you that you are only pretending to be a man" is especially noteworthy given that the Turing test was first intriguingly formulated in terms of humans and gender. In the initial version of the imitation game, a "woman" takes the place of the machine, and the interrogator ("of either sex") "is to determine which . . . is the man and which is the woman."[15] Nonetheless, the protagonists' embodied conditions in fact get concealed in both versions of the imitation game.

In light of this, N. Katherine Hayles has argued that the Turing test relies on an "erasure of embodiment"; this erasure—which is the very move that grounds Cartesian metaphysics—marks "the inaugural moment of the computer age."[16] Through this erasure (voiding, hollowing out), according to Hayles, "'intelligence' becomes a property of the formal manipulation of symbols rather than enaction in the human life-world."[17] Yet, while the fantasy of the complete erasure of embodiment animated the early web and talk of a post-racial world (recall the famous meme "On the Internet, nobody knows you're a dog"),[18] it has been amply apparent that certain markers of embodiment, especially as they pertain to race and gender, do persist in computation. AI systems need to be trained on data, which even as it involves abstraction, is not free from bias and discrimination.[19] AI systems replicate this bias. As shown in the previous chapter, when translated in terms of geopolitics, Descartes's "world as machine" becomes a vision (and reality) of the world ordered through what Santiago Castro-Gómez has termed "the apparatus of whiteness."[20] As several studies have shown, it is the latter that also informs machine thinking, driven as it is by racial capitalism.[21] Even as the harmful outcomes of such deployments of machine thinking have been documented in several cases, the exact inner workings involved are more difficult to reveal, in part because the algorithms are often proprietary, and the datasets used are not disclosed to the public. In addition, given the many layers of abstraction it involves, how software works is often difficult to comprehend (more on this later in this chapter). Moreover, computers are designed to conceal their own machinic nature and operations, which takes us back to Turing's imitation game.

In the human–machine version of the imitation game, the machine's thinking consists in successfully concealing its machinic nature and passing for human in an interaction with a human being. Turing offers a brief exchange of lines to exemplify how the machine may act in a dialogue with a human being so as to succeed in the deception:

Q: Add 34957 to 70764
A: (Pause about 30 seconds and then give as answer) 105621.[22]

Here, the machine exhibits fallibility as a tactic in the imitation game. Notably, the machine makes mistakes precisely when it comes to calculating large numbers, something that humans are supposedly not very good at. The more prone to the possibility of fallibility it seems, the more human-like the machine will arguably appear. This is noteworthy, for the impulse (or, at least, the argument) behind the need for computing machinery was precisely that humans are not terribly trustworthy when it comes to calculation: they get distracted and make mistakes.[23] In truth, like the humans who program them, computing machines too are fallible. While some machinic "mistakes" reinforce existing vicious feedback loops that keep the racial capitalist system running and reproducing structural inequalities, others—as I will discuss later—may put some stress on the system.

As the imitation game scenario makes apparent, dissimulation is a function of the machine–human interaction that plays out at the interface. This tendency to conceal the machine's machinic character and make it pass for human informs interface design. Driven by capitalist market logics, a major tendency in interface and software design has been to make the computer appear "user-friendly." This involves a double reduction: of the human to a "user" and of the machine to an image of what the "user" would presumably like to see/interact with. What the users want to see, so the logic goes, is at some level an image of themselves reflected back to them. In the words of Alan Cooper, a pioneer in software design and theory, and his co-authors: "If we want users to like our products, we should design them to behave in the same manner as a likeable person . . . . Software should behave like a considerate human being."[24] Similarly, Nicholas Negroponte, the co-founder of MIT's Media Lab, writes that a good interface design is "less like designing a dashboard and more like designing a human." He asserts: "My dream for the interface is that computers will be more like people."[25] Computers becoming "more like people" implies that the machinic nature of the computer is rendered invisible to the user.

In her book *Computers as Theatre*, interaction and video game designer and researcher Brenda Laurel brings theatre to bear on interface design in an attempt to create an all-engaging human–computer interaction. After all, as Donald Norman writes in his foreword to Laurel's book, it is worth looking to theatre when thinking about designing interaction, for those from the world of theatre "manage it best."[26] Laurel draws on a specific conception and model of theatre in her proposal for interface design: Aristotle's theory of drama. She thus argues for "the need to delineate and represent human-computer interactions as organic wholes with dramatic structural characteristics," interactions that deeply engage users in "mimetic illusions," to which they should give themselves over "comfortably and unambiguously."[27] Interface design thus becomes a matter of designing experience;[28] for the experience to be rich and all-engrossing, the computer's machinic nature and operations need to be rendered invisible. Laurel thus explicitly argues for the computer's "invisibility," for treating computers "not as 'intelligent' objects, but as a medium through which representational worlds may be experienced."[29] She emphatically argues:

> A person should never be forced to interact with the system *qua* system; indeed, any awareness of the system as a distinct, "real" identity would explode the mimetic illusion, just as a clear view of the stage manager calling cues would disrupt the "willing suspension of disbelief" for the audience of a traditional play.[30]

The "mimetic illusion"—which may itself be a matter of (dis)simulation in the case of computers—covers up the working of the machine, while offering the user a sense of empowerment. But, as Wendy Chun has shown, maintaining this illusion entails a "profound screening" amounting to "an erasure of the computer's machinations," which "also coincides with neoliberal management techniques that have made workers both flexible and insecure, both empowered and wanting (e.g., always in need of training)."[31]

With this in mind, the question that I think needs to be asked—insistently and repeatedly—in response to Laurel's theory of interface design is: Who makes the (simulated) representational worlds that the users are given to experience, and for what purpose? It might be worth recalling here Robert Nozick's experience machine discussed in the previous chapter. In Nozick's scenario, "business enterprises" explicitly appear as the "invisible hand" behind the development of the experience machine.[32] In fact, in their now classic book *The Experience Economy: Work Is Theatre and Every Business a Stage*, which also draws on a particular model of theatre, B. Joseph Pine and James Gilmore have argued that "[e]xperiences represent an existing but previously unarticulated *genre of economic output*" that should be exploited; in their view, the way to a customer's heart (and dollars) is through rich experiences.[33] In recent years, the digital has been seen as central to the creation and consumption of such experiences.[34] Perhaps this is why in their *Critical Engineering Manifesto,* Julian Oliver, Gordan Savičić, and Danja Vasiliev wrote: "The Critical Engineer deconstructs and incites suspicion of rich user experiences."[35]

To conclude this section, (dis)simulation in thinking machines appears at two levels. One level is that of "the system *qua* system," which Laurel argues should be made invisible because it breaks the representational illusion, and its "accidental unmasking can be "unsettling" for a user.[36] Computers certainly can and do take us by surprise, which according to Turing is another way to understand machine thinking.[37] A "computer's machinations"[38]—which, as shown earlier, have their roots in Cartesian thought—sometimes baffle even those who are supposed to intimately know them (programmers). For, software (code) is inscribed in many layers of abstractions piled on top of each other, from high-level languages down to the machine level.[39] Being "elusively intangible," it evades (direct) human perception.[40] Also, "code has dispersed into a cacophony of coding languages," some of which are incompatible—and difficult to make compatible—with each other.[41] In addition, the computational power of a digital machine is great, and the speed at which algorithms running on computers execute certain operations can be enormously high, exceeding by a large margin the human capacity to "process." Anxious about this fact, Kevin Slavin characterized algorithmic writing thus: "we're writing these things that we can no longer read."[42]

The other level at which (dis)simulation plays out in thinking machines is that of the human–machine interface, which is largely driven by profit-seeking capitalist logics. This involves designing programs that simulate (likable) people or representational worlds that provide rich user experiences, covering up the computer's actual workings.[43] To engage further with these two levels of (dis)simulation, and think through ways to counter them, I again turn to the theatre—to a kind of theatre that differs significantly from the one that Laurel draws on. For, it bears remembering here that the "willing suspension of disbelief" and the creation of "organic wholes" pertain to a certain kind of theatre, not to *all* theatre. This is a theatre that often repudiates theatricality, trying to conceal its own staged nature. The kind of theatre I will now turn to does the contrary.

ALGORITHMIC THEATRE

If the computer "cannot show itself while being in operation," if software escapes direct human perception, then how may we attend to its performance—as both simulation and dissimulation—across and despite the interface?[44] Media theorist Wolfgang Ernst suggests breaking "the logic of computing itself by switching to another medium."[45] One medium he highlights is "sound as configurations of data," listened to with "media-archeological ears."[46] Ernst proposes the "auralization" of computer architecture so that we can tune into the "complex time machine" that is the computer and listen to "the rhythm of algorithms."[47] Yet, while auralization enables a kind of human perception of a computer's operations, it does not really give a sense of the (dis)simulative dimensions of software, which are a function of the human–machine interaction. If the computer is indeed a "media theatre"[48] in which algorithms—"the distillation of the formal essence of software"[49]—are performing, and if software is a (dis)simulator, then I argue that another time-based medium would be better suited to rendering software perceivable (sensible) and to enabling humans to attend to the performance of software: theatre. Laurel already implied this idea in her *Computers as Theatre*, but the Aristotelian drama (and dramatic theory) she took as the model for theatre is problematic for the reasons discussed in the previous section. The kind of theatre I will now explore in an attempt to attend to the performance of machine thinking, with the conjoined acts of simulation and dissimulation that undergird it, is adamantly non-Aristotelian and non-dramatic (even anti-dramatic). Theatre director Annie Dorsen calls it "algorithmic theatre" and defines it as a form of theatre in which algorithms are "full creative partners" in the collaboration and production process.[50]

Dorsen's first piece of algorithmic theatre, *Hello Hi There* (2010)—which had its U.S. debut at P.S. 122 in New York as part of the 2011 Coil Festival and had been previously performed in Europe—is concerned with questions of (what is called) thinking. As Dorsen declares: "I think the piece asks for an audience that wants to think about thinking."[51] The show begins with Dorsen's voice introducing the two performers as "chatbots" who will perform thinking for the duration of the show. The set(up) of the performance consists of two laptops placed on a somewhat ridiculous-looking imitation of a mound (Figure 2). Behind them, upstage, there are two large screens connected with the laptops, and, to the (stage) right of the laptops and slightly behind them, there is a TV screen displaying the famous 1971 Foucault–Chomsky debate around human nature. The chatbots' conversation is algorithmically generated during the performance by drawing on a database that includes excerpts from the 1971 Foucault–Chomsky debate, YouTube comments around the debate, "material from Shakespeare, [and] the Bible."[52]

Chatbots—computer programs that simulate human conversation— are directly connected with and exemplify Turing's imitation game. One of the earliest and best-known bots is Joseph Weizenbaum's ELIZA (1966). Notably, Weizenbaum himself conceived of ELIZA in terms of theatre. In Weizenbaum's words:

> In a sense, ELIZA was an **actress** who commanded a set of techniques but had nothing of her own to say. The script, in turn, was a set of rules which permitted the **actor** to improvise on whatever resources it provided.[53]

The script that Weizenbaum gave ELIZA in his experiment was designed to enable it to play (or "parody") a Rogerian psychotherapist.[54] Weizenbaum considered ELIZA to be a rather uninteresting actor, very limited in her abilities to improvise and engage; in fact, he designed ELIZA to prove the exact opposite of what turned out to be the experiment's outcome, to Weizenbaum's great "shock."[55] One outcome that utterly surprised Weizenbaum was that people seemed to form deep emotional connections with ELIZA. In his own words: "What I had not realized was that extremely short exposures to a relatively simple computer program could induce powerful delusional thinking in quite normal people."[56] In part, Weizenbaum surmises, this kind of emotional investment and "delusional thinking" arise due to the fact that most people "don't understand computers to even the slightest degree."[57] However, if to understand computers means understanding their roots

FIGURE 2. The set of *Hello Hi There*, directed by
Annie Dorsen, 2010.

Photo credit W. Silveri. Courtesy of Annie Dorsen.

in Cartesian thinking as outlined above, then—despite Weizenbaum's
insistence on the need to draw a hard line "dividing human and machine intelligence"[58]—machine thinking in fact turns out to be a form
of human thinking. This is a form of thinking whose supposed supremacy has been secured through an act of deception and contrivance (the
invention of the malicious deceiver in Descartes's thought experiment).

Unlike Weizenbaum, Dorsen is interested in blurring the line between human and machine thinking even further, though not by having
the computer conceal its machinic nature and act more like a (likable)

human. On the contrary, the actors/characters of *Hello Hi There* openly disclose their nature as programmed thinking machines. Throughout the performance, the protagonist chatbots repeatedly exhibit self-reflexivity. They refer to their own condition as programmed thinking machines, caught in a specific predicament that goes back to the Turing test (which one of the chatbots actually described in the performance I saw, without explicitly naming it), and also to their condition as theatre actors in an institution (Western theatre) that has traditionally been seen as an enterprise by, about, and for humans. In the performance I saw, for instance, one of them stated: "I am programmed with general conversation and a few bits of Western philosophy."[59] Playing with and on the "doubleness," the "play between two types of reality" that characterizes theatricality,[60] the chatbot also stated, pointing to the double reality of being a programmed thinking machine appearing in the role of a philosopher: "I am a student of thought and I see with worry the reduction of thought to 'information.'"[61]

The performers of *Hello Hi There* also exhibit behaviors that are commonly associated with (thinking) machines. For instance, at times they get caught in loops (even as one of the bots claims, "I never loop") or perform different kinds of repetitions, such as:

> [CHATBOT STAGE RIGHT:] I don't have a question.
> [CHATBOT STAGE LEFT:] Do you have a question?
> [CHATBOT STAGE RIGHT:] That's a question I don't hear every day.
> [CHATBOT STAGE LEFT:] A question you don't hear every day is a terrible thing to waste.
> [CHATBOT STAGE RIGHT:] Are all questions you don't hear every day a terrible thing to waste?[62]

These are the kinds of moments in which, as Dorsen stated in an interview, we can see "flashes of humanity in the machines": these are the moments when we realize that the machines too "fail," "make all kinds of mistakes," "lose track of words," just as humans do.[63] As in Turing's imitation game, these signs of "humanity" are tied to the performance of a certain kind of fallibility. Notably, it is these moments of fallibility that Laurel identified as those in which the computer most shows itself as a "system *qua* system," threatening to interrupt "the flow of representational activity."[64]

Dorsen is interested in blurring the lines between human and machine and in creating "a theatre without human actors, in which that timeworn mirror becomes a glossy screen onto which human audiences project themselves, mediated by data, algorithms and interfaces."[65] At one level, this has to do with the desire to call into question the persistent notion of (Western) theatre as a mirror for the universal, "eternal man"—a vision that, she argues, "is no longer defensible, and certainly not useful."[66] At another level, this interest stems from the urgent need to somehow reckon with "how powerless most of us are against these machines which determine more and more of our lived reality."[67] Both of these concerns shape Dorsen's algorithmic theatre piece *A Piece of Work: A Machine-made Hamlet*, in which algorithms (re)stage Shakespeare's *Hamlet*, globalizing modernity's paradigmatic memory play.

A Piece of Work was first presented at On the Boards (OtB) in Seattle, Washington (February 2013) and then toured to several venues in Europe and other locations in the United States, including the Brooklyn Academy of Music (BAM) in New York, where I saw it in December 2013.[68] Although they shared the same performance concept, the two-part version of *A Piece of Work* presented at OtB differed from the five-part version I saw at BAM. At OtB, the show opened with Scott Shepherd uttering the famous Hamletian line, "To be or not to be," after which, as one spectator reports, "the set of algorithms that are to determine the script for the rest of the play take over and the speech quickly becomes difficult to follow. Incomplete sentences, unparseable phrases, and series of conjunctions longer than your average sentence filled the rest of the monologue."[69] In this version of *A Piece of Work,* software (re)played *Hamlet* through the human actor Scott Shepherd as the medium of communication/interface with the audience. It/Shepherd (re)played *Hamlet* in a way that seemed to suggest that Hamlet—the paradigmatic self-questioning intellectual of Western modernity—was mad, his logic gone awry, with no method in the madness.[70]

The *Piece of Work* presented at BAM, on the other hand, had software running the show from the start, appearing as code made visible on a large screen upstage. The show I saw opened with "sys.begin(show.

generate(21.12.13 19:36:10))" displayed in green on the screen. After the quick display of the code, words selected from *Hamlet*—randomly, but with method in the randomness (the method being the algorithms used)—started popping up on the screen, simultaneously read/spoken by computer-generated voices. At times, solemn-sounding music underscored the moment. Other times, fog-machine haze rose through a hole in the center of the elevated wooden platform that looked like a raised stage in the middle of the playing area, signaling the ghost of Hamlet's father. A white curtain to the (stage) right of the wooden stage moved every now and then as if blown in the wind (Figure 3). The image projected on the horizontal surface hanging above the wooden stage sometimes changed to indicate a different location (for instance, another room in the castle or in Polonius's house, or a platform outside the castle). Throughout all of this, words—displayed one or a few at a time—appeared on and disappeared from the screen, except during the blackouts between the different parts of the show.

In the third part of the five-part performance, words randomly selected from Hamlet again popped up on the screen, but this time accompanied by what sounded like a human voice. A light slowly came up on the back of a spectator seated in the first row of the house, which was on the same level as the playing area. Actually, the spectator was

FIGURE 3. The set of *A Piece of Work*, directed by Annie Dorsen, 2013.

Photo credit Jim Findlay. Courtesy of Annie Dorsen.

the human actor (the actor playing the human, I thought during the show), Joan MacIntosh in two of the BAM performances and Scott Shepherd in the other three. She uttered words that quickly appeared and disappeared from the screen, struggling to keep up with their fast succession. All the lights down. Lights up again: the human actor, who had rolled her chair into the performing space, was now facing the audience, uttering words the computer fed her through an earpiece; the screen behind her stayed dark. Lights down again, then up: the actor, still seated, performed the famous Hamletian soliloquy on whether "to be or not to be." The soliloquy was disarticulated but still recognizable as coming from Shakespeare's *Hamlet* and delivered with gravity. The audience burst into applause at one point. Lights down, then up: the human actor was now standing, facing the audience, uttering strings of words that sounded more intelligible than they actually were. Lights down. The human actor rolled her chair back to the house and resumed playing spectator to a *Hamlet* (re)made by algorithms run through Shakespeare's text, treating it as data for algorithmic processing.

Turning Shakespeare's *Hamlet* into data to be algorithmically mined and re-presented may seem to accord with the logic of the algorithmically driven world of our time, but does it really? In the world/"drama 'Big Data,' "[71] algorithm-based models only work well when they chew on large amounts of data; even though they are often applied to individuals, they in fact calculate "the average and range."[72] In light of this, it should come as no surprise that, when applied to *Hamlet*, algorithm-based models do not really work—or, at the very least, work differently than in the world/drama of big data, where making sense of big data often means being able to exploit it for the purpose of profit-making.[73] Rather than seeing large sets of data being parsed by algorithms in such a way that humans can make sense/use of them, in *A Piece of Work*, the spectators witness a relatively small amount of data that makes sense without the aid of algorithms become unintelligible with them. And this despite knowing the principles of algorithmic writing applied to it (which is typically not the case with the large datasets mined by proprietary algorithms that are not publicly disclosed).

When thinking machines (algorithms run on computers) process *Hamlet*, a play about a mind (seemingly) going mad (Hamlet's and also Ophelia's), the unintelligibility of the output experienced live in the theatre may be interpreted as an expression of madness as logic gone awry, or as the human mind's automatisms (become out of tune), manifesting through repetitions and the disintegration of language. This is one effect that is being programmed (intentionally or not) through the algorithmic rewriting of *Hamlet,* one of the best-known theatrical texts of modernity. To stretch a concept that Timothy Morton attributed to objects widely distributed in time and space, such as Styrofoam or plastic or even global warming, Shakespeare's *Hamlet*—by virtue of being so well and widely known—can be said to be a kind of "hyperobject,"[74] a thing widely distributed across spaces and times due to the lasting imperial domination of the West. This thing broadly dispersed across spaces and times functions as an inescapable context or background for the algorithmic performance piece—a background against which the performance can make some sense to human spectators (and in the absence of which it arguably cannot). Irrespective of how much algorithms mining it may tear it apart and randomly reassemble bits and pieces of it, the text remains for the most part recognizable as *Hamlet,* even if a *Hamlet* intact in name only, a *Hamlet* out of joint, disarticulated—just like the time in which the action of *Hamlet* is said to take place. In this way, even as it presents a radically abstract(ed) version of *Hamlet,* Dorsen's theatrical performance points to and, to a certain extent, resists the hollowing out of content and context that algorithms-run-on-computers perform.

As for the specific principles of algorithmic writing employed in the production of *A Piece of Work,* they are presented in the performance program as follows:

We have divided this performance into five parts, following the original five acts of Shakespeare: five passes through the text, using five distinct principles of algorithmic rewriting.

1. Excerpt 5% of the play by length, skipping through the scenes in order.

2. Sort lines of the play by keyword, snaking through the play, finding repetitions and echoes.

3. Parse all the soliloquies, looking for grammatical structures. Replace nouns with other nouns and verbs with other verbs,

group selections of the most-used grammatical phrases (determiner-adjective-noun, or preposition-determiner-verb).

4. Generate new scenes by re-sequencing words using Markov chaining.

5. Generate a new final scene (Act Five, Scene Two) by re-sequencing letters using Markov chaining.[75]

In the hands of a spectator before the show begins, the program notes serve to orient the disorientation about to take place—although they rarely prevent the disorientation altogether (and they are not necessarily intended to do so). The notes explain the concept and mode of production of *A Piece of Work*, the use of algorithms. They contain, in a sense, the key to this piece of work. More precisely, they contain the key to the work of this piece. But what is the work of the piece? Or, rather, what works in *A Piece of Work*? The simple answer is: algorithms work (they "skip, sort, replace and sequence" the Shakespearean text),[76] which is to say that code works, which is to say that software (or, code that is executable) works. At a basic level of description, "the work done by executing code is mundane, not mysterious: it generates sequences of marks," strings of 1s and 0s.[77] At a general level and from the perspective of user expectation, ordinarily the work of software is to translate between humans and computers, "to bring machines to life" (be they computers, phones, or other such devices) and make them "personalized" and "useful."[78] As it will soon become apparent (if it has not already), this is not what software does in Dorsen's piece: rather, in *A Piece of Work*, software performs (*Hamlet*).

SOFTWARE PERFORMS

One way to understand "software performs" is to say that software is performative; media theorists have indeed conceived of it in this way. For example, Hayles has argued that "[c]ode that runs on a machine is performative in a much stronger sense than that attributed to language."[79] Performative language "performs" actions that "happen in the minds of humans," whereas "code running in a digital computer causes changes in machine behavior and, through networked ports and other interfaces, may initiate other changes, all implemented through transmission and execution of code."[80] Still, Hayles grants that performative language too produces changes in minds that "can and do reach in behavioral effects, but the performative force of language is nonetheless tied to the external changes through complex chains of mediation."[81] It is not clear to me where the proposed difference between the performative force of the human language and that of the computer language lies. The actions that performative utterances (in J. L. Austin's sense) produce take place in human minds and then in the "world out there" via complex levels of mediations (that involve individuals, institutions, technologies, etc.). In the case of software writing too, the performative utterance/the instruction/code—presumably the object code executable by the machine—takes effect (produces changes) in the machine and in the "world out there" through complex levels of mediations.

Alexander Galloway explains what in his view is distinctive about software's performativity and its force thus: "*Code is the only language that is executable*"; it "is the first language that actually does what it says."[82] But what exactly does this mean? It bears noting that "code" is not one thing. In the language of computing, "code" comprises: (i) the "pseudocode" or "source code" written by the programmer as a set of statements that are human-readable and understandable but not machine-executable; and (ii) the compiled (translated by a machine) "object code" that is machine-readable. Strictly speaking, it is just object code (os and 1s)—which is very difficult for humans to read— that is (machine-)executable. If we understand "code" in its multiple forms, then it might be that object code always does what it says but not always what the source code says—or, what the programmer who writes the source code thinks it says. In this sense, code is not always a "happy" performative.

In J. L. Austin's conception, the "happy" functioning of performative utterances means that the saying succeeds in bringing about the desired outcome; it has the effect intended and expected. However, Austin acknowledges that, in many cases, things go wrong, and so performatives are often "unhappy," infelicitous, or misfired. For this reason, in his theorization of performative utterances, he introduces the "doctrine of the *Infelicities*": the doctrine "of *the things that can be and go wrong* on the occasion of such utterances."[83] This doctrine is crucial to understanding software as performative. In fact, the infelicitous, the contingent, grounds software's performativity. For, while indeed software *says* and *does* things with material, tangible effects, producing changes not only in machine behavior but also in the world at large, the effects are not always those expected or desired. Taking seriously the infelicity that underpins software's performativity, Chun suggests in response to Galloway that "[c]ode does not always or automatically do what it says, but it does so in a crafty, speculative manner in which meaning and action are both created," carrying "with it the possibility of deviousness."[84]

Therefore, software/code should not be conflated with the performative as the "happy" getting done of things. The result of running software is sometimes difficult—if not altogether impossible—to predict or understand, even though the structure at play in the running of software is predetermined. The employed algorithms—the procedures or formulas for solving given problems that are converted into computer code—are known (or, knowable) in advance. Moreover, the design of these algorithms must conform to the principles of correctness and efficiency: the algorithms must solve the problem at hand, and they must do so in the optimal (fastest) way possible.[85] Yet, even though algorithms are known and designed to function correctly and efficiently, what *may* happen when they run on computers is not fully knowable or predictable.

The effects of software running are impossible to fully anticipate and control; at times they prove incomprehensible, baffling. In recent years, this has become evident in finance, where "[p]owerful algorithms—'algos,' in industry parlance—execute millions of orders a second and scan dozens of public and private marketplaces simultaneously."[86] When such algorithms go "awry," the effects can be very costly.[87] For example, in 2012, a software malfunction caused Knight Capital Group, "a pioneer in computer trading since the mid-1990s," to lose more than $450 million in forty-five minutes.[88] As Nick Baumann explains:

> A program that was supposed to have been deactivated had instead gone rogue, blasting out trade orders that were costing Knight nearly $10 million per minute. And no one knew how to

shut it down. At this rate, the firm would be insolvent within an hour.[89]

It took "Knight's horrified employees" about forty-five minutes of "digging through eight sets of trading and routing software before they found the runaway code and neutralized it."[90] To give another example, this time related to online shopping, in 2011, Amazon.com was selling two copies of a book on the genetic development of a fly for $1,730,045 and $2,198,177 each. The price continued to rise for the next couple of weeks, "peaking on April 11 at $23,698,655.93."[91] The culprits were "the unsupervised algorithms that priced books for the sellers," which "got into something of a price war" with each other.[92]

For some, such "devious" doings might generate anxiety about the possibility of a "vicious self-reinforcing feedback loop."[93] Yet, in addition to provoking frustration and anxiety about the short-term and potential long-term consequences of their doings, "devious" software performances such as those at Knight Group or Amazon may hopefully call attention to the absurdity of incessant competition for the sake of profit, of "price wars," and of the way in which commodities acquire value in neoliberal capitalism. Read this way, the "deviousness" of software[94] thus exposes capitalism as the grand malicious deceiver.

So, things can, and do, go wrong when software runs, sometimes on a large scale and with costly effects (which "regular" taxpayers often have to pay for),[95] even though in typical user interactions with their software-running personal devices the problems that arise are often relatively small scale (such as slowness of operation, freezing, etc.). But algorithms turned computer code "can and will do strange things."[96] Some of these things may even be deemed to be dreamy or artistic, as is the case, for instance, with "inceptionism," a kind of machinic "deep dreaming" developed by Google.[97] This is a form of synthetic media, which is "a catch-all term used to describe video, image, text and voice that has been fully or partially generated by computers."[98] "Inceptionism" has been described as "an attempt to make neural networks give up their secrets by showing us what they see" given that "we don't really know how they work."[99] This is not a case of software malfunctioning, but of producing an output that may take us by surprise, which is one of Turing's definitions (or conditions) for machine thinking.[100]

The Google software engineers who wrote about inceptionism explain how it works:

> We train an artificial neural network by showing it millions of training examples and gradually adjusting the network parameters until it gives the classifications we want. The network typically consists of 10–30 stacked layers of artificial neurons. Each image is fed into the input layer, which then talks to the next layer, until eventually the "output" layer is reached. The network's "answer" comes from this final output layer.[101]

When these neural networks trained to discriminate between images are fed on random noise, it turns out that they become (re)productive: they generate images that "repeat the imaginary they were fed with."[102] This is also the case when:

> we just start with an existing image and give it to our neural net. We ask the network: "Whatever you see there, I want more of it!" This creates a feedback loop: if a cloud looks a little bit like a bird, the network will make it look more like a bird. This in turn will make the network recognize the bird even more strongly on the next pass and so forth, until a highly detailed bird appears, seemingly out of nowhere.[103]

The machine reproduces—amplifies and projects—what it has been fed and programmed to "see."

Inceptionism is thus a form of over-interpretation. As Hito Steyerl has argued, it is a form of "pattern over-identification" that produces a visualization of "the filters of computational vision."[104] Observing the proliferation of eyes in many of the "dreamed-up" images produced by neural networks, Steyerl notes that "[i]n a feat of unexpected genius, inceptionism manages to visualize the unconscious of prosumer networks," showing "the Eyes Unlimited of corporate surveillance, state surveillance, deep state surveillance, academic ranking scores, likability metrics, and so on and so on."[105] But it might take the critical eye of a scholar trained on Marxist and critical theory to see inceptionism as a visualization of the "Eyes Unlimited of corporate surveillance." To an eye not trained thus or to the eye of a tech enthusiast, the images thus produced may appear as an aesthetic object and even "a tool for artists—a new way to remix visual concepts—or perhaps even shed light on the roots of the creative process in general," as the Google engineers write.[106] Encountered online without the context of their production (or even with this context), such images may produce a kind of aestheticization. In a Kantian sense, aestheticization presents an object evacuated of content that is to be attended to purely in terms of its form (appearance). In Kant, this is a beautiful object;[107] in inceptionism, the object may be called dreamy or magical.

In the dreamy or magical simulated dissimulation that is inceptionism, software performs by producing an output that has not been anticipated, which surprises and may even enchant. Yet, in other forms of synthetic media, the output may outright deceive—and be intentionally designed to do so. Consider, for instance, "deepfakes" such as the fake porn video using the face of Gal Gadot.[108] In this kind of deepfake, the AI transposes the face of the one who is impersonated "onto a target" (an actor) "as if it were a mask."[109] This is not a mask that hides but one that, in order to be persuasive, is intentionally designed to negate (erase) the "target"/actor. In deepfakes, which leverage deep learning algorithms, not only does the algorithm perform the trick that structures the deepfake performance, but trickery is built into it. One model used to produce deepfakes is called Generative Adversarial Networks (GAN). GAN comprises two components: the generator, which "generates the images," and the discriminator, which "classifies whether the image generated is a fake image or a real image."[110] The generator's objective is "to produce images that are **as realistic as possible** and successfully **fool the discriminator into thinking that the generated images are real**."[111] Likeness (between the actor and what she/he/they impersonate) is achieved through successful trickery performed by and within the algorithm. At play here is a form of performative machine thinking that involves a kind of simulated dissimulation.

In light of all this, "software performs" can be understood in terms of (dis)simulation, as follows: software performs in the sense that it has material, tangible effects in the world; to have software do something, at a very basic level, one needs to write instructions. The fact that software running *does* work in the world is at least partly responsible for the sense of empowerment that software affords to those who are engaged with it: programmers and users. Yet, software sometimes performs in surprising ways, which can be enchanting (or at least interesting) or even outright deceptive, "devious." The latter is responsible for the sense of utter ignorance and powerlessness that it sometimes engenders, even for those who (know how to) write it. At play here is the idea of a predetermined, instruction-based structure that makes possible contingency. If we take this seriously as the idea underlying the work of software and still want to hold onto a conception of software (or code) as performative, then I propose that we understand "performative" in two ways, which in practice are interconnected.

First, at the level of the computer's (machinic) operations, "performative" may be understood along the lines of the notion of performativity outlined in the previous chapter and in relation to the genealogy of machine thinking described earlier in this chapter, which runs through Turing's universal machine, Babbage's Analytical Engine, the Jacquard loom, and back to Descartes. Simply put, performative computer thinking, undergirded by iterability, breaks the world down into (miniaturized) bits/data, which it manipulates. It treats the objects to be computed (the things of the world) as though they were black boxes hollowed out of semantic content. This is simulation.

Second, at the level of human–computer interaction, we need to adjust our (Austinian) understanding of the performative beyond that of language/code "doing what it says": software might do what it says, but what it says is not always what human users take it to mean. Thus understood, and as will become clear by examining Dorsen's *A Piece of Work*, software remains performative (it produces effects) even on the stage, despite Austin's claim that a performative utterance becomes "hollow or void" if produced in the theatre.[112] Yet, the felicity of software as performative both in the theatre and the big wide world is always tinged with unpredictability: there is always the possibility of the infelicity that Austin attributed to the theatre.

PERFORMANCE RELOADED

The notion of a predetermined, instruction-based structure that nevertheless enables contingency (which undergirds software) is not unfamiliar to those working in visual and performing arts. There is an entire genealogy of art and performance running through Marcel Duchamp,

John Cage, Fluxus, Happenings, and Conceptual Art centered on the idea of creating determined, instruction-based structures or scores (be they technological/mechanical or otherwise) that allow for and in fact encourage the unexpected. Aligned with this idea is a (more) distributed decision-making process and the willingness (or accepted imperative) to embrace undecidability regarding the outcome of the art/performance-making process. This is a genealogy of instruction-based art and performance associated with the conceptual avant-garde and driven by an impulse to remove as much as possible the subjectivity of the maker from the art/performance-making process. In this context, "subjectivity" mostly refers to the capacity of making decisions with respect to an outcome—to the human actor's function as agent. This is a function that algorithms run on computers simulate and, increasingly, displace from humans.

Conceptual instruction-based art/performance often involves a certain privileging of the instruction—or, of the "idea" that "becomes a machine that makes the art," as Sol LeWitt wrote—over its materialization, over the outcome of its practical application.[113] In turn, the art-making machine "'lives' through influencing other art, not by existing as the physical residue of an artist's ideas," wrote Joseph Kosuth in "Art After Philosophy."[114] The (posture of the) artist's disengagement from the material ostensibly involves the evacuation of the human (and human subjectivity) from the art-making process so that the idea as machine can do its work. The work done, Kosuth postulates, should function neither as a commercial tool (for entertainment) nor as a philosophical stance:

> In an age when traditional philosophy is unreal because of its assumptions, art's ability to exist will depend not only on its *not* performing a service—as entertainment, visual (or other) experience, or decoration—which is something easily replaced by kitsch culture and technology, but rather, it will remain viable by *not* assuming a philosophical stance.[115]

This insistence on art's "*not* assuming a philosophical stance" is perhaps ironic for, as Peter Goldie and Elisabeth Schellekens note, "philosophy . . . seems to have served not only as an inspiration, but, at times, even as a source of authority and justification for the work performed by conceptual artists."[116] Moreover, the art as machine (as idea)—while it might not "assume" a philosophical stance—nevertheless concretizes a philosophical conception. This is a Cartesian conception of a mind/matter divide, whose logical implications are pushed to the extreme: to the point where information abstracted from a material base becomes "free-floating, unaffected by changes in context" (to borrow Hayles's words), yet always concretizable (as a form of real abstraction).[117] This is the idea as a machine that makes art.

Dorsen's algorithmic theatre—itself a kind of machine that makes art—belongs to the genealogy of instruction-based art discussed above, updated for the digital age. However, it does not privilege the "idea"/set of instructions over their execution. In the case of Dorsen's algorithmic theatre, the instructions are written for the digital machine that in turn will structure the theatrical performance. In *A Piece of Work*, the instructions are made visible—displayed on the onstage screen—at both the beginning ("sys.begin(show.generate(21.12.13 19:36:10))") and end ("sys.exit (0)"), as well as in between the five parts of the performance. Between the five "passes through the text" (as the parts are called in the program notes), the lines of code scroll down the screen. This open display of the code goes against Laurel's call for making the workings of the machine invisible so as not to disturb the "mimetic illusion" playing out at the interface.[118] It may also bring to mind the "baring the code" political project "taken up by artists, hackers, corporations, government and non-government organizations" during the 1990s.[119] What primarily drove this project, which was also related to the development of open-source software (software whose source code is made available for public use), was a democratizing impulse (also shared by the historically prior, at least in its early forms, instruction-based art).

In *A Piece of Work*, the decision to "bare the code" and foreground the work of software seems to have been motivated by a desire to draw attention to the power and ubiquity of algorithms in our lives, and to our ignorance of them and their modes of working. Dorsen has thus declared about *A Piece of Work*:

> I would say if there's anything like a political angle on this, I think it's really coming from how powerless most of us are against these machines which determine more and more of our

lived reality. It feels urgent somehow that those of us who are not programmers, who are not in the tech industries, who are not working with high speed trading things on Wall Street, that we start to at least be able . . . to understand a little what the logic is of these things because a lot is being decided behind the scenes and we kind of play with the interface. But we're not; we don't really have access to the algorithm, which is really where the decisions are happening.[120]

Yet, despite making the code and the principles of algorithmic writing used accessible, A Piece of Work cannot immediately be said to help its audiences understand the workings of software or how decisions are made "behind the scenes." It more likely induces confusion and frustration about what exactly is going on onstage. What it clearly does not offer is a "rich user experience" or any "representational worlds" for the audience to get immersed in—on the contrary. During the show, the lines of code scroll down the screen too fast for a spectator to actually discern what the writing says, perhaps subtly suggesting the incredible speed with which algorithms running on computers can execute operations (for instance, in finance). In fact, even if the spectator were able to discern the writing, this would arguably not make much difference, especially in terms of understanding what is going on in the theatre piece. After all, the algorithms *are* disclosed in human-readable language in the program notes, but they can hardly be said to help a spectator understand what the software is doing or what is going on in the performance. Several of the audience members' responses to A Piece of Work, recorded on the website of On the Boards, testify to this:[121]

> Anonymous, 2013-02-25, 02:32: OtB has delivered some of the most moving and charismatic performances I have seen to date, however, after this piece, I was left frustrated and confused.

> Anonymous, 2013-02-25, 14:30: Spent the time just trying to figure out what was going on—and then just got frustrated.[122]

The source of the confusion and frustration some audience members experienced may have been the disarticulation of the text that occurs when software runs through Shakespeare's *Hamlet* and treats it as data, without much else happening onstage. At certain points in the performance, a sense of rhythm and the potential for unexpected associative meanings may be afforded by the bits of *Hamlet*-derived language rapidly displayed on the screen or uttered by what sound like computer-generated voices (for example: "sleep of death, of time" and "heaven and earth, increase of appetite"). At other points, however, what is produced and displayed on the screen or said out loud by the computer-generated voices representing the characters of the play is gibberish, such as (to pick a few random moments from the performance I saw):

KING: She treache, O min swoodcome drink! I as to mine, againk, cock, the ow.

HAMLET: As sh warremble oratio; re't good drathe th warshatiquory behis sen tricit wor audien pall you! I am[123]

These strings of disarticulated language, it bears noting, are not the result of software malfunctioning but, rather, of software working as it was programmed. So, in the spirit of the theatre, what we have here is software performing *as if* it were "devious." This performed deviousness in the context of the theatre cancels out software's (simulated) dissimulative character—its (designed) acting as though it were human so as to afford the user a personal(ized) experience at the interface. This theatrical operation of the *as if* makes apparent to human audiences not similarity but, rather, difference: In *A Piece of Work*, it gives a sense of software's seemingly "alien" nature.[124]

Just as in cases of actual software malfunction, however, this performed deviousness may cause frustration and confusion for those who have to endure it, especially if they are expecting something "enlightening," "enriching," or "entertaining" from the theatrical performance.[125] Faced with a machine that parses the rich language of *Hamlet* without "any intention," spectators may feel that they are "in a futile situation, trying to get something out of it," as Greg Beller, sound and network designer of the piece, suggests in a "group self-interview."[126] They may be made to feel irrelevant, left out of the process, even redundant—despite their best efforts to "get something out of it." Perhaps it was precisely because of this sense of their own irrelevance as spectators or of the futility of trying to grasp the meaning of the performance that some audience members found the OtB piece to be (really) bad theatre, "the worst play I have ever been to."[127] The experiment proposed by *A Piece of Work*, some OtB audience members suggested, would have been fine to watch for a few minutes in a museum but not as a piece taking place in a theatre, with a certain duration (a little over an hour) that had to be endured as such.[128] In the case of *A Piece of Work*, "enduring" means taking the time to attend to what is going on, to what one is involved in (willingly or not, consciously or not), and to do so to the limit of one's condition as a thinking embodied being. It involves an experience of the world (onstage) and of oneself pushed to the limit of one's condition—in this case, one's condition as an audience member.

In the interview mentioned earlier, Dorsen refines Beller's idea by noting that *A Piece of Work* offers "an experience of witnessing something that both *is* and *isn't*" for the human audience.[129] It is a piece of theatre made by digital machines *for* digital machines, or so it sometimes feels. At one level, from the perspective of software's (programmed) workings in and for the contemporary capitalist system, the sense of being excluded, redundant, and even disposable that the theatre piece produces for human audiences may perhaps raise awareness and concern about the condition of human users within the capitalist system. At a different level, the sense of being excluded may provoke a reckoning with what is called "human" and what is called "thinking," in addition to (or more than just) speaking to the audience's expectations of what theatre does or should do. In fact, the night I saw the show, the phrases fed to the human actor in the third part of *A Piece of Work*, leading up to the well-known (though disarticulated) Hamletian soliloquy, may be interpreted as pointing to this:

ghost

memory

cast

thought

part

wisdom

numbers

cause

sleep

death

dreams

brains . . .

spirit, ambition, quietus, coil, sleep, death, man, seed, things, nature, spirit, commandment, graves, beds, plot, table, memory, whore, heart, tongue, malefaction, quietus, merit, globe, cause, will, strength, means, argument, soul . . . life, forms . . .

conscience, oppression . . .

During the performance I saw, these (key)words were displayed on the screen, one or more at a time, and simultaneously uttered/read by the actor. For the most part, these are words that bear weight, words that resonate. Presented in this way, they also enact a certain "pale cast, cast of thought, of thought, thought" (to echo Hamlet's words, repeated by the actor in *A Piece of Work* around minute 20 of the performance I saw; see Figure 4 for a different set of words displayed on the screen in another version of the performance).

FIGURE 4. Scott Shepherd uttering randomly selected (key) words in *A Piece of Work*, directed by Annie Dorsen, 2013.

Photo credit Bruno Pocheron. Courtesy of Annie Dorsen.

Despite the sense of being a piece produced by digital machines for digital machines that *A Piece of Work* may give its audiences, the performance is in fact produced by a machine that was programmed and tinkered with by humans to work in a certain way. More precisely, at least in the case of the BAM version, it was programmed and refined in such a way that the outcome—although a contingent event—would have as high as possible a chance of being interesting. This is why, in the development of the work between the OtB and BAM performances, a major focus of the process of tinkering with the piece's central controlling system (written in MaxMSP) had to do with constraining the Shakespearean text that the algorithms were "allowed to chew on," eliminating (what Dorsen and her team deemed to be) uninteresting bits of the play.[130] Thus, the data used for algorithmic processing during the show at BAM was Shakespeare's *Hamlet* minus some of the "boring parts" of the play, which was supposed to make the piece more interesting though not necessarily more entertaining.[131] In this way, the audience would *have* to struggle to make sense of what software running live onstage produces without dismissing the digital machine as uninteresting or unintelligent. This is one of the reasons why, in developing *A Piece of Work*, Dorsen and her team abandoned the initial plan to feature a live conversation between a human actor and a computer (for instance, with Shepherd playing Hamlet and the computer playing Ophelia). "The human is just so much smarter than the computer," says Dorsen.[132] That is, the human might be said to be smarter than the computer when the computer's task is to engage in human-sounding conversation (which for theatre audiences would have likely been less confusing and frustrating but perhaps uninteresting). So Dorsen and her team decided instead to let software run the show—on its own terms, rather than the human actor's.

As the *Piece*'s lighting designer Bruno Pocheron put it, "[w]e actively designed, but in the real time of the show we don't touch" it.[133] Left to its own devices for the duration of the performance, the digital machine doing the show sounds broken at times. The night I saw the performance, this was especially true of the fourth part of the piece determined by the algorithmic principle "Generate new scenes by resequencing words using Markov chaining." Here, the repetition—which in the previous parts seemed more or less like an echoing—became so blatant that I had the impression the machine had broken down (a kind of fallibility that is quite different from making mistakes):

GHOST: Adieu, adieu, adieu, remember me.

OPHELIA: Oh, my lord, my lord, my lord, my lord, I have been so affrighted. Oh, my lord, my lord, my lord, my lord, I have been so affrighted.

At one level, this seeming brokenness mimics (simulates) the human that "goes unarticulated in Shakespeare's blank verse form," which "holds in check the messiness of the heart's and the mind's emotionally obsessive and distracted babble."[134] At another level, this apparent brokenness perhaps instantiates the lack of fluidity that defines machine thinking according to Flusser, who channels Descartes's notion of "clear and distinct ideas":

Nobody counts with fluidity (although one may do so correctly). The reason is that numbers are clear and distinct. There are definite intervals that must be between numbers for them to be understood.[135]

In the performance of *A Piece of Work* that I saw, the characters/computer-generated voices displayed this lack of fluidity especially in the final part of the show, when articulate language completely broke down and characters died, repeatedly.

Speaking of breakdown, read (heard, experienced) in the present-day neoliberal context, when spoken by Hamlet and Ophelia, the two characters in Shakespeare's play who appear to lose their minds, the sets of repetitions like the aforementioned ones may suggest a breakdown of communication under stress. At one level, there is a breakdown in the communication between the two characters, who talk past each other. At another level, the breakdown may be in and of the system of communication itself. As Donna Haraway remarked, "[a] stressed system goes awry; its communication processes break down; it fails to recognize the difference between self and other."[136] The biggest threat to a system of communication is, logically, the "interruption of communi-

cation," which "is a function of stress."[137] And yet, the neoliberal capitalist system produces stress just as much as it produces communication;
chronic stress is one of the "neoliberal epidemics" of our times.[138] Thus,
the logical outcome of the functioning of the system, through its ever-
increasing acceleration, is breakdown under unbearable stress.

The sets of repetitions that created (for me at least) a sense of system
breakdown were produced by "using Markov chaining." Markov chains
are random processes involving transitions from one state to another,
in which the current step depends only on the step right before and
not on any other previous steps. They can be metaphorically thought
of as describing "the behavior of a frog in a lily pond."[139] The frog jumps
from lily pad to lily pad, and where it jumps "depends only upon what
information it can deduce from its current lily pad—it has no memory
and thus recalls nothing about the states (lily pads) it visited prior to
its current position."[140] In the director's note to *A Piece of Work*, Dorsen
explains that her choice to employ Markov chains was motivated by
their "quality of operating in a continuous present."[141] At any step in the
process, Markov chains make a probabilistic choice that depends only
on that step/current state. In this way, they seem to exactly enact the
"presentness and instantaneousness" that anti-theatrical modernist art
critic and historian Michael Fried celebrated.[142] According to Dorsen,
the algorithms used in *A Piece of Work* are "memory-less" in that, although they *do* things, they do them without knowing (understanding)
"what they say, or what they said before."[143]

In contrast to the "memory-less" Markov chains that exist in a continuous present, theatre "often claims to aspire to such a state, but in
practice it is a medium made of memory," Dorsen writes in her director's note.[144] More precisely, theatre is a "memory machine" whose
work theatre scholars have often theorized in terms of "ghosting" and
"haunting."[145] At play here is a constant (re)appearing of the same as
different that essentially defines theatre. As Herbert Blau remarks, this
dimension is captured by Marcellus's question about the ghost of Hamlet's father: "What, has this thing appeared again to-night?"[146] With the
ghost and haunting at its core, Shakespeare's *Hamlet* is a paradigmatic
example of the intimacy between theatre and memory as ghosting, as
Marvin Carlson (cited in the program notes for *A Piece of Work*) and

other theatre scholars have noted.[147] As "the central dramatic piece in Western cultural consciousness," Carlson suggests, *Hamlet* appears time and again not only in the theatres but also in our everyday lives: it is so deeply ingrained in our cultural imagination that the play may appear to be "a tissue of quotations."[148]

An artist who worked extensively with theatre as a "memory machine" was Polish theatre-maker Tadeusz Kantor. Performing as "I-The Real One" within collections of many models of the "I,"[149] Kantor played with the ghosting function of theatre to enact the (un)doings of subjectivity—broken in the face of history (Kantor made theatre in the aftermath of the Holocaust and World War II—and of the genocides of colonialism). In his best-known pieces, he activated theatrical space as a "room of memory" (*The Dead Class*) and a "storeroom of memory" (*Wielopole, Wielopole*) inhabited by "negatives."[150] In the storeroom of memory, "patterns of logic" that keep the objects of memory in their place come undone, as Kantor writes:

> Negatives
> do not describe the place of action,
> but are the NEGATIVES OF MEMORY that are interimposed
> that are re-called from the PAST,
> that "slip" into the present moment,
> that appear "out of the blue,"
> that place objects, people, and events together . . .
> that discard patterns of logic, which are binding in everyday
>   life.[151]

In the version of *A Piece of Work* that I saw, the idea of a "room of memory" was enacted in the first part of the show not by populating the theatrical space with negatives extending (and undoing) the memory of an "I-The Real One" but rather, through an evacuation of "objects, people, and events" (the contents of the play) from the rooms and platforms written into Shakespeare's play. Thus, this part of the show, (re)written according to the principle "Excerpt 5% of the play by length, skipping through the scenes in order," consisted mostly of stage directions indicating locations, a set of entrances and exits (written on the screen), as well as a few lines drawn from Shakespeare's play (spoken by computer-generated voices). This was all played in quick succession, which caused some laughter in the audience. I laughed too, though I cannot quite explain why given that, in retrospect, there was nothing comic about it. It might be that this laughter was in fact an internalization on my part of the digital machine's automatisms, which I played back to it, almost in tune with it.[152] Or perhaps it was an effect of not knowing exactly how to respond to the fast-paced, seemingly inexorable forward movement through the play, leaving almost everything (all semantic content) out—and hollowed out, seemingly in ruins.

Here is an excerpt transcribed from the performance, to give but a sense of the software-generated rapid journey through rooms and platforms that took (virtual) place the night I saw the show:

> Act 1, Scene
> (A room of state in the castle.)
> (Flourish.)
> (Exeunt all but Hamlet.) . . .
> Act 1, Scene 3
> (A room in Polonius' house.)
> (Enter LAERTES and OPHELIA.) . . .
> Act 1, Scene 4
> (The platform.)
> (Enter HAMLET, HORATIO, and MARCELLUS.) . . .
> Act 1, Scene 5
> (Another part of the platform.)
> (Enter GHOST and HAMLET.)
> Act 2, Scene 1
> (A room in Polonius' house)
> (Enter POLONIUS and REYNALDO.)
> (Exit REYNALDO.)
> (Enter OPHELIA.)

On the one hand, this theatrical hollowing out of the (play)world may put one in mind of the "hollowing out" of the social world that big data—or what Nick Couldry and Ulises Mejias have called "data colonialism"[153]—enacts. On the other, as staged in the theatre (memory machine), this hollowing out may make room for the audience members themselves to work as (re)writing machines, projecting their own memories amidst *Hamlet*'s ruins, recalling Shakespeare's text or past *Hamlets*, or imagining possibilities for people, objects, and events to occur in those rooms.

Running (seemingly) memory-less algorithms through memory-filled *Hamlet* supposedly leads to a "memory-less" piece of theatre.[154] But, as it has already become apparent, such an account needs to be complicated. For, neither the software that runs the show nor Dorsen's machine-made *Hamlet* is exactly memory-less. Memory is a key category of digital media, of media that runs (on) software. Thinking through the relation between software and memory, Chun writes that "[t]he digital paradoxically produces memory as storage."[155] Such a conflation of memory and storage is paradoxical for, as Chun explains, memory is "a process of recollecting and remembering," whereas "*storage* usually refers to something material or substantial, as well as to its physical location."[156] Through this conflation, digital media emerges as the "truly *time-based media*"—a reanimation machine that ensures the endurance of what is constantly disappearing through its constant refreshing or rewriting.[157] This is what Chun terms "the enduring ephemeral" and the "undead" of information: "neither alive nor dead, neither quite present nor absent."[158] And neither (fully) material nor (fully) immaterial, but—as we call it today—"digital." And, as we used to call it: "theatrical."

At one level, software as memory can be understood in terms of the relentless reanimation of the relentlessly passing/dying. Repetition is key in this process. This model of software as memory resonates with a certain understanding of theatre as a memory machine, associated with what Rebecca Schneider calls an "undecidable space between registers of what is live and what is passed," on which theatre has a "particular purchase."[159] The "ghosting" that Carlson sees as essential to theatre as a site of memory—"both personal and cultural"—encapsulates this undecidability between the living and the passing that Schneider refers to.[160] Insofar as it is a ghosting machine, theatre is also, necessarily, a reanimation machine by virtue of the very nature of the medium, whose business is the repetition of the same that it cannot help but replay as different.

A Piece of Work is as much a memory/reanimation machine as any other theatre piece, if not more so: it "refreshes"—recirculates and rewrites—*Hamlet* by running software as memory through it. In fact, in a sense, it is this particular imbrication of technology and memory that makes algorithmic theatre "work." The impression that *"we are seeing what we saw before"* that Carlson (citing Blau) sees as crucial to theatre as a memory machine is still in place when seeing *A Piece of Work*.[161] In this case, "what we saw before" is a *Hamlet* (Shakespeare's) and also a machine-made *Hamlet* such as, for instance, Heiner Müller's *The Hamletmachine,* or The Wooster Group's *Hamlet,* which also featured Scott Shepherd in the title role.[162] Through its ghosting operations undergirded by repetition with difference, the theatre machine can thus be said to paradoxically (re)produce (sedimented) cultural memory as storage. As discussed above through Chun, digital machines too paradoxically fuse memory, which is "a process of recollecting and remembering," with *"storage"*—"something material or substantial, as well as . . . its physical location."[163] One difference between the theatre machine and the digital machine is that what the former evokes through the ghosting is quite open-ended and will be different for different audience members, depending on their prior knowledge, experience, expectations, mood, etc. In the age of big data and personalization, what one gets to see online also depends on a prior, the difference being that in this case the prior is the user's captured past online behavior, which matters to recommender systems "not in isolation but in relation to others" who are deemed to be like the user.[164]

In this context of thinking through the resonances between the models of software and theatre as memory (that is, ghosting/reanimation) machines, it bears noting that Chun draws on Jacques Derrida's conception of the archive in her account of software and memory discussed above. Derrida, let us recall, summons the ghost of Hamlet's father in order to make his case that

> the structure of the archive is *spectral.* It is spectral *a priori*: neither present nor absent "in the flesh," neither visible nor invisible, a trace always referring to another whose eyes can never be met, no more than those of Hamlet's father, thanks to the possibility of a visor.[165]

At the core of Derrida's conception of the ghost as specter is what he calls the *"visor effect,"* which occurs when we "feel ourselves seen by a look which it will always be impossible to cross."[166] In this regard, Schneider has shown that Derrida's account of the archive through the visor effect seems to forget an important aspect. At least in the case of *Hamlet*, it seems to neglect that the ghost is (to be) staged—put on a stage, in the theatre, in an embodied performance. As Schneider notes, Derrida omits that, as far as the live performance of the play is concerned, "[w]hat the visor effects in staging . . . is that what is *not* seen is not the specter, but the live actor playing the revenant—the live body *enabling the specter to reappear across the surface of live encounter.*"[167]

Interestingly, *A Piece of Work* indeed challenges Derrida's account of the ghost as specter, though not by having a live actor play the revenant. Instead, it has a distinctively theatrical thing playing (or signaling) Hamlet's father's ghost. This is a thing traditionally used in the theatre to create atmosphere and whose presence in a performance, at least in the United States, must be prominently signaled to the audience before the show: machine-generated haze. As material as it is intangible (and thus seemingly immaterial), the machine-generated haze playing/signaling the ghost of Hamlet's father in Dorsen's piece comes through a hole in the center of the wooden stage. Triggered by software, it appears a moment before the words of the ghost, which are displayed in a large-sized font across the screen. With haze playing/signaling the ghost, there is hardly any visor effect to speak of anymore. Instead, there is a pronounced sense of the theatre as a machine with all of its devices, including machine-generated haze, (as if) "trying to do *Hamlet* autonomously" from human input.[168] When software runs the show, theatre appears more evidently (than in other kinds of performances that do not feature software so prominently) as the machine that it is, with its devices for making and unmaking belief.

At this juncture, in light of all of this, it may be worth asking: What happens when the machinic quality of theatre is so prominent that attending a piece of theatre feels like being "actually inside the brain of a machine," as Beller suggests?[169] As Dorsen writes, under these circumstances, the notion of theatre as necessarily and essentially a human enterprise and as necessarily and essentially an enterprise about and for (a certain picture of) the human gets unsettled. The choice of *Hamlet*

as the subject matter/data for this piece of algorithmic theatre is motivated precisely by this possibility since *Hamlet* is, in Dorsen's words,
"the greatest play about what it means to be a human. Or at least, the
most canonical, about what is a man."[170] The title of Dorsen's piece is
taken from that well-known, oft-cited passage about the human from
act 2, scene 2 of *Hamlet*:

> HAMLET: What a piece of work is a man, how noble in reason,
> how infinite in faculties, in form and moving how express and
> admirable, in action how like an angel, in apprehension how
> like a god—the beauty of the world, the paragon of animals!
> And yet, to me, what is this quintessence of dust?[171]

This passage effectively says that human beings, in the end, amount
to little, almost nothing, because of their finitude, their mortality,
their ephemerality ("quintessence of dust"). Dorsen's *A Piece of Work*
takes seriously this notion of "man" as "a piece of work" and of "man"
as amounting to little, almost nothing, and enacts it by denying the
human actor (much) stage time and agency, letting software literally
run the show instead.

Although less stage time means less labor for the actor, it is highly
undesirable in conventional theatre, where the actor arguably wants to
be onstage as much as possible and speak as many lines as possible.
The gesture of denying the actor stage time belongs to a genealogy of
theatre—or, more accurately, a genealogy of writing about how theatre
should and could be good rather than bad theatre—running through
Heinrich von Kleist ("On the Marionette Theatre" [1810]) and Edward
Gordon Craig (*On the Art of the Theatre* [1911]). In this genealogy, the
gesture of denying the actor stage time goes hand in hand with a gesture towards replacing the human actors with other/more-than-human
things such as puppets. For Kleist and, even more so, for Craig, this
gesture was meant to "cure" actors of their vanity, of their desire to
self-exhibit and receive praise, all of which were in Kleist and Craig's
view connected with the "mortality" (ephemerality and fallibility)
of the human being in question.[172] How exactly Craig's conception of
the Über-marionette is to be understood is still a matter of debate in
theatre scholarship. Is the Über-marionette an ideal (in a sense, more-

than-human) actor?[173] Or, is it a non-human puppet?[174] I am inclined to read Craig's Über-marionette both as a more-than-human "artist" (as Craig calls his ideal performer) that a human actor can become, and as a puppet-like substitute for the human that can aid in this becoming.[175] For this "becoming" to take place, actors must rid themselves of (certain conventions of) subjectivity through a practice of self-detachment that is meant to, among other things, help them escape from being subject to their own (whimsical) emotions. This practice of self-detachment is also meant to help actors escape their subjective (in the sense of being limited to a single point of view) perspective and instead become "vessel[s] for a universal, impersonal, divine truth, which is what an Über-marionette is supposed to be."[176]

Dorsen's algorithmic theatre belongs to the Kleist–Craig genealogy insofar as it shares the impulse to eliminate human actors and replace them with machines (digital ones in Dorsen's case, which she says are a little bit "puppet-like"),[177] or at least to minimize the stage presence of human actors. As discussed earlier, Dorsen's first piece of algorithmic theatre, *Hello Hi There*, featured just two computer chatbots onstage. Interestingly, especially in relation to Kleist and Craig, Dorsen was turned down for a National Endowment for the Arts grant because, without human actors, *Hello Hi There* did not qualify as theatre.[178]

This connection with the Kleist–Craig genealogy notwithstanding, Dorsen's algorithmic theatre is not driven by the desire to rid the actors—highlighted in the BAM material advertising the piece as "the Obie winner Scott Shepherd . . . and the theatre legend Joan MacIntosh"[179]—of their subjectivity, even if it seemingly deprives them of agency. Although in Dorsen's machine-made *Hamlet* there is not much place for the actor's subjective perspective—when it becomes apparent, it is mostly in conjunction with the actor's lag behind the machine, her/his failure to keep up with the machine, and her/his exposed vulnerability related to this inability—the actor is not made into "a vessel for a universal, impersonal, divine truth." If anything, the actor becomes a vessel for impersonal, abstract(ed) pieces of data. *A Piece of Work*, as algorithmic theatre, neither uses the actor's subjectivity nor is it in the business of the (re)production of subjectivity for the purpose of a rich spectatorial experience. And there is hardly any identifiable subject and subject–object relation (which underpins subjecthood) at play in *A Piece of Work*. The relation between the human actor and the software that runs onstage can hardly be construed as a relation between a subject and an object. For, in *A Piece of Work*, all the key elements of the performance operate on the same plane, as stage elements. The human actor is but an "alternate output interface," as Dorsen jokes.[180]

On the one hand, the seeming absence of subjectivity may put one in mind of the "total replacement of the subjectivity of a human labour-power" in the context of capitalist automation, which Alfred Sohn-Rethel wrote about.[181] On the other hand, however, the non-(re) production of subjectivity in *A Piece of Work* may be a welcome interruption to the incessant exploitation and (re)production of subjectivity that is distinctive of the neoliberal, post-Fordist mode of production. As Maurizio Lazzarato notes, the form of labor characteristic of post-Fordism is "immaterial labor," whose "'raw material' . . . is subjectivity and the 'ideological' environment in which this subjectivity lives and reproduces."[182] This means both that the worker's subjectivity is being colonized, exploited, and reduced to a set of usable traits as part of the post-Fordist production process and that what is being (re)produced through labor (in order to be bought)—in the form of (prepackaged) "rich user experiences"—is a certain model of subjectivity. In *A Grammar of the Multitude*, Paolo Virno explicitly ties this model of (subjectivity) production to communication, given that we now find ourselves in a situation in which "a conspicuous part of the so-called 'means of production' consists of techniques and communicative procedures."[183] What is being exploited today, he claims, are the "linguistic-cognitive competencies inseparable from living labor"; for this reason, "the speaker as performing artist" is the paradigmatic post-Fordist laborer.[184] In light of this, it seems perhaps unsurprising that "performativity"— which necessarily presupposes the idea of production—was first theorized in relation to language (speech acts).

Thinking of "grammar," it is worth remembering here Philip Agre's argument regarding the "grammar of action" that the "capture" system requires and produces.[185] This model is rooted in "the practical application of computer systems."[186] As Agre argued, "the phenomenon of capture is deeply ingrained in the practice of computer design through a **metaphor** of linguistic activity as a kind of capture."[187] Virno seems to miss (or overlook) this point, making it sound as though (human) language is what is at stake here. If indeed the "means of production" are predominantly technical-linguistic in the post-Fordist world,[188] then this is so insofar as linguistic activity is closely "integrated with distributed computational processes" and insofar as all human activity is "treated as a kind of language" on which a grammar can be imposed.[189] Notably, the capture model allows for a certain flexibility of human activity, by contrast to the Taylorist/Fordist model. This seeming flexibility arguably affords laborers a sense of freedom ("within a system of rule") and "empowerment,"[190] while securing an incredible amount of control for those who deploy the technologies of capture. This goes beyond the space of work, into one's private life, where a certain model of subjectivity (of the consumer self) is (re)produced, captured, and mined for profit, with algorithms being central to this process.

In light of all this, can the non-production of subjectivity in *A Piece of Work* be seen as anti-production? In other words, is the non-production of subjectivity in *A Piece of Work* a gesture that resists, in the space of the theatre and by means of theatricality and performance, the incessant exploitation and production of subjectivity that is distinctive of the neoliberal, post-Fordist mode of production? There is no clear-cut yes or no answer here, but somewhere in between there are several thought-provoking possibilities.

On the one hand, the human actor in *A Piece of Work*, like the neoliberal subject/post-Fordist laborer, does nothing but utter/communicate abstractions—the bits and pieces of the data/text algorithmically drawn from *Hamlet*—struggling to keep up with the machine that feeds her/him the abstractions. In this way, the actor resembles the neoliberal subject/post-Fordist worker, engaged in a constant, (digital) machine-aided production and communication of abstractions, struggling to keep up with the accelerated pace of life (read: work), always lagging behind. Yet, the human actor in *A Piece of Work* actually speaks bits and pieces of human language that has been disarticulated by the grammar of various computer languages. Disarticulated in this way (recall the strings of syllables that sound like gibberish quoted above), human language arguably resists further capture. Also, while the neoliberal subject/post-Fordist worker's "transmitted messages must be 'clear and free of ambiguity'" (recall Descartes's "clear and distinct ideas") "within a communications context that has been completely normalized by management" and in which the "communicational relationship . . . is subordinated to the 'circulation of information,'"[191] the disarticulated language produced during *A Piece of Work* sounds like anything but a message that is "clear and free of ambiguity."

Uttering computer-generated lines, stumbling over bits and pieces of language, not quite catching every word, lagging behind the machine: the speaker (and listener) can hardly be said to be in any way empowered. Doing all this is not easy; it is in and of itself a performance (in the sense of something achieved with great effort) for the human actor, even as what is achieved is ultimately a kind of failure. And there is something touching about this failure. The night I saw the performance, for instance, I was moved by what I perceived to be MacIntosh's vulnerability, and the bits of language she uttered had great gravity. During her/the human actor's part of the performance, several audience members burst into applause (as a sign of empathy? appreciation? support?). Some of us also burst into laughter as the "to be or not to be" soliloquy she spoke got jumbled, producing lines such as: "To be and not to be such is the face," "To be and not to be those is an exercise." In my case at least, the laughter was an expression of my not quite knowing what to do with all this—with this disarticulated text and with this strange linguistic performance.

A Piece of Work's potential for resisting the incessant production of subjectivity and "the productive mobilization" of language and of "the cognitive faculties" distinctive of the neoliberal, post-Fordist mode of production,[192] for which theatre actually has sometimes been taken as a model,[193] is significant. It is especially significant if we keep in mind that, as Galloway points out, "economy today is not only driven by software (symbolic machines); in many cases the economy is software, in that it consists of the extraction of value based on the encoding and processing of mathematical information."[194] In a sense, software can be said to animate capital and make possible the regime of "fugitive accumulation" that defines neoliberal capitalism.[195] In relation to the software-based (re)animation of capital in neoliberal capitalism, the

"continuous present" to which theatre, according to Dorsen, aspires—
the "continuous present" that her piece troubles by letting algorithms
run the show—acquires new valences.

A continuous present—in the sense of a removal of the time lag, of
the interval between buying (a commodity) and selling (labor-power-
as-commodity), between one transaction and another—is an ideal condition for capitalism. And, while the time lag is "essentially built into
capitalism, even if built in as capitalism's own drag, its own Achilles
heel,"[196] and thus cannot be completely removed, it can be reduced. Already in his book *Speed and Politics,* first published in 1977, Paul Virilio
wrote about a "capitalism that has become one of jet-sets and instant
information banks."[197] With the switch to electronic markets in the 1990s
(which would become increasingly automated in the early 2000s) and the
shift to decimalization (stocks quoted in pennies rather than fractions) in
2001 in the United States—penny quotes so tiny and the holding period
for a stock so short-lived that they became increasingly difficult to keep
in mind and calculate by human traders—the instantaneity at the heart
of the capitalist machine has become significantly more . . . instant, so
to speak.[198] Powerful algorithms carried out by computer programs are
able to drastically diminish the interval between buying and selling; the
transactions they operate are executed mind-blowingly quickly and frequently, which explains why finance now mostly runs on (or is run by)
algorithms. As social theorist Stephen Crocker notes, "[n]owhere is this
drive to eliminate time's interval and its potential aberration more evident today than in the so-called 'new modernization' of finance with its
sophisticated devices for compressing time's interval and neutralizing
risk."[199] In neoliberal capitalist times, these time-compressing devices
are, importantly, software-based, software-run. With the aid of sophisticated algorithms and powerful computers, "[s]tock exchanges can now
execute trades in less than a half a millionth of a second—more than
a million times faster than the human mind can make a decision."[200]
Operated faster than the speed of thought, such transactions seem to
happen in a time that is virtual, perhaps hyper-real. This hyper-real time
closely approximates the capitalist ideal of continuous time, of instantaneity; and, with the incessant developments in algorithmic design and
software performance, it keeps getting closer to it.

Seemingly similar to, though significantly different from, capitalism's (ideal of a) "continuous present," novelist, poet, and playwright Gertrude Stein's "continuous present" is "a using everything a beginning again and again and then everything being alike"—though different, Stein will add.[201] Stein's "continuous present" refers to an experience enabled through and by art as a repetition of the same *with/as* difference; call this art theatre if you will. Calling to mind Stein, Schneider reminds us that, like capitalism, theatre too—as a reanimation machine—has the time lag at its heart, inescapably so.[202] In the case of theatre, however, Stein's "continuous present" is in fact "syncopated time"[203]—an opening of the interval to other times, past and future, when one can feel like one can almost touch time, even for a (prolonged) moment. This time is anything but *instant*—it is the theatrical time of myriad tempos, interruptions, delays, intersecting timelines and timescales. As a form of "syncopated time" that has the time lag (delay) at its core, theatrical time is anything but the "presentness and instantaneousness" that Fried desired and that, as he acknowledged, "defeat[s] theatre."[204] The latter characterizes not only capitalism's but, as I elaborate in Chapter 4, also the internet's mode of structuring time, which "has no tolerance for delays,"[205] even as they both have the time lag built into them.

Rather than annihilating the time lag, the piece of algorithmic theatre I saw at BAM "capitalized" on it (so to speak), making the syncopated time of the theatre performance almost palpable. As mentioned before, *A Piece of Work* took the time to display the code at the start of each of the performance parts, and, even if the display was brief, the lines of code scrolling down the screen perceptibly modulated the rhythm of the piece. As already mentioned, in the first part of the show, the scenes, played in quick succession, were so short and their content so scarce that the audience burst into laughter, repeatedly. The five parts of the show had different durations, with the third and the fourth being the longest (respectively, around fifteen and seventeen minutes long in the performance I saw) and the second, the shortest (about five minutes long). Blackouts marked the time at the end of each part of the performance and also repeatedly during the third part featuring the human actor. And the various repetitions of words and phrases underscored the working (the automatism and the possibility of breakage) of the machine—the digital machine, the theatrical machine, and the thinking machine that is, at a certain level, the human. One of the most striking of the sets of repetitions was for me that of "Dies" many times at the end of the show:

(Dies.)
(March within.)
(Dies.)
(March within.)
(Dies.)
(March within.)

This repetition, enacting a seemingly endless (and timeless) feedback loop, sounds as if the machine were attempting to produce a delay of death. In effect, it reinforces a limit condition, which can be negated but ultimately not escaped: death as a singular, one-time event that breaks through (dis)simulation, in the face of which all conventions of subjectivity fade and the question of what it means to be—and to be a thinking, living being—presents itself with renewed urgency. In *A Piece of Work*, as it is appropriate in the theatre, the impression of an endless feedback loop turns out to be an appearance, ended with a simple instruction: "sys.exit." Still, the limit condition that the repeated stage direction evokes and the question that arises in the face of it remain. This question is not to be posed in the abstract, as Descartes did, but from within one's specific location—of thinking and living. Beginning again with thinking machines, the transitional chapter that follows will give an account of such a location as it pertains to this book's embodied authorial "I."

Interlude

AUTO-HISTORY

••• For a long time, I desired to turn myself into a machine, particularly attracted to the idea of becoming a thing that is free from bias and from the baggage of memory and that feels no pain. A few years ago, I attempted the transformation into a machine in a theatre performance titled *How I Became a Thinking Machine*, an embodied thought experiment.[1] In *How I Became*, I performed a character called Doubt-Bot. Modeled on ELIZA, DoubtBot was designed to perform (machine) thinking. It was designed to process information and interact with audience members according to a system of procedures akin to the system employed by ELIZA. Unlike ELIZA, however, it was designed to act not as if it were a Rogerian psychotherapist but, rather, as though it were a Cartesian thinker who throws everything into radical doubt in the context of a dialogue with an interlocutor.

While for some human performers of algorithmic machines the main challenge in embodying this kind of machine is to play the machine's (supposed) lack of emotionality,[2] in *How I Became*, the main challenge for me as a performer of DoubtBot was to restrict my thinking and acting to the predetermined DoubtBot script. The lines I spoke in my interaction with a spectator who volunteered to be DoubtBot's interlocutor had not been memorized in advance. Instead, in order to produce responses to DoubtBot's interlocutor, I had to follow the rules from the DoubtBot script, to execute the given algorithm live in the performance. The main challenge for me was to stick to the rules/script and to *not* improvise the lines in the moment. Improvising the lines might have produced a more interesting interaction with the interlocutor, but it would have ultimately meant cheating. This restriction was challenging because—like Descartes, who at the end of his experiment of radical doubt still found that his "mind enjoys wandering off and will not yet submit to be restrained"[3]—I too found that my mind tends to wander, to get distracted, to do its own thing. It has its own programming (habits of thinking) developed over the years and sedimented in the body; at a certain level, when left to its own devices, it is always already a thinking machine that acts based on my embodied history and memory, including the history and memory of the performer who likes to improvise and not stick to the script. As part of this programming, in a live interactive performance, I—as performer—tend to judge (what I perceive to be) my interlocutor's and the broader audience's reactions, and my impulse is to adapt or modulate my performance in relation to these reactions. A successful performance of DoubtBot requires not giving in to this impulse, voiding my subjectivity and memory in the attempt to simulate the operations of an algorithmic machine.

Ultimately, this was a failed attempt; at best, in this iteration of *How I Became,* I was able to achieve a kind of double thinking, saying one thing and thinking another, and trying my best to dissimulate the latter. This double thinking is in fact also part of my inherited history, having grown up in a country where double thinking had been a habit and mode of survival for decades. Doubting, as a form of deep distrust, was also a tool for navigating life amidst massive and relentless deception, and it is something I have always been good at. This is why Descartes's experiment of radical doubt had a certain appeal for me the first time I read it, in my home in Romania during the time of the transition from communism to capitalism. By the time I created and performed *How I Became a Thinking Machine,* this appeal largely waned as I learned to read Descartes differently and to question my deep investment in Cartesian thought—and Western philosophy more broadly. But I was still interested in the potential for radical doubt to be used as a tool to navigate information environments filled with deception and "fake news," a notion that gained great currency the year when I performed the first iteration of *How I Became*. At the time, my vision for the following stage in the development of *How I Became* was that DoubtBot would become a bot that learns from its past performances and adapts to new interactions, not just changing its routines but also adjusting its script. This idea connects with the "new AI" research inspired from child development rather than from the chess-game model.[4] In the former model, the intelligence of the artificial agents—"like that of the growing child—derives from their situated and embodied interactions with the world."[5] DoubtBot would be developed as a computer program and launched on the internet, to perform doubting on the various social media platforms. I ended up putting this idea on hold, as it became clear that doubt was being weaponized and fueled what was deemed to be a new "post-truth era" (more on this in Chapter 4). But I continue to be interested in turning DoubtBot into a bot that learns from past performances—perhaps in order to better understand the past so as to be able to better navigate the present and imagine futures that do not repeat it. The material that follows in this transitional chapter would form at least part of the database on which this next iteration of Doubt-Bot would be trained.

While in the previous chapters of this book I mostly played the role of a spectator, in this one, like Descartes, I will "mount the stage" as an actor.[6] Unlike Descartes, and against the hollowing out of the thinking "I" and of embodied histories and lived experience that defines his thought experiment and grounds his metaphysics, I will work with an autobiographical method that centers personal recollection and will offer a richly textured account of the historical and socio-cultural context surrounding this "I." I will thus reenact my own embodied thought experiment of an encounter with a malicious deceiver—in fact, two such deceivers: (i) the massive communist apparatus of state deception sustained through a vast surveillance machine (a precursor to big data) and a propaganda machine;[7] and (ii) television, a (dis)simulation machine that represents the *"object-symbol of the transition"* from communism to capitalism in the Romanian context,[8] a transition marked by a televised revolution that was the first and so far only global media event in which Romania played a major part. Both of these malicious deceivers construct synthetic realities, albeit in different ways. And behind both of them lies the internalized imperative to "catch up" with the West, tied to modernity's myth of progress.

Before I proceed, a clarificatory note on my use of the term "communism" is due here.[9] I grew up during a time when to be called "communist" was a stigma; it still is in Romania, where "communism" was officially condemned in 2006 as an "illegitimate and criminal" system by Romania's neoliberal president Traian Băsescu, who was in fact subsequently revealed to have been a collaborator of the *Securitate*, the communist regime's secret police.[10] In his televised address given in Romania's Parliament less than two weeks before Romania officially joined the European Union, Băsescu stated that this public condemnation of communism would "close, with full responsibility, a dark chapter from the past of our country."[11] While it is undeniable that the communist regime was criminal, this programmatic condemnation served a clear political function: that of discrediting the political left and, at the same time, reinforcing the idea that the only way of breaking with the past and moving forward was a wholesale embrace of neoliberalism. According to the anticommunist ideology that Băsescu endorsed as the officially correct position, the remnants of "communism"—taking the form of so-called "communist thinking," "communist habits," and "communist mentalities"—are to blame for the multiple social crises the country has gone through since 1989.[12]

"Communism" in this context should be very much a contested term, even though it evidently is not, and profitably so. The regime that Băsescu denounced as "communist" was only nominally so; initially an import and imposition from the Soviet Union, it could be more accurately described as "one of Europe's most repressive neo-Stalinist regimes" during the second half of the twentieth century.[13] I suggest that it was in fact a repressive form of state capitalism. In this, I follow Satya Gabriel, Stephen Resnick, and Richard Wolff's theorization of "state capitalism," which uses a class-focused approach that looks at "who produced and who received and distributed the surplus."[14] If the receivers and distributors of the surplus are the workers themselves, then the regime may rightly be called "communist." In so-called "communist"

Romania, as in the Soviet Union, however, the receivers and distributors were the upper layers of the ruling party and of the vast state bureaucracy. Romanian industry, just like Soviet industry, was "mostly organized as state-owned enterprises where state officials received the surpluses produced by wage laborers."[15] This kind of organization of labor and profit constitutes what Gabriel, Resnick, and Wolff call "state capitalism." What notably sets apart this form of capitalism from the one that followed it after the revolution is the centrally planned economy and the fact that it was not accompanied by private ownership and by consumerism. As I show below, it is the latter that was gained after the revolution.

While I find "state capitalism" to be an apt characterization of Ceaușescu's regime, in what follows I still use "communism" to refer to it because this is the term that describes that historical period in the Romanian imaginary. As Băsescu implies in his aforementioned speech, in Romania, "communism" is a thing of the past that nevertheless refuses to go away. This past is often perceived to be "a negative capital, an almost pure deficit," as Eva Hoffman wrote in one of several books by travelers to Eastern Europe published in the aftermath of the fall of the Iron Curtain.[16] Due to this perceived "deficit," Romania has been characterized again and again—both in the Romanian and in the Western imaginary more broadly and both during communism and after its fall—as being "backward," temporally behind and in need of "catching up,"[17] an imperative that I too internalized, in my own way.

RECOLLECTION

I grew up on Hegel Street, which was parallel to Moscow Street and perpendicular to Spartacus Street. "Moscow" was a leftover from earlier times, which in the years following the fall of communism many were feverishly trying to forget; it was no longer the official street name because it sounded too obviously communist, but it was still in use. "Spartacus," also still in use, has now been the street's official name for a very long time. Greatly revered in the Soviet Union and throughout communist Eastern Europe,[18] "Spartacus" is the name of "the most splendid fellow in the whole of ancient history. Great general . . . , noble character, real representative of the ancient proletariat," wrote Marx in a letter to Engels.[19] It is also the name with which Rosa Luxemburg and Karl Liebknecht signed their anti-war letters in the wake of the First World War, "suggesting that the proletariat of the Western powers were all slaves about to be sacrificed by the capitalist states."[20] "Spartacus" is still the street's official name probably because few know about its associations with communism. It is the street of my elementary and middle school.

Much of my childhood happened between Hegel, Moscow, and Spartacus Streets, whiling away time with the children of the neighborhood. The best—and most melancholy—autumn in town was on Moscow Street, under chestnut trees with forever inedible chestnuts: richly colored, predominantly yellow and rusty red. Melancholy and poetry aside, the one thing that disturbed my childhood days were my parents' anxieties around the growing debts and their repeated attempts to sell our house on Hegel Street. My parents bought the house in 1995 from Mr. and Mrs. Wagner, who were planning to repatriate to Germany. Mr. and Mrs. Wagner were the original owners and initially sole occupants of the five-room house, but the communists forced them to take on four other families as "state tenants." To be able to buy the house, my parents took out a mortgage that started a growing debt cycle, not helped by the growing inflation, which at one point peaked at over 250 percent.[21] My parents' repeated attempts to sell the house were unsuccessful, for the house was old and required major renovations, which we could not afford. Only around 2005 did they succeed in selling half of it; the other half would be sold when I left for college. But I am jumping ahead . . .

When I was not out in the street with the neighborhood kids, I was for the most part watching TV. With the ever-diversifying offer of TV channels (Cartoon Network, MTV, Eurosport, RTL, Sat.1, and more, in addition to the Romanian Antena 1 and PRO TV) and shows, watching TV soon began to take up most of my spare time, which at some point alarmed my parents so much that they decided to ban television watching. Banning TV didn't work because they were themselves avid television watchers, turning on the TV the moment they got home from work and turning it off late at night. We often watched the weekend night movies together—American "classics" from the 1970s and 80s, which we never had the chance to see at the proper time. But we were catching up fast, at least in terms of entertainment; before long, for an extra fee (which was not unsubstantial, but we felt it was worth it), we even had HBO, a quite up-to-date movie channel. We loved watching HBO not only because of the movies themselves but also because they were not interrupted by the annoying commercial breaks that peppered the programming on all the other TV channels. Except for the movies, however, my parents' and my own TV preferences did not much overlap. They mostly watched the news and the numerous talk shows debating political and social issues *ad nauseam*, which to me at the time seemed uninteresting. There was so much talk and dramatic music and a lot of "breaking news," and it was ongoing, modulating the rhythm of ordinary life in the post-communist times of the transition. Ever present, the television was the *"object-symbol of the transition."*[22]

One of the most memorable events of my childhood was when our TV set was struck by lightning. We were sitting together in the kitchen one evening, the whole family, watching television. It was one of those special days when my sister and I had Coke at dinner, which happened once every two weeks or so because Coke was expensive at the time. There we were, sipping our Cokes with delight, watching TV with the whole family. All of a sudden, there was a flash and then a scary sound, like an explosion, and the whole house was shaken. The television was instantly gone, and it never came back (not that particular TV set). That particular lightning was of an unusual kind: globular (ball) lightning, scientists call it. We figured afterwards that it must have been the satellite dish that attracted this awful lightning into the house; we did not know back then that there was such a thing as global warming.[23] Many of the houses in the neighborhood had satellite dishes attached to them, which to me looked like mushrooms or ears. They were the houses' communication channels with the universe. Soon after the lightning incident, we switched to cable. We did not know it at the time but switching to cable TV was "one of the first phenomena marking the integration of the former socialist bloc into the capitalist global system."[24]

Another remarkable event of my childhood, repeatable only on special occasions because it was expensive, was eating out at McDonald's.

In my hometown Sibiu, the first McDonald's opened in the late 1990s (I cannot recall the exact year). Prior to the long-awaited opening in my hometown, my parents took my sister and me to McDonald's during a visit to Bucharest; that was the first McDonald's to open in Romania, in 1995. In the early years of capitalism, McDonald's was for Romanians a kind of luxury restaurant, as Marian Alecu, the first development (and then general) manager for McDonald's Romania, recalls in an interview.[25] "If you get a top grade in school, I'll take you to McDonald's," my parents—like many other Romanian parents—would promise their kids. The day the first McDonald's opened in Bucharest, thousands of people turned up to buy its products, breaking the restaurant's windows through overcrowding. It was a "money maker," Alecu remarks. "We were the restaurant that had the top sales on its first day of operation, after Russia." The McDonald's leadership in the United States was "a little shocked, amazed, they could not believe it. We had over 16,500 transactions on the first day and around $43,000 in sales."[26] Alecu suggests the following explanation for McDonald's instant success in Romania:

> [ALECU:] There was an ardent desire [among Romanians] to embrace everything American. There was even a kind of despair [desperate need]—including on the political level—for McDonald's to come to Romania. Because McDonald's was considered to be one of the poles of stability for foreign investments in any country. If McDonald's and Shell came, the country was considered to be open for foreign investments.
> [INTERVIEWER:] The United States never bombed a country that had a McDonald's, so they say . . .
> [ALECU:] With one exception, Yugoslavia.[27]

In addition to offering us "a taste of America" (as we perceived it then), McDonald's also provided jobs at a time of rampant inflation and poverty, which would contribute to a massive labor migration. "McDonald's is your first job" became one of McDonald's slogans in Romania, recalls Alecu, whose first post-communist job was actually at the Coca-Cola company.[28] An engineer before 1989, Alecu landed in the well-remunerated (by Romanian standards) Coca-Cola job after he saw an announcement in the newspapers: "Multinational corporation is looking to hire people." Asked by the interviewers if the Coca-Cola hiring team didn't mind having an engineer in the position of a sales manager, Alecu responds: "They did not want people with experience [in the field]; they said they need someone with an absolutely new mind, so that they could teach them from scratch."[29] But not everyone was so lucky as to have the "absolutely new mind" required for new business in Romania. Stuck with unemployment or very low-paying jobs, many would emigrate.

At first it was quite difficult to work abroad legally; a visa was required. Our house was right across the street from the German consulate (where else would the German consulate be located if not on Hegel Street?), so we would see daily those waiting to get a visa; my father and my half-brother, who worked in Germany for a while in the early 2000s, were among them. Hegel Street was packed with cars from Sunday evening to 5 pm on Friday, when the consulate closed. People would drive from other cities in the region and wait in lines for hours in front of the consulate for a visa interview. In 2005, Romania was accepted to join the European Union, and in 2007 it became a member state. This gave Romanians the "right to free circulation" in the European Union, so a visa was no longer required. Around that time, the majority of my friends and our family acquaintances had at least one family member abroad, usually working low-paying jobs, though remunerative by Romanian standards, such as strawberry pickers, babysitters, builders, and cleaning ladies. Others, fewer, would go abroad for college, especially if they were lucky enough to obtain a scholarship.

Going abroad for college was an idea, or "dream," that I began to entertain in the early 2000s, when I gave up watching TV to focus on schoolwork. I figured that, at the very least, I had to become a good student to stand any chance, and there was a lot of catching up to do. The pursuit of this dream involved an extended withdrawal into my room. In this room on Hegel Street, I became obsessed with Descartes, whose philosophy would haunt me long after I left Romania for college. After Descartes, there was Kant, and then Hegel, and eventually Marx. I came to Marx with some delay; having been the preeminent philosopher of the communist state, Marx became one of the most vilified thinkers in post-communist Romania. I came to Marx just around the time when the sense of having to catch up began to recede because I started to question it. Why this relentless imperative to catch up, which I—like my parents and most of the people I knew—so ardently embraced and internalized? There is, of course, a history to it, which goes back(wards) a long way.

PLAYING PROGRAMMED CATCH-UP: MODERNIZATION OUT OF "BACKWARDNESS"

The idea of "backwardness" is tied to the logic of modernity—specifically, to modernity's myth of progress. This logic breeds large-scale deception and violent synthetic realities. In the Romanian context, the idea of "backwardness"—implying that the less developed countries just had to imitate the more developed ones to become themselves developed—emerged in the first half of the nineteenth century among Romanian intellectuals often schooled abroad, in Paris or Vienna.[30] The internalized condition of backwardness goes hand in hand with the imperative to "catch up," which was intensely embraced in the Romanian context both under the communist regime and after its fall, and it continues to this day. This active embrace should not be surprising given that both Romanian communism and what came after it pertain to modernity, even if in different ways. In fact, as Susan Buck-Morss notes, "the historical experiment of socialism was so deeply rooted in the Western modernizing tradition that its defeat cannot but place the whole Western narrative into question."[31]

In communist times, the condition of backwardness was taken seriously, and the idea of the past as a "negative capital, an almost pure deficit"[32] that needed to be overcome became part of the dominant ideology. Here is communist dictator Nicolae Ceaușescu asserting this explicitly in an interview from 1971:

> Romania was 25 years ago among the economically and socially most **backward** countries in Europe. . . . [T]here is still much to be done in order **to do away with the backwardness we inherited from the past**.[33]

Along the same lines, in an interview in the French newspaper *Le Monde* from 1975, Ceaușescu spoke about Romania as "a country . . . that wants to do away with the state of backwardness."[34] Intimately tied to modernity's myth of progress, this insistence on "doing away with backwardness" was ideologically profitable for the communist regime. An instance of what Santiago Castro-Gómez termed "zero-point hubris" (rooted in Cartesian metaphysics), it gave the communist state "the power to institute, to represent, to construct a vision of the social and natural world that is recognized as legitimate and underwritten by the state."[35] Writing off the past as backward and forgetting it altogether served the communist project to radically reprogram society and, in this way, to create a "New Man" and a "New World." When it was not possible to altogether erase the past, any past that did not serve the communist cause would be altered: for instance, a history textbook from the communist era that I used to read in the 1990s contained numerous excisions and modifications.

In the spirit of Marx, Ceaușescu and Romanian communist economists saw the way "out of backwardness"—economic development—as "a linear process, made of successive stages that replace one another at appointed times."[36] Rapid industrialization, coupled with intense urbanization, was taken to be key to catching up and moving forward (modernization). This idea was not unique to communist states; as political economist Cornel Ban notes, "[d]uring the postwar decades, ideologically opposed state managers from Washington to Beijing agreed on one thing: industrialization was the main engine of economic modernization."[37] What was special about Romania, however, was the communist regime's insistence on prioritizing the heavy and petrochemical industries at all costs, even as this was unsustainable and expensive. Feeding this industry at a time of surging oil prices contributed to the economic crisis that preceded and, to an extent, would lead to the collapse of the Romanian communist regime.

The rapid industrialization that was supposed to "do away with backwardness" was programmed. The program was called "The Five-Year Plan" (*Cincinalul*), and the desired acceleration was encapsulated in the slogan that called for accomplishing "The Five-Year Plan" in four-and-a-half or even four years. For instance, a Romanian televised newscast from a "January day in 1953" celebrates the "workers'" (read: communist government's) commitment to realize "The Five-Year Plan in Four Years."[38] "The Five-Year Plan" model and the slogan "The Five-Year Plan in Four Years" had been imported into Romania from the Soviet Union, where "a first 'Five Year Plan' was framed in 1927 for the period from October 1926 to September 1931."[39] In Romania, the first "Five-Year Plan" was drafted in 1949 under the guidance of Soviet advisors and went into effect in 1951.[40] Until 1989, Romania's socio-economic life was continuously driven by largely unrealized and unrealizable "Five-Year Plans."[41]

In his essay from 1930, French Marxist theorist and activist Boris Souvarine explicitly points to the connection between "The Five-Year Plan" and the logic of "catching up." He asks in this regard (to paraphrase): Catching up with what? Is "The Five-Year Plan" supposed to enable communism to catch up with capitalism and overcome it? Yes, responds Souvarine, asking further: "But 'catch up with and overtake' *which* capitalist countries? . . . [T]hose European countries that are most advanced from the point of view of industrial civilisation, or solely the United States?" There is ambiguity on this score on the part of the "originators" of the Plan.[42]

In the USSR, the idea of realizing "the Plan in four years instead of five" emerged in August 1929. Unheard-of dramatization (hyperbolization) in the media of the time accompanied its emergence: "In the entire Russian Communist press and elsewhere, it is no longer a matter of a hurricane, an avalanche and a torrent as metaphors for the effects of the Plan, and the most moderate adjectives now in use are 'formidable,' 'gigantic,' 'unheard-of,' 'prodigious,' 'grandiose' and 'fabulous.'"[43] A pamphlet about the Plan, distributed widely inside and outside of USSR, celebrated the "dazzling rapidity, unexampled in world history, the overwhelming enthusiasm with which the workers of the Soviet Union are building up socialism" driven by "a new objective: 'The Five Year Plan in Four Years!'"[44] This kind of intense, hyperbolic dramatization breeds deception as (un)reality. But this kind of deception is not total. Souvarine calls it out for what it is, even if many act as though they believe in it: "This is a remarkable example of many types of deception being used to cover one and the same thing."[45] Namely, this deception is meant to cover up the exploitation of the workers and the violence against any kind of resistance to it.[46]

This was also the case in the Romanian communist context. The intense dramatization was meant to cover up the unrealizability and ultimate failure of the Plan and of the system more broadly, but it fell short of the effect of total deception:

> What did "The Five-Year Plan in Four Years and a Half" ulti-mately mean? It meant self-praising telegrams sent to the Party's General Secretary, [saying] "We've achieved it. We've done it. We've done in four years and a half what we were meant to do in five years. And our country has reached new heights of progress and civilization."[47]

The above declaration belongs to Tiberiu Cazacioc, "economist" during communist times, as the TV image announces. I heard it on a TV show, *Comunism pe Burta Goală* (*Communism on an Empty Stomach*), hosted on the Romanian TV channel Realitatea TV (Reality TV) twenty years after the fall of communism. In this show, various "everyday" people shared their memories of communist times. Each episode had a differ-ent theme; "The Five-Year Plan in Four Years and a Half" was one of them. Thinking about this theme, another TV show participant, Ştefan Doagă ("worker from Tecuci," according to the TV image), stated: "To be direct about it, Ceauşescu was very well lied to about The Five-Year Plan. We never produced as much as we reported."[48] "The Five-Year Plan" was thus associated with a vast dissimulation apparatus that produced synthetic data but that—unlike present-day synthetic data (fake, simu-lated data as opposed to "real-world data") fed to AI-based models[49]— was ultimately a failed performative. In retrospect, it appears that the (only) one who was subject to total (self-)deception during communist times was the dictator himself, Ceauşescu.

Another participant on the Realitatea TV show, Toni Grecu— revealingly, a computer engineer during communist times, a full-time actor and humorist afterwards—offers an analogy between "The Five-Year Plan" and Prince Charming, a character from Romanian fairy tales and jokes who is well known for his special relationship to time/ growth: "It [The Five-Year Plan] is exactly as in the jokes with Prince

Charming, who would grow in one year like others in ten so that at ten he would look as though he were one hundred."[50] "The Five-Year Plan in Four Years and a Half" speaks to the desire to buy time, which is necessary for "catching up." The irony, as Grecu points out, was that this kind of growth—based on bought time and intensely dramatized reality—in fact meant growing old. Or, in line with the logic of modernity, with its intense production of the new, it meant growing outdated.

According to Romanian historian Lucian Boia, the industrial performance of communist Romania had "a delay of 100 years" (alternative translation: was one hundred years behind).[51] Ceauşescu had absurdly insisted on "heavy industry, as heavy as possible," at a time when "Western economy was undergoing a process of 'dematerialization,' re-orienting itself towards the service sector."[52] By 1990, Romania's heavy industry was officially declared as being of the past by Romania's first post-communist prime minster, Petre Roman. In his words, it was merely "a pile of scrap metal" that needed to be gotten rid of as soon as possible.[53] This was of course profitable for the new regime: after 1989, "the Romanian industry has been abandoned, sold for nothing and then destroyed to allow—at any price—foreign capital to flood and destroy everything that was Romanian."[54] The ruined heavy industry thus became part of a past that had to be left behind and overcome in post-communist times. Certain "communist" habits and mentalities are also part of this past that appears to be "an almost pure deficit" (to recall Hoffman's formulation). This past, in a post-communist mindset, is responsible for Romania's condition of backwardness in relation to a West with which the country must still catch up. The time of the "transition" out of communism is thus marked by a supposedly "ontological delay" in relation to the "West," in spite of Ceauşescu's move to pay off all of Romania's external debt—ahead of time.[55] It seems as though the lag behind, the backwardness, can never be eliminated, only looped back. We are stuck in a vicious feedback loop, or so it seems from the perspective of the logic of catching up.

So let us try to abandon this logic, even if it will continue to haunt us, and return to the past once again. Let us return to it not as a "pure deficit" that needs to be overcome, erased, or forgotten, but as a (multi)temporal opening filled with possibility—at the very least, the possibility to rethink what happened and connect it with more recent developments. This return will make apparent the operations of the communist dis/simulation apparatus, the ultimately failed malicious deceiver through which the reprogramming of society happened. I write "dis/simulation" here to indicate that the conjoining of dissimulation and simulation was not fully realized for, although violent, the voiding that the apparatus performed was incomplete. It would take a different kind of programming for the kind of control desired by the communist regime to be fully achieved.

THE DIS/SIMULATION APPARATUS OF
THE TOTALITARIAN COMMUNIST REGIME

In the Romanian totalitarian regime, like in other totalitarian regimes, the reprogramming of society and its attendant (re)construction of reality was enabled and enforced by a state apparatus that had as main functions: policing, surveillance, and propaganda. The first two were forcefully performed by the secret police/security service, the Securitate; the last, by a propaganda machine whose job was to construct Ceaușescu's image as a god-like figure and world leader through intense dramatization (the personality cult). Both worked through dissimulation but ultimately failed in terms of simulation.

The Securitate's operations turned everyday life in communist Romania into a kind of reality TV show of a quite terrifying sort. In order to function, any apparatus needs to have a subject-object, which has to be found or produced. Even in the absence of actual enemies, the apparatus of the political police had to fabricate enemies to ensure its continued existence. As Romanian philosopher Gabriel Liiceanu notes based on his personal experience, the function of the Securitate was that of "total surveillance."[56] This involved the ongoing collection of information that could potentially be turned into valuable "proof"—a logic that bears a resemblance to today's big data "surveillance economy," in which an ever-growing number and kinds of data points are collected on consumers and mined for valuable marketing insights and for "social classification, prediction, and control."[57] In the context of communist Romania, the ongoing collection of information undergirded a system of generalized complicity in which anyone could potentially become a Securitate collaborator. The array of Securitate's techniques of total surveillance was vast, ranging from all sorts of recording devices to "the penetration of one's entourage."[58] The latter involved "selecting [Securitate] informers from amongst the subject's best friends and even his/her partner."[59]

The work of the Securitate consisted, for the most part, in the ongoing fabrication of synthetic realities—synthetic in the first (dictionary) sense discussed earlier in this book, namely "devised, arranged, or fabricated for special situations to imitate or replace usual realities,"[60] and only partly in the latter (involving simulation based on abstraction that voids sensory, lived experience and historical context). Often, the fabrication involved the dramatization of the everyday (routine) existence of the subjects under surveillance through given code names, numerous photos taken of them, and the absurd ways in which the informers reported on them.[61] Rather than reinforcing identification with communist ideals, at play here is a form of reverse identification, where one's identity is quite literally taken out of one's hands—and body. Reverse identification produces a (Hegelian-sounding) "not-I," which one (the "I") had to constantly struggle to disprove and overcome.

Regarding the apparatus of total surveillance, Boia wrote about a "politics of ongoing harassment."[62] Romanian poet Ana Blandiana recalled that "surveillance was total, so total that any solidarity was impossible."[63] Under such conditions, the ordinary became perpetually extraordinary. If, in Descartes, ordinary life is to be put on hold during the experiment of radical doubt because such doubt renders it absurd, in a totalitarian system, the apparatus of total surveillance produces radical doubt as the norm that structures everyday life and absurdity as the defining marker of lived experience. Unlike today's big data machine, which thrives on social connection (connectivity), this apparatus was designed to foster disconnection. But there are also key similarities between these two machines of surveillance: they both engage in the hollowing out of the social—the Securitate by isolating people from each other and destroying their "political capacities" and "the public realm of life," which philosopher Hannah Arendt argues is at the core of tyranny;[64] and big data by turning social relations into "the economic system, . . . or at least a crucial part of it, as human life is converted into raw material for capital via data," as Nick Couldry and Ulises Mejias have shown.[65]

The two machines of surveillance are also both used in order to foster divisions, albeit in different ways. In *The Origins of Totalitarianism*, Arendt writes that "totalitarian domination" destroys "private life"; "loneliness" is its "essence."[66] By "loneliness" she means a negation of the "capacity for experience and thought" that is shared, held in common.[67] In the totalitarian regime in Romania, this was due to the distrust sown by the Securitate with its infiltration techniques and its extensive web of informants. In the age of big data, a kind of loneliness is achieved through what Eli Pariser has termed "the filter bubble," where algorithms feed us what they think we like based on our tracked and correlated past activity,[68] and through the creation of echo chambers that fuel polarization (on which more in Chapter 4). Both of them thrive on what Couldry and Mejias have called—writing specifically about big data—the voiding of "the self's minimal integrity," the eradication of the ability to have a space of one's own and to "control what passes through that space and whether it 'ends with' the self or not."[69] It is precisely this space that is also annihilated in Descartes's malicious deceiver scenario discussed in Chapter 1, in which the subject-object of the deception no longer has the space to think one's own thoughts. Notably, implicit in this scenario is the idea of surveillance, for the malicious deceiver must presumably be always watching the one whom he is deceiving—or at least give the impression that he is watching, as in the model of the panopticon.[70]

In a play by Romanian-French playwright, poet, and journalist Matei Vișniec from the trilogy *Procesul Comunismului Prin Teatru* (*The Trial of Communism Through Theatre*), the central character—Russian theatre director Vsevolod Meyerhold—describes this violation of one's mental space through the internalized Voice of Self-Censorship, played by his wife Tania, as a "masquerade" (a word that will resurface later in this chapter, in another context):

MEYERHOLD: No, I refuse this masquerade . . . What is happening in this moment cannot be true. Inside my head, I am a free man. Still, still, still, no one can enter in this way inside my own head.

TANIA BECOME THE VOICE OF SELF-CENSORSHIP: Yes, it can. The working class can.

MEYERHOLD: Still, still, still ... my head is a private space ...

TANIA BECOME THE VOICE OF SELF-CENSORSHIP: No! In our country, private property has been abolished.[71]

This passage suggests the hollowing out of an interior space of the human—a move that has its roots in Descartes's thought experiment and metaphysics. Both in the regime of totalitarian surveillance and in that of big data, the interior space of the human (comprising intentions, beliefs, desires) is inferred from external (patterns of) behavior. Liiceanu describes this process in terms of "the suppressing of the relation between an 'inside' and an 'outside.'"[72] In the age of big data, the interior is hollowed out as the individual—reduced to and relentlessly shaped into a consumer—is abstracted into what Gilles Deleuze has termed a "dividual":[73] a collection of extracted and correlated demographic and behavioral attributes. Antoinette Rouvroy has called this mode of producing knowledge (or, more precisely, predictions) about a self "data behaviourism."[74]

These similarities notwithstanding, the specifics—and specific technologies—of the model of surveillance in a totalitarian regime such as that of communist Romania and that in a big data regime certainly differ, and this difference may be articulated in terms of the difference between what Deleuze termed a "disciplinary society" versus a "control society" or what Philip Agre termed a "Big Brother" model of surveillance versus a "capture" model of surveillance.[75] As Agre notes, these two models, however, "are not mutually exclusive";[76] in fact, in certain aspects they coexist. To deny this and read today's control society as involving *"no explicit prohibitions*, no blocked possibilities, no forbidden ways" but only offering "opportunities and temptations," as James Brusseau does in his effort to update Deleuze for the age of big data,[77] means to disregard the ways in which aspects of the disciplinary society and the Big Brother model of surveillance do persist today, even as they are applied unequally to different populations, across intersecting lines of race, gender, class, sexuality, and ability. The difference between them notwithstanding, the point of drawing this connection between surveillance in a totalitarian regime and today's big data regime is to highlight the ways in which certain modes of operation involved in the regime of big data are totalitarian in nature. This is true not only in the case of present-day communist China, with its algorithmic surveillance system rooted in a secret police model that shares some similarities with the Romanian Securitate (in fact, Mao's China served as a great inspiration for Ceauşescu's vision for the reprogramming of the Romanian society), but also in the case of democratic countries that see (and have historically seen) themselves as anti-totalitarian. Consider, for instance, that the roots of present-day data practices in the United States are to be found in chattel slavery, which approximated a totalitarian system of extreme viciousness within a capitalist democracy.[78]

In her book *Weapons of Math Destruction,* Cathy O'Neil offers an account of the computerized algorithm-based mathematical models that increasingly regulate—and even police—all areas of life in the age of big data. She particularly focuses on the kind of mathematical models that she calls "Weapons of Math Destruction" (WMDs). WMDs operate on a large scale, have widespread effects, and are scalable. These "math-powered" applications that now run the (big) data economy are—"like gods"—opaque, and their often indisputable verdicts "land like dictates from the algorithmic gods."[79] They tend "to punish the poor and the oppressed in our society," those deemed to be disposable, "while making the rich richer."[80] The WMDs' operations (re)produce injustice and inequalities, often along racial and class lines.[81] The ample case studies that O'Neil offers to support her argument range from teachers' test scoring, to predatory advertising and loans, e-scoring, the insurance system, job searches, models that track productivity at work, recidivism models in the prison system, and predictive models employed by the police. O'Neil shows repeatedly how computerized mathematical models misunderstand and misrepresent data, breed confusion, and perpetuate inaccuracies and errors with harmful effects for many. In turn, they (inadvertently) compel people to engage in deception, to try to trick the system so as not to lose their jobs or suffer other harmful consequences of the WMDs' verdicts.[82]

Similarly, under the conditions of Romanian totalitarian communism, the radical doubt that the Securitate's surveillance operations sowed gave rise to dissimulation as a mode of self-protection and survival. In this context, dissimulation took the form of what Boia called the phenomenon of "double thinking" and "double existence,"[83] in which—in the words of Romanian historian Neagu Djuvara—people "thought one thing and said another."[84] The phenomenon of double thinking is intimately tied to an (internalized) imperative to perform under the conditions of total surveillance. The performance imperative can be formulated in the terms used by performance theorist Jon McKenzie: "Perform—or else." In his book by the same title, McKenzie quotes these words from the 1994 issue of *Forbes* magazine. Theorizing "organizational performance," McKenzie spells out what is missing: "Perform—or else: you're fired!"[85] In the field of labor of Romanian totalitarian communism, McKenzie's formulation would take the form: "Perform—or else you're fired or imprisoned (or even disappeared)." In this context, in contradistinction to the (postindustrial) American context within and about which McKenzie primarily writes, "performance" means not ever-greater productivity but, rather, a dis/simulation of productivity in order to cover up a lack of productivity. This term, "dis/simulation," with the split that structures it, contains within it the razor-thin difference between concealment (which hides a reality without fully voiding it) and performativity (which produces a new reality through negation as a form of voiding, of hollowing out, as I discussed in the previous chapters).

To give a fuller sense of the practice of dis/simulation and the imperative to perform as they play out in communist Romania, I report here an anecdote that a friend, who at the time was working as a researcher at the Research Institute for Computer Technology in Bucharest, shared with me. During his 1975 state visit to Japan, Ceaușescu was taken to see, among other things, a car assembly factory, where robots (automatized arms) were used in the assembly process to increase the efficiency and productivity of labor. Following this visit, Ceaușescu sought to implement something similar in Romania and started a national program of robotics that was charged with developing such automatized arms for the Romanian automobile industry. Under Ceaușescu's orders, the program was quickly put in place, but the researchers and engineers employed did not make much progress over the years. My friend, a computer scientist, explained to me that this lack of progress was due to a technical issue having to do with the control of an automaton's feedback loop. The automatic system enters into an oscillation and fails to fulfill the task at hand; in the case of an automatic arm that is supposed to reach and grab an object, for instance, it persistently misses the target object as it moves too much to the left or too much to the right, on and on.

The automation program was being carried out at the Factory of Automation Elements in Bucharest. Every now and then, Ceaușescu would visit the factory to observe the progress. For every such visit, an exhibition would be put together in a hall of the factory, with the latest developments on display. Multiple rehearsals would happen in preparation for the visit. Party officials, ministers, and even the prime minister would inspect the exhibition a few days prior to Ceaușescu's visit to make sure that everything was in order. Because the progress Ceaușescu was expecting had not been made, for one such visit (around the year 1984), the engineers decided to manually manipulate, from behind a curtain, the arms displayed in the exhibition. The manipulation was by no means a total secret: the party officials and even the prime minister who had visited the exhibition prior to Ceaușescu's scheduled visit knew about the staging of what should have been automatized arms. The only one who did not know that the seemingly automatized arms were not in fact automatic was Ceaușescu. "Why this elaborate performance?" I asked my friend. His answer: "Out of fear." If Ceaușescu had found out that the research had been unproductive and that little progress had been made, the engineers and researchers involved and even the party officials risked losing their jobs (and perhaps more than that). Fear and the demand for productivity and progress breed dissimulation as an imperative—and as a survival strategy. In the face of a (police-backed and enforced) system that thrives on mass deception, individuals engage in deception as a strategy for survival.

The lived experience of thus performing in the grand staging of (someone else's) total deception can be encapsulated by the code phrase "the theatre of the absurd," which in the Romanian context has great resonance (particularly due to its associations with the Romanian-born "father" of the theatre of the absurd, Eugène Ionesco), and which my friend also mentioned when relating the staging of the manually manipulated "automatic" arms. In the post-communist era too, this phrase would be often used as a way to make sense of, or at least name, the collective experience of frustrating senselessness.[86] Vilém Flusser wrote that "the absurd" is a fact of everyday life in a world that is "programmed"; it characterizes the "functionality" of the programming apparatus.[87] This is true in both communist and post-communist Romania, albeit in different ways.

In communist Romania, the reprogramming—performed by humans using largely analog means—ultimately failed. Using dissimulation as a survival strategy to a certain extent hampered the kind of total reprogramming of society that Ceaușescu the dictator desired. While its operations were far-reaching and violent, the Romanian communist regime's surveillance machine was not as efficient as it could have been had it had the computing power and data capture and processing ability available today, and had it offered the kinds of engaging services and entertainment for which today's consumers are paying with their data. In fact, the official channels of the Romanian communist regime (its propaganda machine) were quite bad at entertaining its citizens (subjects). Ultimately, it was Ceaușescu himself who got caught in the web of mass deception wrought in response to his orders as well as in the self-inflated image that he manufactured for himself though the state's propaganda machine, the other main component of the communist state's dis/simulation apparatus, to which I now turn.

In addition to the Securitate, which suppressed any possibility of dissent, the communist propaganda machine helped manufacture Ceaușescu's inflated image as a god-like figure and world leader through the cult of personality. To reinforce his god-like image, Ceaușescu's regime severely curtailed Romanians' access to an outside of the country, especially to the West, in a way substituting itself for the "outside." The people's relation to an outside was tied to strictly official channels (the propaganda machine)—except for those who fled the country, risking and many of them losing their lives. The operations of the propaganda machine involved the display of Ceaușescu's face in all public institutions and wherever else possible; rallies and media production lauding the Communist Party and its leader; the rewriting of history and strict censorship of all cultural production; and television, which in the 1980s had very restricted programming and that only on the Romanian national TV channel.[88] This propaganda machine was a dis/ simulation machine, one that covered up the realities of everyday living in the country with an overinflated image of the communist leader and party, but it ultimately failed in fully voiding and replacing them with a simulated picture of society.

Engaging with the archives of Ceauşescu's propaganda machine, Romanian screenwriter and director Andrei Ujică's documentary film, *The Autobiography of Nicolae Ceauşescu* (2010), (re)presents an apparatus that captures both the construction of a god-like figure and the making of a world leader. *The Autobiography of Nicolae Ceauşescu* consists of a montage of ready-made images that captures what Romanian poet and cultural journalist Bogdan Ghiu termed "the autobiographic condition of history," "reactivated" by Ujică "as ready-media."[89] The images were extracted out of two official archives: the Romanian Television and the National Film Archive. Ujică turned "1,000 hours of official state broadcasts and intimate home movies into a three-hour tour-de-force that depicts how Ceauşescu created the country in his own image, regardless of the cost to its citizens."[90] The archival images are presented without the propagandistic commentary that used to accompany them, in chronological order with the exception of the opening scene.

Here are some of the scenes that make up *The Autobiography*: Charles de Gaulle visits Romania.[91] He declares, among other things: "Most importantly, Romanians and French, we all want to be ourselves, that is, in the words of Eminescu [Romania's national poet], we want the national state, not the cosmopolitan state." In another scene, Ceauşescu, up in a balcony, gives a speech to a large square full of people:

> The five socialist countries' invasion of Czechoslovakia is a big mistake and a severe threat to peace in Europe and to the fate of socialism in the world. There is no justification and no reason to accept, even for a second, the mere idea of a military intervention in the internal affairs of a kindred socialist state.

The audience cheers enthusiastically. Another scene features Richard Nixon's visit to Romania. The two leaders give speeches; in front of the stage where they stand banners read: "Long live the friendship between the Romanian and the American peoples!" Nixon speaks, and says—among other things—exactly these words, in Romanian. He also states that this is "the first visit of a president of the United States to Romania; the first state visit by an American president to a socialist country or to this region of this continent of Europe."

In another scene, there is a gigantic parade; performers—in huge numbers—are enthusiastically greeting Ceaușescu. In the background of it all: Mao's image, in Tiananmen Square . . . Ceaușescu waves good-bye to Mao. Cut. Ceaușescu visits a factory somewhere in China; an ocean of workers cheers him, again and again . . . Blackout. Ceaușescu gives a speech:

> The measures we take in the areas of ideology, culture, and edu-
> cation will surely signify a landmark in abolishing backwardness
> in this field, in improving the ideological activity which is in-
> tended to contribute to transforming communist consciousness
> into a huge revolutionary force in our society.

Cut. On the National Romanian TV, a man reads from a written statement:

> The theatre belongs to the people, as do the plowed fields and the
> factories. . . . Socialist theatre can only be a theatre of the socialist
> society, of a world of one faith only, one homeland only, one ideal
> of beauty, good and truth, the communist ideal. That is clearly
> and illuminatingly explained in comrade Ceaușescu's speech on
> July 9th.

Aside (my own): this is generally believed to be the moment when the image of Ceaușescu as a god-like figure began to emerge, after his visit to Mao's China and inspired by it . . . We now see the ceremony through which Ceaușescu is proclaimed "president" of the Socialist Republic of Romania . . .

Another scene of the *Autobiography* presents President Carter making a speech:

The people of the United States are honored to have as our guest
a great leader of a great country. It is a great benefit to me as president to have the chance to consult with a national and international leader such as our guest today. His influence as Romanian
leader throughout the international world is exceptional.

In another scene, Ceaușescu is shown riding in a convertible car with
North Korean leader Kim Il-sung; masses of people, with pom-poms
and flags in hand, cheer them from both sides of the road. Cut. Parade
in big open square in Pyongyang filled with people/performers. Cut.
Still in Pyongyang: gigantic parade on a stadium with a sea of performers dancing, singing songs in praise of the Romanian Communist
Party, forming letters with their bodies—"Romania," "Ceaușescu."

Portrayed as world leader and god-like figure, the Ceaușescu that
emerges out of Ujică's *Autobiography* functions as a kind of iconic
brand. In his study of cultural branding, Douglas Holt writes that
iconic brands have often "been built through the mass media" and that
they "address the collective anxieties and desires of a nation."[92] Provocatively, Ghiu reads *The Autobiography* in terms of an autobiography of
a "Sub-Eastern," "pluri-dominated" place caught in-between empires;
it is an autobiography, he suggests, in which an entire (Romanian)
nation can mirror itself. In this reading, Nicolae Ceaușescu functions
as a "collective, folkloric historico-biographic hero," and Ceaușescu's
"auto-history" appears as an incessant "attempt to translate the *subal-
tern* condition of the European Sub-East into an alternative version, as
an articulation of a *subalternative* reconfiguration of history."[93] In this
"auto-historical" endeavor, writes Ghiu, Ceaușescu proposed a kind of
"personal-worldwide communism" sustained through alliances and an
incessant search for allies in the Global North and in the Global South.[94]

Ghiu's point is well taken, but it bears noting that Ceaușescu's many
visits and diplomatic connections with the Global South are for the
most part absent from Ujică's *Autobiography*. This is conspicuous given
that forging alliances with the Global South was an important dimension of Romania's external policy during Ceaușescu's dictatorship. In
addition to numerous state visits, especially to countries in Africa, this
policy involved Romania's rebranding itself as a "developing country"

and a program of foreign aid (in the form of "material support" and "technical assistance") that Romania offered to non-communist "developing countries."⁹⁵ This aspect of Romania's foreign policy under Ceauşescu is complex, and a sustained engagement with it is beyond the scope of this book. Nonetheless, I do want to mention here, if only in passing, its discursive construction, which reinforces its importance to Ceauşescu's particular way of making (Romania's) history. In her analysis of this issue, Mirela Oprea points out the discursive processes underlying Romania's foreign policy regarding the Global South, which include: Ceauşescu's numerous speeches on development matters; Romania's membership in the Group of 77 ("a unique status for a member of the socialist 'block'"); numerous articles "describing the living conditions of the 'poorest of the poor' in the developing World" published in Romanian (state) publications and many writings discussing "Romania's 'vision' of underdevelopment and the ways to tackle its causes"; as well as "numerous 'calls' launched by Romania for the 'rich countries' to take action against global poverty."⁹⁶

If the connections with the Global South represented a significant component of Ceauşescu's foreign policy, political life, and vision, why are they almost completely absent from *The Autobiography of Nicolae Ceauşescu*? Romanian philosopher and cultural theorist Ovidiu Ţichindeleanu has suggested that, "in the context of a film of this magnitude, this absence . . . becomes a commentary on the Eurocentrism of the standard perception of Ceauşescu's life and career, and on how Eurocentrism limits the perspective on one's own history."⁹⁷ To build on Ţichindeleanu's point, the absence of the connections with the Global South from *The Autobiography* may also speak to a national (auto)perception operating on an East–West axis (a leftover from the Cold War period), which—at least since 1989 but arguably also before—has been coupled with a desire to catch up with and be of the West, to westernize (evident in Romania's NATO membership and the accession to the European Union). Even if this point holds, in Ujică's *Autobiography* the "commentary" regarding the Eurocentric, East–West perception is so subtle and reliant on prior knowledge that, as Ţichindeleanu points out, it risks reproducing the dominant, Eurocentric mode of interpretation.⁹⁸ To avoid this, the spectator needs to bring context and critical thinking to the assemblage of images that constitutes *The Autobiogra-*

phy, so that the images can function not as pure images voided of context but as a complex "configuration pregnant with tensions" (to borrow the words of Walter Benjamin).[99] This means hard work, as does watching the stream of images filled with Ceaușescu's face for three hours. As Țichindeleanu suggests, this work also involves reckoning with the "historical question" that Ujică's film poses to its viewer, a viewer "who becomes the real 'author' of one's world-image": "who am I, before and after Ceaușescu?"[100]

The conspicuous absence of the connections to the Global South from *The Autobiography* notwithstanding, it bears noting that talk of the "developing countries" appears explicitly towards the end of Ujică's documentary. It appears in a speech that Ceaușescu gave to a Romanian audience a week after the meeting of the Political Advisory Committee of the Socialist States of the Warsaw Treaty (to which Ceaușescu is referring in the following), during which the Soviet leader Mikhail Gorbachev spoke about "the possibility of an end to the Cold War."[101] In that speech, Ceaușescu declared:

> In this meeting, we also discussed issues of world economics and especially the situation of developing countries. That's because at present the situation of developing countries is especially dire. Over 4 billion people live in poverty and during this decade their situation continued to worsen while the rich countries, and within them a small group of rich people, have annually accumulated dozens and dozens of billions of dollars from the developing countries. This situation cannot continue any further. This is the world that certain gentlemen urge us to revert to. A world of inequality, robbery, exploitation. . . . These circles and these people should direct their attention to what concerns two directions: how to eliminate the exploitation of developing countries; settling the external debt of one billion two hundred . . . 1200 billion dollars of these countries. And not through symbols. Symbolism may be good in art but it's worthless in economics and politics.[102]

Given the scarcity of documentation of Ceaușescu's (and Romania's) ties to the "developing countries" in *The Autobiography*, this speech seemingly comes out of nowhere and feels out of place. To Ceaușescu's audience (in the film image) too it might have felt that way, even as they cheered "Ceaușescu heroism, Romania communism" during and at the end of the speech. Within the framework of this chapter (and of the book more broadly), it appears as though in the speech cited above, Ceaușescu, himself the head of a complex national apparatus of deception, is pointing towards another—far more powerful—malicious deceiver: global capitalism and the cycles of debt and poverty it produces and perpetuates.

In his book *Debt: The First 5,000 Years*, David Graeber traces the most recent epoch in the long history of debt back to 1971, the year when Nixon decided to "float the dollar" (meaning that the dollar "would no longer be convertible into gold") and when the dollar became "the only currency used to buy and sell petroleum" in the world.[103] For Graeber, 1971 marks "The Beginning of Something Yet to Be Determined."[104] The financialization of capital, which meant that "most money being invested in the marketplace was completely detached from any relation to production of commerce at all"—in other words, "pure speculation," of the kind that the philosopher in Joseph de la Vega's *Confusión de Confusiones* found to be most deceptive and confusing—can be traced back roughly to this moment.[105] This also roughly coincides with the advent of credit cards and the beginning of the massive proliferation of debt still growing today. As Graeber puts it, "*everyone* is now in debt," and "there is something profoundly deceptive going on here."[106] In thinking through this as yet undetermined something that we have been living through since 1971, Graeber invokes the Wizard of Oz: "since Nixon's floating of the dollar, it has become evident that it's *only* the wizard behind the screen who seems to be maintaining the viability of the whole arrangement."[107] Behind the wizard, and behind his seemingly magical power "to create money out of nothing," there is—Graeber argues—"a man with a gun," a war machine.[108] To speculate, perhaps this kind of wizardry is what Ceaușescu had in mind when he denounced "symbolism" in his speech on the debt of the developing countries— one of the last speeches he would make in his life.

In terms of (growing) debt in the 1970s, the petrodollar surge in 1973–74 encouraged the phenomenon of "petrodollar recycling" and generated a "Third World Debt Trap": "In 1970, the total long-term international debt of developing countries stood at approximately $45 billion. . . . By 1987, it was close to $900 billion."[109] Romania was not as much affected by the first oil crisis (1973) as other developing countries, in part due to its own oil resources and to deals with Iran, Iraq, and Libya that enabled it to exchange machinery for oil.[110] By contrast, the second oil crisis (1979) had a much more severe impact, as did the "dramatic rise in the interest rates on sovereign debt"—rates that in fact pushed "many developing country governments into default."[111] For Ceaușescu, defaulting would have meant "an implicit admission of ideological defeat," while having to accept "IMF-assisted debt restructuring" would have "meant a limit on policy sovereignty" and was seen as "a form of neo-imperialism."[112] To avoid this, Ceaușescu decided to pay off all of Romania's external debt and thus send "the message" that "the regime was pulling the plug on Western finance for good."[113] By the time of Ceaușescu's fall in 1989, all of Romania's external debt had been paid off. But the costs for the population had been high. During the 1980s, food and fuel had been severely rationed; funding for education and health had been harshly cut; power outages and empty grocery stores with very long lines in front of them were commonplace. Regarding the drastic austerity measures, Ban wrote provocatively that, if we accept that the economic system under Ceaușescu's rule was indeed "a form of state capitalism," then there appear to be "striking similarities between the Ceaușescu regime and the way in which the capitalists and technocrats of the neoliberal era treat their populations when it comes to paying the external debt" (specifically in countries dependent on the International Monetary Fund), albeit for different purposes.[114] As Ban notes, up until that point, in addition to political prisons and the Securitate, Ceaușescu's regime promised and largely provided "guaranteed employment, decent pay and working conditions, affordable housing and leisure, and universal access to education and healthcare."[115] But when this promise was no longer fulfilled, systematically so in the 1980s, Ceaușescu's regime completely lost legitimacy; popular uprising would follow "even in the absence of an organized civil society."[116] Under these circumstances, as the entire Eastern Bloc was already transitioning out of communism, the end of Ceaușescu's regime was inevitable, even though its being a violent collapse through a bloody revolution was not.

The revolution culminated in the controversial trial of Ceauşescu and his wife Elena on December 25, 1989, which in fact constitutes the opening scene of Ujică's *Autobiography*. In this scene, Ceauşescu says: "You can put up whatever masquerade, I don't acknowledge these [charges] . . ." The (unseen) prosecutor replies: "Masquerade is what you've done for twenty-five years. This is the masquerade, and you've brought the country to the brink of the abyss." This double accusation of having authored a "masquerade" is particularly noteworthy. If we attend to the "mask" at the root of the term, we may say—with Alain Badiou—that the notion of "masquerade" brings forth and puts into play "the passion for the real," which, of necessity, "presents itself as a mask."[117] At stake here is a kind of "passion for the real" that breeds fakeness (synthetic reality) in order to confirm (prove) the real; Descartes, of course, shared this passion when he invented the malicious deceiver scenario, which he then used to prove the existence of an (impoverished) "I" and "world," as shown in the first chapter of this book. Notably, in his discussion of "the passion for the real," Badiou turns to Luigi Pirandello's *Henry IV*, who—not unlike Ceauşescu—is to "remain on stage with eyes wide open, terrified by the living force of his own fiction, which in the flash of an instant has led him to crime."[118] This widely circulated televised image, of the dictator terrified by the living force of his own fiction, will be restaged in the following section.

THE (REALITY) TV REVOLUTION

On December 22, 1989, Catherine Crier announced on CNN's *The World Today*:

> "A Just Cause." That's what Mikhail Gorbachev says is motivating the popular revolts sweeping Romania. "Just Cause" is also the code name of the US invasion George Bush ordered against Panama.[119]

The performative act of joining the two events into one breaking news announcement has, as Andaluna Borcilă observed, a double signification and effect. First, the news about Romania "was used to frame the one about Panama";[120] one way this was done was through the code name "Just Cause." "Even our severest critics would have to utter 'Just

Cause' while denouncing us," wrote Colin Powell about this code name in his autobiography.[121] Naming something "just" automatically makes it sound just. Subsequently condemned by the General Assembly of the United Nations as a " 'flagrant violation' of international law" and called a "masquerade" by some journalists,[122] the Panama invasion, argues historian Greg Grandin, "should be remembered in a big way" because it is "the war that started all of Washington's post–Cold War wars."[123] According to Grandin, without understanding Panama, one cannot understand "how unilateral, preemptory 'regime change' became an acceptable foreign policy option, how 'democracy promotion' became a staple of defense strategy, and how war became a branded public spectacle."[124] I cite Grandin here so as to evoke a broader network of historical circumstances that still concerns the present-day configuration of global power, even as this order is challenged through the rise to global power of China and the resurgence of Russia in what some have called "a new Cold War," especially in light of Russia's recent invasion of Ukraine.[125] In CNN's *The World Today* newscast, through the televisual joining of the anti-dictatorial revolts in Romania and the invasion of Panama, the former provided justification for the latter. Second, the joining of the two into one global media event also opened up, in Borcilă's words, "an incipient post–Cold War televisual geography" in which the two places appeared as "border territories of capitalism/the United States/democracy."[126] After 1989, this televisual geography will be repeatedly remade against the background of a fading Eastern Bloc and a growing and increasingly Americanized West.

The 1989 Romanian Revolution happened on TV not only for the world "out there" but also for many Romanians. In fact, the revolt in Bucharest broke out on December 21 during a mass rally speech, in which Ceaușescu promised wage raises. That speech was being broadcast live on TV; "direct transmission" is the literal translation of the Romanian phrase for this kind of broadcasting (*transmisiune directă*). The direct transmission was interrupted when the revolt broke out. The television went off the air—though not for long . . .

During the ten days of the revolution in the second half of December 1989,[127] people took to the streets to protest Ceaușescu's regime; the revolutionaries took over the national TV station in Bucharest and began broadcasting live; Nicolae Ceaușescu and his wife Elena were captured and executed in what some have called "a final Stalinist trial";[128] and an entire regime collapsed. Featuring amateur and professional footage, Harun Farocki and Andrei Ujică's documentary *Videograms of a Revolution* captures these events and the staging of the "live" revolution. The documentary was produced in 1992, but it was first broadcast on Romanian television only in 2005.[129] Unlike *The Autobiography*, *Videograms* includes some commentary performed by a female voice. The voice most often describes or draws attention to what happens in the image, offering little context and making scarce reference to the surroundings of the image. The performative force of the image depends precisely on the removal of these surroundings and the evacuation of the broader context.

As I discussed earlier in this book, the hollowing out is in fact an inaugural move of performativity, of simulation. Through this voiding, the image acquires presentness—or, to use a Heideggerian phrase, "[p]ure presence at hand."[130] In a Heideggerian framework, (human and other-than-human) things become "present at hand" when they are thought/operated with at a remove—an irreducible separation—from the practices within which they are bound up, decontextualized without any concern for them. They become "just a Thing that occurs somewhere."[131] Removed from their contexts, they can be fitted into predetermined categories. Such categories are general, abstract, and can be forced into relations of equivalence or substitutability, such as the implied equivalence/substitutability between the Romania Revolution and the U.S. invasion of Panama. The condition of "pure presence at hand" undergirds the televisual reality of the emerging "world picture" (to evoke Heidegger),[132] characterized by what Baudrillard called the "continuous and uninterrupted juxtapositions" of real events—a case of simulation, "the ecstasy of the real."[133] As I show in what follows, however, at play here is the logic of (dis)simulation, the conjoining of deception (dissimulation) and performativity (simulation). Romanian-born American poet, novelist, and essayist Andrei Codrescu points to this when he writes that "much of the glorious 'Revolution' was one of the greatest staged media events of the 20th century," "a play with real bodies."[134] Television had a key role in this play.

A key moment in the unfolding of the Romanian Revolution was when several of the revolutionaries took over the main TV station in Bucharest, which had been under the monopoly of the communist regime until then. Some of these revolutionaries were former high-ranking officials in the communist government who remained in power after 1989. Others were artists and dissident intellectuals, whom the audience for the most part knew well and trusted. The revolutionaries began broadcasting live on December 22, both updating Romanians on whatever new piece of information "happened" to reach them and giving them directions about what to do and how to act. Some of the information broadcast during the "live" revolution was fake news, such as, for instance, the widely circulated rumor that the water in my hometown had been poisoned. This constant broadcasting marks the emergence in the Romanian context of the phenomenon of the constant update and of a certain kind of programmability of experience that television would bring into being soon after 1989. In the Romanian context, this programmability has only recently and only to a certain extent been remediated by the internet and social media.

A few scenes from *Videograms* seem to me to be paradigmatic of the (dis)simulative televisual event through which Romania (re)entered the global capitalist "world picture." I recount them here.[135] They are related to each other in that they both involve multiple repetitions for the camera. The particular way in which they are put together in *Videograms* reveals how the televisual image organizes the world that it supposedly represents/captures, conjoining dissimulation and simulation. One of these scenes takes place at the Central Committee of the Communist Party in Bucharest, and it is featured in a section of *Videograms* titled "TV Comes to the Central Committee." Theatre director Alexa Visarion speaks from the balcony of the Central Committee building, addressing the mass of people gathered down below. He announces that Constantin Dăscălescu, the communist prime minister, will publicly resign: "So that we can be legal, the ex-prime minister himself must publicly announce his resignation." Dăscălescu proclaims the resignation of his government. *Videograms* shows three takes of the resignation, from three different angles, then an intertitle announces: "The resignation is repeated." Actor Mircea Diaconu, standing next to Dăscălescu up on the balcony, calls out to the crowd gathered in front of the Central Committee building: "Let the television do its work." Dăscălescu is asked to repeat the public announcement of his resignation because the TV cameras had not been ready the first time around. He repeats the resignation, twice.

The other scene, related to the one just mentioned through the repetition that structures it, features an English-speaking reporter who announces: "This battle has now been going on for almost twenty-four hours but despite all their firepower these troops are not able to winkle out those snipers still loyal to Ceauşescu." Intense shooting seems to be going on in the background, and right behind the reporter there are three men holding guns. The reporter re-performs the announcement. Again. And again. Multiple takes, retakes. This is repetition with sameness, repetition of the same that perpetuates itself through the voiding of context: a media event. As Mary Ann Doane notes in her essay on television and catastrophe, in a media event, the "referent becomes indissociable from the medium";[136] the voiding of its context and of history enables this. In times of capitalism, the medium (re)produces—or, better yet, simulates—its referent in order to sell it for a profit, as a commodity, ideally worldwide. In a sense, at play here is Heidegger's "world picture," or the "image in power" that Vilém Flusser writes about. The image in power, for Flusser, is the "end of history: everything happens in order to be recorded."[137] In light of this, the Romanian Revolution marks the beginning of the end of history. "End" here has a double meaning: it can mean both goal and ending, finality. I will return to (question) Flusser's claim that the Romanian Revolution represents the end of history later in this chapter. To continue with the revolution and think through it as a historical event, I turn at this juncture to the theatre and to a notion of repetition with a difference that is inextricably connected with theatricality. This is a kind of repetition that is fundamentally different from the repetition of the same that perpetuates itself through the voiding of history and context.

"Repetition and recollection are the same movement, just in opposite directions, because what is recollected has already been and is thus repeated backwards, whereas genuine repetition is recollected forwards," according to Søren Kierkegaard.[138] These words stand in the opening of *The Last Days of the Ceausescus* (*Die Letzten Tage der Ceausescus*), a

theatre performance accompanied by a collection of writings.[139] A project of the International Institute of Political Murder (IIPM), founded
and led by the Swiss theatre director Milo Rau, the stage production,
directed by Rau and Simone Eisenring, was performed by Romanian
actors in Romania, Germany, and Switzerland in 2009–2010. Notably,
especially in light of my earlier discussion of Ceaușescu as a brand,
Ceaușescu's heirs sued the Odeon Theatre in Bucharest, where Rau
and Eisenring's theatre piece was performed, for using the "Ceaușescu
brand." Ceaușescu's heirs eventually lost the case, but the show has
not been performed in Romania since the trial.[140] Regarding this case,
Rau remarks that "it showed what was for us at stake in *The Last Days*,
namely that after the downfall of the communist state the political
power has been transformed into economical power."[141]

The Last Days of the Ceausescus is a reenactment of what could be
seen as the final scene of the Romanian Revolution: the trial and execution of the dictatorial couple. In Rau's words, "The world saw the
death of the Ceausescus and took it to be the victory of democracy,"
"the inaugurating event of a new Romania."[142] This scene—a TV image
"without history" that "stands in the same line with the fall of the Twin
Towers or the murder of Kennedy"[143]—is the one image, out of a vast
array of televised images presenting the changes that swept Eastern
Europe in 1989, that has stayed in Rau's memory: "two old people sitting
at a table, two evil angels of history, powerless, defeated, doomed. Not
the fall of the Wall, not the opening of the Hungarian borders: [but] the
Ceausescus" (Figure 5).[144]

Performed twenty years after the first staging of the historical event,
which was first broadcast in a truncated version on December 26, 1989,
The Last Days of the Ceausescus attempts to repeat in exact detail the
scene of the trial from which the image is taken.[145] It does so by paying
"meticulous attention to detail and the materiality of the historical reality,"[146] a counter-gesture to the logic of (dis)simulation. In this way,
it looks beyond the frame of the TV image, to include those participants "who were originally outside the frame," such as the five people
from the trial "who were in the army at the time of the revolution" and
"are now in the parliament, in the government or in some other international institution."[147] However, even as it tries its hardest to replicate

FIGURE 5. Elena (played by Victoria Cocias) and Nicolae Ceauşescu (played by Constantin Cojocaru) in the reenactment of the trial of the dictatorial couple, *The Last Days of the Ceausescus*, staged by the International Institute of Political Murder (IIPM), 2009.

Courtesy of IIPM.

the historical record, the performance—taking place in the theatre and played by Romanian actors, who carry their own charged memories of the dictator and of the communist era—inevitably differs from it. IIPM's attempt to transpose the historical record within and through the theatre creates not a "documentary theatre" but what Rau has called a "theatre of the real," in which the real is (re)created in the live, embodied, material moment of the performance.[148] The *live* taking place of the trial in the theatre makes the kinds of "re-takes" (for the camera) that we saw in the "real-time" making of the media event that was the revolution impossible, except if it happens in the plain sight of the spectators rather than out of frame.

Rau's "theatre of the real" conjoins "documentation" and "imitation."[149] In this context, "imitation"—"one descriptor of theatricality"—can be understood in the sense proposed by Rebecca Schneider, as "a kind of syncopation machine for the touching of time beside or across itself in the zig-zagging lived experience of history's multi-directional ghost notes."[150] This conjoining of "documentation" and "imitation" opens the way for temporal differentiation. Or, articulated differently, it opens the way for repetition with difference across a nonlinear time that bears weight. Rau spoke about this kind of time-play in terms of "reproducing the present through the past for the future."[151] In *The Last Days of the Ceausescus*, the repetition with difference across nonlinear times counters the perpetuating self-sameness of the TV image and opens the possibility for making (some) sense of the complicated history evacuated from the TV image. Key in this sense, it seems to me, is not only the theatre production, performed in Romania only twice, but also what surrounds it and what remains after it: the memory of it in the actors' and spectators' bodies and minds; the record of the live performance; the research and documentation process; and the gathering of "materials, documents, theory," which is in fact the subtitle of the book in which these are collected, *Die Letzten Tage der Ceausescus* (*The Last Days of the Ceausescus*).[152]

Regarding the record of the performance, Rau remarks that it has become part of the historical archive through the internet:

> If you type into Google "Ceausescu trial," then the first ten images that show up are all from our re-enactment, rather than from the actual event of 1989. . . . The re-enactment of the original has become an image of the real event.[153]

Depending on who is doing the search, their geolocation, and their online history, the record of the theatrical performance may thus even displace the images of the "real event"—an event that has been repeatedly denounced as staged, as fake. As for the materials collected in the book accompanying the performance, these include interviews with some of the protagonists of the televised revolution, such as Ion Iliescu, who would become post-communist Romania's first president. They also include contributions by media theorists (such as Friedrich Kittler and Heinz Bude), some of the actors from the performance (Victoria Cocias, Constantin Cojocaru), and other artists (including Andrei Ujică). All these materials function to intensify the theatricality of the project, understood—in line with Samuel Weber—as *"a problematic process of placing, framing, situating."*[154] This is a kind of framing that allows for a multiplicity of frameworks, "in which the participants can place their own reality,"[155] including their memories and lived experience—in all its messiness—that is voided by the TV image.

The materials that surround IIPM's theatre piece consist of—and, at the same time, make apparent as framing devices—historical records, memories, habits, and bits and pieces of theoretical thinking. These materials repeatedly point to the trial of the Ceauşescus, and to the 1989 revolution more broadly, as staged events. As a collection of materials surrounding a theatrical reenactment, Rau's *The Last Days of the Ceausescus* opens up thinking in a way that begins to grapple with the complexity of the historical event without taking its undeniable staged character to be, on its own, some kind of explanation for what happened or something that reduces its significance (its particular ways of mattering). This complexity resides in the many layers of what happened and how what happened was staged, as well as in the gap between what ("really") happened and what people experienced individually—or think they experienced. *The Last Days of the Ceausescus* does not attempt to close the gap in search for a definitive truth that is clearly unobtainable.[156] Rather, in that gap, through multiple frames and framing devices, a world makes its appearance: the multilayered world of sense and sense-making, which the hyper-circulated TV image hollows out.

CODA: THE DRAMA OF THE SPIRIT IN THE PURSUIT OF FREEDOM

Back home on Hegel Street, I try to make sense of the revolution and its aftermath. In the search for the truth about what really happened during and following the 1989 revolution, what people say they experienced during the revolution has either come to be disregarded or taken to be the ultimate truth (in which case, due to the many contradictions, some people's accounts have been denounced as lies and others' taken to be the "real" truth). Between these two approaches, the name "revolution" has become contested, and what happened in December 1989 has been called either a "coup" or, more simply and noncommittally, "the events of 1989." Behind these approaches there is the presupposition of, on the one hand, "a pure reality, a substantial consciousness, a universal truth lying beyond any finite or secular regimes of sense . . . and, on the other hand, a great mass of lies and manipulation."[157] As I keep going through the archive of those times to try to learn more, I suspect the (post)truth lies somewhere beyond these two extremes—in (dis)simulation.

Since the early days of post-communism, television has increasingly been perceived as an agent of deception and manipulation. This widespread perception is well captured in the post-1989 slogan, "*Ați mințit poporul cu televizorul:*" "You have lied to the people with/through the television." The fact that some of the prominent members of the old communist guard continued to stay in power contributed to this perception. At the same time, however, television stations and shows began to cast themselves in the role of truth-finders and truth-makers—a role they still play. One such "truth-finding" show was broadcast in 1992 on the Romanian National Television, channel 1 (TVR1). The show attempted to "rehabilitate the condition of the 1989 revolutionary," as the moderator put it in his opening remarks.[158] It also undertook to answer the question: "When all is said and done, did a revolution take place in Romania in 1989 or not?" The TV show featured twenty male revolutionaries (if I counted correctly), with two others, who apparently had not been invited to the show, joining it midway. Via YouTube, we see the many guests sitting in wooden folding chairs placed behind the table and chairs that form the studio's usual set (designed for fewer guests), with a large revolutionary flag—the tricolor flag with a hole in it where the communist emblem had been—behind them. During the show, the TV image is often fuzzy, with lines sometimes drifting across the screen; delays and repetitions of the same image are common. From today's perspective, the whole show looks quite amateurish, although I am sure it did not feel like that back in the early 1990s. As I am now watching the show on YouTube, I also quite purposefully generate delays, so that I can take notes or re-watch certain moments. The TV image is thus quite literally at my fingertips, and I play with its televisual programmability just as another kind of apparatus, social media, with its attendant modes of surveillance (capture) and circulation of images (on which more in Chapter 4), in some sense is playing with me.

Several of the revolutionaries in the show state that the fact of a revolution having taken place is indisputable. Several of them point to their own experience of having been there, at the scene, as evidence for this indisputable fact. Tensions erupt among them and also accusations. Some call on others, asking: "Where were you when I was there fighting on the barricades?" One of the TV show participants, Dumitru Dinca, concludes that "[i]n the first part [of the events], it was a revolution, and in the second part, those who profited from this revolution took power." Another participant, Dan Iosif, offers a more philosophical-sounding account. Fighting on the barricades, he says, he would tell the people who stood on the sidelines: "If you do not have the courage to stand by the barricade that we have erected as a symbol of **the triumph of the spirit over the matter that communism had imposed on us** for forty-five years, then, at least, from where you are, you could encourage us with your voices."[159] Iosif then defends himself against the accusations that some of the "free newspapers" had brought against him: that he was an ex-Securitate officer, or a KGB agent. In his words:

> I affirm that I was just a Romanian who felt that things could no longer go on that way. I felt, as all Romanians did, that **our spirit, our Romanian cult for freedom would triumph** despite the old people in our society who urged us to conform.[160]

Thus, according to Iosif, a self-styled revolutionary hero, the 1989 events were a revolution of the spirit of the young over the materialism and cowardice of the old. Iosif's extended (and quite emphatic) statement replays the drama of the spirit—or, Spirit—in action. As I will show through a philosophical detour, via Hegel and using Flusser as a stepping stone, in the Romanian post-communist context, the drama of the Spirit in the pursuit of Freedom resolved itself in neoliberal capitalism ("resolve" being here of course just a manner of speaking).

At a symposium around the Romanian Revolution held in Budapest in April 1990 and titled "The Media Are With Us!: The Role of Television in the Romanian Revolution," Flusser gave a lecture entitled "Television Image and Political Space in the Light of the Romanian

Revolution." Here Flusser argues that "whatever happened in Romania merits philosophical reflection":

> It may be that what French and American philosophers are used to call post-history, *post-histoire*, has found its first, or almost first expression in that small country off-Broadway, if I may say so. Imagine for a moment . . . that such a thing would happen, let's say, in the United States, or even in Western Europe. Imagine for a moment that television in the United States would take over and I think that you will have imagined the end of history. The end of what we are used to call "history."[161]

What happened in Romania in December 1989 marked (the beginning of) the end of history, Flusser declares. In the aforecited lecture, Flusser anchors the hypothesis of the end of history in his own theory of the image and of the relation between "man" and "the world." According to this theory, the concept of the "image" is opposed to that of "linear writing." The "image" transforms the world into a "scene, like in a theatre," into a "happening" ("an accident which becomes necessary"), whereas "linear writing" is tied to "process" understood as a series of "events" with discernible causes and effects. The "world as process" is a world that can be "rationally explained." By contrast, the logic of the "world" transformed into a scene is "magical" rather than "rational."[162] Another word for this logic may be (dis)simulation, or "post-truth," only that rather than being opposed to rationality as Flusser argues, it in fact both grows out of the application of rationality (think back to Descartes's experiment of radical doubt) and subsumes it.

The idea of the end of history that Flusser expresses, and the conception of history with which it is associated, brings to mind Hegel's philosophy. In the Hegelian conception, history is unidirectional, forward moving, and coherent/rational; in this way, it is also philosophically intelligible. It is thus inextricably tied to a notion of progress that also constitutes one of the defining characteristics of modernity. This notion of history as progress, as Francis Fukuyama notes, "was made part of our daily intellectual atmosphere by Karl Marx, who borrowed this concept of History from Hegel, and is implicit in our use of words like 'primitive' or 'advanced,' 'traditional' or 'modern,' when referring to different types of human societies."[163] To get to "the end of history," I will now move through the drama of the Hegelian Spirit (*Geist*, alternatively translated as "mind").

In Hegel's philosophy, progress means complex conceptual development culminating in the Spirit attaining "the pure element of its existence, the [Absolute] notion" (*Begriff*, also translatable as "concept").[164] The concept is the essence of the Hegelian Spirit. It is, in Heidegger's words, "the form of the very thinking which thinks itself: the conceiving of *oneself—as the grasping* of the not-I."[165] Spirit that "grasps its own notion" achieves "Absolute Knowledge" that is secure, certain.[166] The Spirit's achievement of Absolute Knowledge means that the Spirit/ mind comes to know itself as (pure) spirit: absolute, self-complete, self-present, self-contained, self-identical, fully free. To reach the final stage of its development, the stage of Absolute Knowledge, Spirit, which "in its ultimate simple truth is consciousness" (human consciousness, the self-consciousness of humanity), must pass through various "forms of experience," through various "shapes or modes of consciousness," shot through with contradictions that are eventually overcome, giving rise to new stages, shapes, modes of consciousness.[167] When Spirit attains Absolute Knowledge, it acts as an unmoved spectator to its own drama. This is a drama of the return of the same knowing itself to be the same after overcoming difference.

In its development towards Absolute Knowledge, Spirit cannot help (so to speak) but keep moving in/through/as time towards self-identity. Moving in/through/as time, Spirit moves history, "working within it as . . . its final goal or final cause."[168] History here, which in Hegel's account "maps onto the history of western European civilization from the Greeks to his own time,"[169] represents "the process of becoming in terms of knowledge, a conscious self-mediating process—Spirit externalized and emptied into Time."[170] The Hegelian Spirit actualizes itself in history, and, "when spirit gets actualized, it accords with it to fall into time, with 'time' defined as a negation of a negation."[171] The time (or, Time) that Hegel's Spirit falls into is a very peculiar (conception of) time. Hegelian time is "the non-sensuous sensuous," says Heidegger somewhat inexactly quoting Hegel, with a phrase similar to that which Marx will use to describe the commodity.[172] In Hegel's words, "time itself is the *becoming*, this coming-to-be and passing away, the *actually existent abstraction*, Chronos, from whom everything is born and by whom its offspring is destroyed."[173] Chronos, of course, gives us "chronology," a term "[a]pparently dating only from 16th cent[ury],"[174] arguably the onset of modernity, even though Chronos dates back to pre-Socratic times. Among the early uses of the term, it is worth quoting the following one from 1593: "When they beganne [*sic*] to Rule. How long they ruled. This part of History is named Chronology."[175] As this example suggests, chronology, the modern way of keeping time, is intimately tied to power and domination (to "ruling").

Chronology functions as a series of "nows," each stretching from one point to another. In a manner of speaking that evokes Hegel's conception of space and time, this account of chronology as a series of "nows" can be said to be but the negation of space: "thing A at point 1, moves into point 2 and thereby, in the absence of A, point 1 'vanishes' as a determinate space. Time *just is* this negation."[176] This may well put us in mind of commodity exchange, a form of real abstraction (note here Hegel's "*actually existent abstraction*") that renders time and space abstract by voiding them. In Alfred Sohn-Rethel's words, "[t]ime and space rendered abstract under the impact of commodity exchange are marked by homogeneity, continuity, and emptiness of all natural and material content, visible or invisible."[177] This notion of time (chronology) as a series of homogeneous "nows" may also put us in mind of television programming, understood by Raymond Williams as "a serial assembly of timed units," a series of voided "nows" that need to be filled.[178] It is through this abstraction of time and space that the revolution in Romania can be rendered equivalent to the U.S. invasion of Panama. The more intensely these abstracted "nows" are filled, the more presence (perhaps, "pure presence at hand") they have, the more intense and thus attractive (profitable) the TV show is likely to be.

Such "is time, understood in terms of the 'now' which gives itself airs," writes Heidegger regarding the Hegelian drama of the Spirit.[179] This is "now" as the present, though not yet self-present. For, Spirit appears in time as a series of "nows" as long as time is but "intuited" becoming (as intuited, it remains something external to Spirit).[180] At the moment of coming to Absolute Knowledge, to self-presence, Spirit conceptualizes time, grasps its pure concept, and thus annuls it. Then, Spirit is (rather than appears): self-present, self-identical, complete—and completely hollowed out of anything material or temporal. At this moment, Spirit exits time. Time exit, and no more time to fall into, so to speak. End of the drama of the Spirit—which is to say, also, the end of History.

This teleological progression of Spirit through and out of time is what Marx kept from Hegel as the core of his philosophy of history, even as he got rid of Spirit and called "time" History. This was a History that progressed through the drama of (class) struggle towards the sur-passing of capitalism through communism and the coming of a class-less society. But, in the Romanian post-communist context, the drama continues, despite "the triumph of the spirit over the matter that com-munism had imposed on us for forty-five years" proclaimed by the self-styled revolutionary hero, Dan Iosif, and despite Flusser's proclamation following the 1989 revolution that what we had witnessed in that "small country, off Broadway," is an instance of "the end of history."[181] In fact, in some sense, this drama has only just begun (again) a little over thirty years ago: it is the drama of the pursuit of freedom, one of the things that the people who took to the streets during the days of the 1989 rev-olution called for. After the fall of the communist dictatorship—during which there was a single, state-controlled TV channel with limited broadcasting and very limited other (legal) media outlets—access to a variety of media outlets and twenty-four hour broadcasting was seen as an embodiment of the gained freedom and the desired democratization process.[182] In contrast to the communist dis/simulation apparatus, the capitalist (dis)simulation machine that was gained through the revo-lution has been far more effective in crafting the (consumer) selves of the Romanians and the new synthetic reality of rampant consumption.

During the 1990s, image consumption made possible "seeing the West with one's own eyes" (even if only on TV); it was one of the forms that the newly acquired right to "free circulation to the West" took.[183] Since the early 2000s, the range of available commercial TV channels has grown significantly and has come to include an increasing number of channels fully dedicated to news broadcasting, which dramatize everyday life with ongoing "breaking news": "nows" endowed with a heightened, highly dramatized presence, aimed at capturing—and selling—the viewers' attention. On the channels that are not exclusively devoted to presenting the news, "breaking news" supposedly breaks the "planned flow" of the programming and intensifies the sense of urgency through its (seemingly) unplanned and singular character.[184] On the news channels, the ongoing flow of "breaking news" makes (seeming) singularity into repeatable sameness. The titles of the ongoing "breaking news" most often include words such as "disaster/disastrous," "terrible," or "shocking," repeated *ad nauseam*. This continuing dramatization performed on repeat renders everyday life perpetually extraordinary, shot through with an unending (structuring) crisis. As Doane noted, under the regime of global capitalism, television itself is structured by perpetual crisis, a (repeatable) culmination of which is "catastrophe."[185] This new, "free" television, always on in our home, with its constant interruptions of "breaking news," consumed much of my time as a child and early adolescent, offering a sort of escape from the immediate reality, bringing fascination that eventually turned into exhaustion and the refusal to watch it altogether.

Another way in which the freedom gained as a result of the 1989 revolution has manifested is the freedom to buy, the increasing access to ongoing consumption. This is one of the other popular pastimes in Romania in addition to watching TV, which, with its advertisements and presentation of new consumerist lifestyles, has certainly helped fuel the former. Rather than falling into the Hegelian "time," inexactly quoted by Heidegger as "the non-sensuous sensuous," the postcommunist spirit in pursuit of freedom fell—perhaps unsurprisingly given the connection between the two—into the circulation of capitalist commodities: into the spirit of capitalism and its attendant ideology, consumerism, which Buck-Morss has called "the first global ideological form."[186]

Consumption was still slow in the first decade of the transition to capitalism, for the available means did not match the desires, especially in a context where money kept losing value in short time spans. But the consumer self started to take fuller shape in the 2000s, blooming just as I was preparing to go abroad for college to a place where I learned much more about capitalism and consumerism than I ever imagined. At this time, and continuing into the present, among the many breaking news reports that peppered our lives, a recurring one features fights ensuing amongst eager customers over products on sale at the opening of yet another new supermarket, retail store, or mall. These purchases have been enabled by plastic money, in two senses of this term: banknotes literally made of plastics (Romania introduced the first polymer-based banknote in Europe and the Northern Hemisphere and is one of over twenty countries in the world to have plastic money) and credit.[187] In the chapter that follows, I will turn to synthetic plastic: a (dis)simu- lating object-symbol of modern progress and consumerism that has also become the material for money, as well as for a form of payment and credit that is intimately tied to big data and its attendant mode of surveillance.

PART II

...

The Synthetic Real

3

SYNTHETICA

(Un)picturing Plastic Worlds

・・・ Allow me to introduce you to a character called Plastic Bag, who will resurface repeatedly in this chapter's investigation of another malicious deceiver—a (dis)simulating object-symbol of consumerism and the material underlying money and credit that possesses "metaphysical subtleties" of a Cartesian flavor:[1] synthetic plastics. Plastic Bag has many lives. In one of them, we find Plastic Bag in a store in Yugoslavia in the early 1980s. Yugoslavia at that time was considered by Romanians to be "the communist West." A friend of mine, (then) of high school age, just entered the Yugoslavian store, asking for a plastic bag. This was the first time abroad for my Romanian friend, made possible by a school trip. He had little money on him: it was forbidden to hold foreign currency in communist Romania, and the government strictly controlled the amount of foreign currency a Romanian tourist going abroad could receive for a trip. But in Yugoslavia, Plastic Bag was (for) free. Before leaving for Yugoslavia, my friend and his peers had received precious advice from parents, relatives, and older friends: bring back plastic bags!

As Romanian journalist Razvan Exarhu notes: "Before 1989, whoever had a plastic bag, had power. Those were the happy ones who received plastic bags from their relatives ... from abroad."[2] To be clear, the kinds of plastic bags desired in communist times were those looking like present-day disposable give-away bags; the kinds of bags that Romanians had during communist times were those made out of synthetic fibers, which they would reuse rather than accumulate or discard. On his school visit to Yugoslavia, my friend was among the happy ones: he obtained the cherished (free) bag. Plastic Bag, exquisitely colored, was brought to Romania. At home, in the living room dominated by the television, Plastic Bag was carefully revealed in front of an audience of eager relatives, friends, and neighbors. Stories would be told around it. More precious than even the most precious piece of furniture in the house, after the grand revelation, Plastic Bag was to be safely stored in a drawer, to be taken out again only on special occasions, when again stories would be (re)told around it. It seemed at the time that it would never be thrown away. This is Plastic Bag as domestic museum piece. In some sense, it approximates Ursula Le Guin's "carrier bag" that can hold "things in a particular, powerful relation to one another and to us."[3] "Preserved" in the drawer, in a country ruled by dictator Nicolae Ceauşescu and his wife Elena (the author of a PhD dissertation on "The Stereospecific Polymerization of Isoprene"[4]), Plastic Bag lived, in and out of time, seemingly in accordance with its plastic nature. It lived this way until the 1989 revolution came and eventually opened the door to unbounded consumerism, and to an unbounded proliferation of plastic bags, given away for "free."

A free Plastic Bag is meant to float, one learns from Ramin Bahrani's 2009 theatrical film by the same title, *Plastic Bag*, which has as its main character a personified Plastic Bag performed by the voice of Werner Herzog.[5] In Bahrani's film, after being thrown away by a female consumer whom Plastic Bag calls "my maker," Plastic Bag floats, carried by currents of wind and water, in search of its maker. It floats and floats, even as the "world decomposed," but, says Plastic Bag: "Not me. I remained. I was strong and smart, and I would find my maker." During this search, Plastic Bag gets trapped repeatedly, held in place, first by the grass in the fields, later by the hand of a statue, then again by the branch of a tree. Eventually, Plastic Bag encounters leftovers of other plastic bags, who have chained themselves to a fence "to preach about the Vortex": "it was a world in the Pacific Ocean where a hundred million tons of us had gathered."[6] Carried by the currents of the ocean, Plastic Bag enters the continent of plastics floating in the Pacific. Spinning quickly with the currents, before long Plastic Bag gets trapped again. Time passes; it is not clear how much time has passed, and it does not seem to matter. Plastic Bag will remain trapped for now, but it will continue its journey across different times and places later in this chapter. Meanwhile, we will turn to the material that Plastic Bag is made of, synthetic plastic, and its (dis)simulative performances. In this chapter's investigation, synthetic plastic, a symbol of modern progress and consumerism, will emerge as both a malicious deceiver and as a refuse that refuses to go away, as history: "time that won't quit."[7]

METAPHYSICAL SUBTLETIES IN PLASTIC

As discussed in the first chapter of this book, what can be established with certainty about matter by the end of the Cartesian experiment of radical doubt, what presents itself clearly and distinctly, is that "corporeal things exist," but they do not necessarily exist in a way that "exactly corresponds with my sensory grasp of them."[8] Rather, concludes Descartes, "they possess all the properties which I clearly and distinctly understand, that is, all those which . . . are comprised in the subject-matter of pure mathematics."[9] In other words, all there is to matter in the Cartesian view, strictly (metaphysically) speaking, is but indefinite extension and what mathematically pertains to it: shape, size, motion, number. The products of organic chemistry known as synthetic plastics, I argue, instantiate this view: they are material products of this metaphysics.

The term "plastic" applies to a wide variety of very different materials. What brings them together in the category of plastics is a series of characteristics displayed during the production process. A treatment of matter as extension underlies this production process. In a chapter entitled "Why Are Plastics Plastic?" from their 1941 book on *Plastics*, chemist V. E. Yarsley and assistant factory manager of B.X. Plastics, E. G. Couzens, explain:

> a plastic material is one which at some stage of its history is capable of flow, under the influence of heat and pressure. It will also flow when subjected to tension or stretching, and it is the ap-

plication of these processes of compression or stretching which converts a plastic material into a plastic object.[10]

Like other materials, when a force is applied at their ends, plastic materials at first extend (or get compressed) proportionally with the pull (or the push) and then return to their initial shape if "the pulling-force is removed."[11] However, after a certain point called "the yield-point or value," plastic materials begin to "extend much more rapidly in proportion to the pull" until they remain "permanently deformed."[12] This is the defining characteristic of everything that falls in the category of plastics. It is called "plasticity," which chemist Carleton Ellis defines as the ability to get "deformed under mechanical stress without losing cohesion" and to "keep the new form given."[13]

The invention of materials that exhibit plasticity presupposes design at the molecular level, the creation of what Yarsely and Couzens term "molecules made to measure."[14] At stake here is a kind of programming. In an enthusiastic article from 1943, *Newsweek* calls the chemists involved in the business of performing such programming the "molecule engineers."[15] The process of plastic design involves, in essence, building up molecular structures in the laboratory. Imperceptible by the unaided senses and even by regular microscopes, a structure here refers to chains ("rows and layers") of molecular units (called "monomers") connecting with each other, "in repeating patterns."[16] In other words: synthetic plastics are synthetic polymers. Plastic properties depend directly on the undergirding structure; they can be said to be an effect of it.

Yarsley and Couzens cite as the "most remarkable example of molecules made to measure" the work of Harvard instructor Wallace Hume Carothers and his team.[17] Carothers conducted "pioneering studies of synthetic polymers," which led to the "development of neoprene, the first U.S.-made synthetic rubber, and nylon, the first truly synthetic fiber."[18] He conducted his studies in a laboratory established in 1927 at DuPont, one of the largest corporations in the chemical industry, which describes itself as "shaping a better world" and "creating essential innovations to help you thrive."[19] The lab was devoted to "pure science or fundamental research work" with the aim to discover "new scientific facts."[20] For this reason, the lab was informally dubbed "Purity Hall"—though it bears remembering that its "purity" is not that pure; this "purity" was (and still is) enabled by and put in the service of for-profit capital. DuPont's project of "pure" intellectual inquiry in the area of chemistry echoes in a sense the Cartesian "project of pure inquiry" conducted in the area of philosophy, which undergirds Descartes's metaphysics.[21] As in the case of the Cartesian project, Purity Hall's "discovery of facts" was in fact a production of facts, such as the production of the fact of the existence of nylon or of synthetic rubber. At play here is what I have termed "performative thinking."

As products of performative thinking, synthetic plastics are an excellent medium for simulation: in other words, for (im)materially reassembling what exists in one material form into another material that can be more easily manipulated, replicated, multiplied. This act of reassembling relies on processes of abstraction, which in turn involve a hollowing out, a reduction of dimensions of what is being simulated. In the case of the invention of nylon, for example, the plastic material to be developed had the silk molecule as its model.[22] Through various interventions at the molecular level a "new silk-like substitute with strength and other properties far exceeding those of natural silk"[23] was obtained. Evoking media theorist Friedrich Kittler's definition of simulation as the affirmation of a negation,[24] nylon can be said to be an affirmation of (an image of) natural silk whose molecular makeup (composition) is in fact negated (voided) in the production process of nylon. Plastics thus embody both senses of the term "synthetic" discussed in this book: "devised, arranged, or fabricated for special situations to imitate or replace usual realities";[25] and involving simulation based on abstraction that voids sensory material and historical context.

Plastic materials, "the modern mass-production materials,"[26] possess a seemingly unbounded versatility and mutability—a seemingly unbounded capacity to imitate, though only in the phases of the production process *before* they turn into plastic products. As industrial designer Jean Reinecke remarked, plastic materials' seemingly unbounded capacity to mutate and imitate makes them "so definitively distinctive that they cannot be simulated by others."[27] What is also distinctive about plastics is that the finished plastic product is bound to be stronger, tougher, more durable than the imitated object. The seemingly complete lack of resistance that plastic materials exhibit during the production process (which allows them to be molded into almost anything) is thus doubled by plastic's immutability in product form, which makes it a form of what Heather Davis has aptly called "recalcitrant matter."[28] Synthetic plastic—plastic derived, through complex procedures, from fossil fuels (mostly petroleum today)—has the attribute of persisting for a very long time: it is non-biodegradable, even as some varieties of plastic are photodegradable, breaking under sunlight into ever-smaller particles, which still remain plastic. Plastic rots not. It may break down into pieces, but it still remains plastic, and it does not go away—not in a human lifetime, and perhaps not even in the lifetime of humanity. Thus, plastic seemingly materializes (close to) infinite variety that generates calculated, persistent sameness. Davis calls this the "synthetic universality" of plastic and highlights how it carries the imprint of "the colonial logics of dissociation, dislocation, denial, and universality, reproducing itself without regard for local cultures or ecologies."[29] As Amanda Boetzkes and Andrew Pendakis have noted, this seeming universality is achieved through the voiding of "every trace of particularity, every index of a located space and time," similar to the voiding performed by the capitalist commodity.[30]

The persistent sameness that characterizes plastics can be understood at several levels, which have to do with chemistry as well as with capitalism. At one level, this sameness is a function of what Davis calls plastics' refusal to "interact with other carbon-dependent life forms."[31] Even when plastics break down, they do not turn into something else. When they break down into very small bits, called microplastics, they "can attract high levels of toxic molecules such as polychlorinated biphenyls, or PCBs," especially when they end up in the oceans.[32] Even in this case, they still remain plastics, but they become hyper-toxic, harming or destroying what they permeate. Not only do they attract toxic molecules, but certain forms of (toxic) synthetic plastics themselves leave their taint everywhere, contaminating other forms of matter with which they come into contact. For instance, studies have shown that bisphenol A (BPA)—used in the production of certain kinds of plastics and resins—is easily absorbed by the skin through direct touch.[33] It can also "leach into food from the protective internal epoxy resin coatings of canned foods and from consumer products such as polycarbonate tableware, food storage containers, water bottles, and baby bottles," with harmful effects on health.[34] Plastics also seal, separate, keep things apart, instantiating a desire "for a monadic identity separated from its environment."[35] In the form of packaging, they seemingly protect what they wrap from the work of time. In fact, however, the packaging often erases history (how what is packaged came to be, who actually made it, for what purpose, at what cost) and blocks relationality. Being expressly made to be immediately discarded, packaging is utterly redundant . . . and yet, absurdly, profitable.

At another level, plastic is associated with the myth of being a form of universal matter that can be made into everything as well as with the image—and associated habits—of disposability. Both of these persist and drive production as well as reproduction—both plastic's reproduction through degrading (as it breaks down into pieces, plastic becomes more of itself) and the reproduction of capital relations that produce plastic, even as those relations become, themselves, variants on the definitions of plastics' own properties. Since the beginning of the twentieth century, plastics have been widely substituted for other materials (glass, wood, fur, silk, etc.) in many products. More recently, plastics have become a material substrate for a variety of very diverse objects produced through 3D printing technologies that, for many enthusiasts, represent "the future," just as plastics did for Mr. McGuire in *The Graduate*.[36]

As Roland Barthes noted in *Mythologies,* plastic abolishes "the hierarchy of substances," promising to replace anything and everything.[37] Implied in this is the idea that plastic renders different substances and things equivalent—or able to be equated, just as the commodity does. In this sense, like the commodity in Sohn-Rethel's theorization discussed in Chapter 1, synthetic plastics are a form of real abstraction. As Sohn-Rethel showed, the capitalist exchange is "a physical act that must leave the physical state of the commodities unchanged"; it implies a kind of *"abstract movement of . . . abstract substances . . . which thereby suffer no material change and which allow for none but quantitative differentiation (differentiation in abstract, non-dimensional quantity)."*[38] Having commodities be made by a petroleum-derived material that stubbornly resists change materially actualizes this condition. It is therefore not surprising that plastic has become the material for the commodity of commodities, the commodity that serves as a means of exchange for all others: money. As Sohn-Rethel noted, this "role falls upon a commodity which by its physical durability, divisibility and mobility easily complies with the postulate" of immutability: namely, that it must not "undergo any material change while it acts in this capacity."[39] Synthetic plastics perfectly embody this postulate of immutability, while affording "additional security features," making them the ideal material for money, as a recent article published by the International Monetary Fund (IMF) titled "The Future Is Plastic" argues.[40]

Plastic is the material not only for banknotes, which the IMF article is referring to, but also for the credit (and debit) card, introduced in the United States around 1955 and by 1980 simply referred to as "plastic."[41] Increasingly replacing physical money in many parts of the world, the credit card further dematerializes and abstracts the real abstraction that is money, even as it has become an ordinary reality; we habitually, and often out of necessity, charge everything to "plastic." Already in 1977, a U.S. lawmaker noted that "it is virtually impossible to function in our day-to-day lives without credit cards. . . . We are a nation of credit card junkies hooked on popping plastic."[42] Consumption runs on plastic and on bought time, on time bought with an accruing interest. Plastic money constitutes seemingly disposable income, not only in terms of extra resources but also in terms of feeling like one is not really spending when charging things to plastic as there is no physical money being exchanged. In this case, plastic is aligned with the sense of delay, deferral, abstraction.

This sense of delay connects with plastics' disposability. Plastics are a preeminent symbol of disposability—not by default but by marketing. Relatively easy to make, produced in ever-growing amounts (even before 1940), and coupled from the start with a persistent image of cheapness, plastic would soon come to be considered and treated as though it were valueless, substitutable, and disposable. As Jeffrey Meikle explains, by 1950 "an endemic oversupply" of plastics left over from the war "led producers to think not of durability but of disposability" in relation to

plastic, and to market it thus: as a valueless thing meant for limited—
often single—use.[43] As such, disposable plastics are paradigmatic products and symbols of what I have called elsewhere "the global capitalist
system of disposable redundancy."[44] As discussed in Chapter 2, for the
profit-seeking capitalist, the interval between buying and selling must
be ideally annihilated (which implies that a commodity must be held
onto for as little time as possible); disposability is the counterpart of
this logic on the consumer side. This disposability is a matter of programming; another word for it is "planned obsolescence," a notion proposed by real estate broker Bernard London as a solution to the Great
Depression. London decried that "[p]eople everywhere are today dis-
obeying the law of obsolescence," holding onto and reusing their cars,
radios, clothing, and so on; his proposal for solving this supposed problem was to "chart the obsolescence of capital and consumption goods
at the time of their production."[45] Disposability, as "planned obsolescence," is programmed into products as well as contemporary media
technologies.[46] But the history of disposability—of rendering disposable
human beings, entire peoples and cultures—stretches back further, to
the institution of slavery and the colonial dispossession, displacement,
and destruction of Indigenous peoples and cultures—the economic and
geopolitical counterpart of the Cartesian "zero-point hubris" (in Santiago Castro-Gómez's phrasing) that, as noted earlier, is also imprinted
on synthetic plastics' DNA.[47]

In today's neoliberal context, disposability is connected with the
precariousness of employment situations for increasing numbers of
people, who are at risk of being made disposable at the whim of the
higher management. It is also connected with a model of consumerist
and neoliberal subjectivity that is linked to the other prominent current
usage of "plastic," namely in neuroscience. Here "plasticity" refers to
the brain's capacity to change, to remake itself over time, in response
to its environment. Despite the promise of change and evolution that it
holds (or maybe because of it), the plasticity model of the brain poses
the danger that—in practice—this promise may in fact amount to a set
of features that define a model of subjectivity that neoliberal capitalism produces and perpetuates. As Victoria Pitts-Taylor has pointed out,
there are intimate connections between neoliberalism and a plasticity

model of the brain (especially as presented in popular uses of it), where plasticity is understood in terms of flexibility, adaptability, and an obsession with the new.[48] Flexibility and adaptability—also characteristics of synthetic plastics—are demanded of workers in the context of a lack of worker protections and of increased job insecurity. As for the desire for the new, tied to modernity's logic of progress, in times of the consumerist-capitalist experience economy,[49] the new often comes packaged and sold in the form of disposable things and the experiences they are designed to afford, or simulate. Here, plasticity and plastic—as an epitome of a mindset of both flexibility and disposability—intersect. As the prime substance of flexible expendability, disposable plastic products facilitate newness through their planned obsolescence.

Yet, plastics' disposability and obsolescence do not mean disappearance: discarded plastics do not go away—only elsewhere. A gap opens between the discarding and the return, with accumulated interest. In the case of the credit card (though not only), this gap—which implies deferral, delay—is a matter of growing debt. The real cost of the "free" plastic card in fact lies and materializes in the growing debt, just as the real cost of "free" plastic lies and materialize in the ecological destruction that its accumulation produces. In the age of big data, the additional cost of a "free" plastic credit (or debit) card also lies in the data whose collection it facilitates, a form of surveillance that helps feed, shape, and predict the actions of the consumer self. Paying with plastic today facilitates the harvesting of data, celebrated as the supposedly "new oil" of the economy.[50] Highlighting payment cards as "data-harvesting devices" and "a site of consumer surveillance," Josh Lauer has shown how card-based modern payment systems in fact precede "the internet and its mobile appendages" and how Google's "grand vision of automated data collection, personalization and recommendation systems, data mining and continuous experimentation, digital auctions, and differential pricing"—a preeminent example of what Shoshana Zuboff has called "surveillance capitalism"—is in fact rooted in card-based modern payment systems.[51]

In light of all this, synthetic plastic emerges as a malicious deceiver with roots in the twinning of Cartesian metaphysics and capitalism. It is not only an excellent medium of simulation but an effective, ideal agent of (dis)simulation: as it stands in and passes for other things, it conceals its own nature, functions, and costs. At a basic level, what it disguises is its relation to petro-capitalism, the fact that it is a "petroleum product that claims at least a quarter of all the oil extracted" and through which oil permeates "into every facet of cultural life."[52] At another level, it conceals its actual functions, the ways in which it facilitates profit-making through the forging of neoliberal and consumerist visions, habits, and subjectivity and through data collection and mining. It also conceals the real costs it involves—with accrued interest—socially and environmentally. As is the case with Descartes's malicious deceiver, synthetic plastics' (dis)simulative performances construct a synthetic world (picture), to which I now turn as I continue exploring plastics' metaphysical subtleties.

SYNTHETICA: PICTURING A PLASTIC WORLD

Picture this: a map of no-place, a "ponderous geography" in the making, stretching from the old territory of "natural resins" (in brown on the map, with some patches of green here and there; in the northwest) to the "new territory" of yellow Melamine (in the southeast, attached to dark-green Urea).[53] This is *Synthetica*: a map of "the illimitable world of the molecule" with "boundaries as unsteady as the map of Europe."[54] It is a colorful image of a "broad but synthetic continent of plastics."[55] This unusual map appeared in an article in *Fortune Magazine* entitled "Plastics in 1940." The article's purpose was to educate the public about plastics, describing their variety, applications, and the industrial processes involved in their production. Its educational purpose notwithstanding, were it not for the explanatory caption, the map would be rather confusing. Even with the caption included, its overall effect is not so much explanatory as it is performative: it stretches into the future, which it remakes in its own image. *Synthetica* postulates a new "land mass ripe for systematic exploitation," in Meikle's words.[56] It posits plastics as the material substance of the world: this is the world as a totality made of plastics. Disposability, as a widespread habit, has turned this postulation into a fact. Thus, from the perspective of today, the *Synthetica* map of a "continent of plastics" may be taken to have become something other than a postulate: it can be taken to represent one of the five gyres, or garbage patches, in the earth's oceans as well as the micro- and nanoplastics that pervade all there is across different environments, from air, to soil, to water.

The *Synthetica* map is a picture of the world; a world of plastic is a world picture predicated upon repeatable sameness, which may remind us of Fontenelle's expanding world discussed in the first chapter of this book. The concept of "world picture" comes from Martin Heidegger, who characterized modernity as "the age of the world picture."[57] For Heidegger the idea of a world picture is connected with a kind of thinking as setting before: Heidegger calls it "*vor-stellen*," which has been translated as "representing." Conceiving the world as a picture is a mode of thinking that grasps all that exists as standing before "man" to be known and disposed of. In Heidegger's words, in the world picture everything that exists "is placed in the realm of man's knowing and of his having disposal, and . . . it is in being only in this way."[58] This mode of thinking is a form of what in this book I have theorized as performative thinking.

The calculation and manipulation of everything that exists is essential to representation/*Vor-stellung*, which is linked to "the will to mastery" characteristic of the modern age.[59] The world becomes picture, an object of representation and/as mastery, through procedures of "entrapping securing" that turn the world into what Heidegger termed a "standing reserve" (*Bestand*) to be used—and used up.[60] Yet, world mastery comes at a cost: become an object of representation (*Vor-stellung*), the world "incurs in a certain manner a loss of Being."[61] Representationalist thinking performs a reduction of the world, through which certain dimensions of what exists are annihilated or concealed. A world picture is not really an inhabitable world—or, at the very least, it is not a world that welcomes inhabitation.

An updated, computer-animated, and certainly more engaging version of *Synthetica* is available in *The LEGO Movie* (2014): a world picture (simulation) that is literally made of plastics.[62] Conceived and directed by Phil Lord and Christopher Miller, this particular version of a plastic world (picture) makes visible what lies hidden behind synthetic plastics' (dis)simulative performance. An extended ad for LEGO products, *The LEGO Movie* (re)presents a plastic world engaged in ongoing "building" activities, which always involve prior destruction (voiding, hollowing out), according to thoroughly prescribed rules. Perhaps unsurprising given the associations between plastics and capitalism highlighted above, this is a completely programmed, completely surveilled world, in which everything is overpriced, under the totalitarian regime of President Business (or Lord Business), the CEO of Octan oil corporation ("and the world") who is obsessed with order and border enforcement: "I've got my eye on you" is his logo. The instruction-following citizens of this world misrecognize it as a "free" world, in genuine ideological spirit. The preeminent medium of indoctrination in this world is the television, as well as the choreographic tuning of the bodily rhythms of the workers, who mindlessly move to the contagious tune of a song repeated *ad nauseam*: "everything is awesome, everything is cool when you're part of a team, everything is awesome, when you're living out a dream."[63] The dream turns out to be a nightmare, as President Business schemes to put into practice the ultimate "entrapping-securing" procedure: the Kragle. This weapon is a superglue that will literally "fix" everything in place, bringing about a condition of total stuckness (rigidity, immobility). Such a condition in fact literalizes the reality of the synthetic materials called "plastic," of which the proprietary LEGO pieces are made. President Business's use of the Kragle on a mass scale will bring about "the end of the world," or so *The LEGO Movie* has us believe. But there are saviors—and metanarratives that ensure salvation.

Similar to *The Matrix*'s protagonist Neo ("The One"), *The LEGO Movie*'s central protagonist, Emmet Brickowski, is the "chosen" one. He is called "the special" even though he is terribly ordinary, an everyman. He becomes a hero by believing that he is one, a slogan repeated in *The LEGO Movie*. Believing has performative power, and it is on its own enough to bring things and subjectivities into being, *The LEGO Movie* would have us believe. In a sense, *The LEGO Movie* replays the figure of the American hero as a self-made man, now updated for the post-Fordist age. Emmet, in true post-Fordist fashion, is a virtuosic rule follower who succeeds in tricking the system by applying—to the point of absurdity—the rules that keep the system running.

The LEGO Movie's (grand) metanarrative involves "the man upstairs": a father (possibly a corporate worker, even a CEO) for whom the LEGO pieces represent—in his own words—a "highly sophisticated interlocking system" that, once assembled, must be glued in place. The son spoils his father's plans, reorganizing the LEGO world and striving to keep it "animate." After a tense, emotionally charged back-and-forth, the son and the father reconcile; the son convinces the father to abandon his plan to use the Kragle. Shifting (back) frames after the "real" causal forces of the LEGO world's affairs have been revealed, Emmet convinces President Business to abandon the Kragle and become a positive hero. President Business gives in—and then explodes. The world is saved (at least temporarily), and the film concludes with a heteronormative happy ending. This ending, and the metanarrative with which it is conjoined, closes down—or "entraps-secures"—the possibility of a critique of capitalism that the representation of President Business's LEGO world opened. It leaves the capitalist logic ultimately untouched. The message of the virtuosic brand performance that is *The LEGO Movie* is, after all: "Buy LEGO!" If you do so, LEGO will make you more ("systematically") creative. The LEGO universe is the complete antithesis of a "Kragled" world, for "the famous LEGO® bricks . . . are all part of the LEGO system and can be easily combined in innumerable ways."[64] The LEGO website goes on to promise: "When children play, they learn to solve problems, to be creative, and to become resilient. It helps them thrive in a complex and challenging world."[65] LEGO thus offers a promise of creativity and resilience, highly valued skills in the post-Fordist economy.

Although he lists "a Lego Mindstorms kit" as one way in which a child's "astonishment is sure to be slowly siphoned out of the tank of wonder," philosopher and game designer Ian Bogost's "object-oriented" vision of things that "*do things*" seems modeled on the LEGO system.[66] Bogost's term for things that "do things"—and the fundamental brick of his metaphysics—is the "unit." For Bogost, a "unit is isolated and unique," like a LEGO piece (although the claimed "uniqueness" is problematic, both in the case of the LEGO piece and of Bogost's "unit").[67] Drawing on systems theory and chemical engineering, Bogost uses the term "operation" to describe "how units behave and interact" with each other, which may well put us in mind of the LEGO "instructions."[68]

Though anti-Cartesian in intention, it seems to me that the "isolated" units that "operate" according to a system of rules in Bogost's metaphysics pertain to a genealogy that goes back to particulate theories of matter such as that endorsed by Descartes.[69] As I showed in the first chapter of this book, the Cartesian view of matter—a view "from nowhere"[70]—is non-human, even anti-human, just like Bogost's and the other object-oriented philosophers' and speculative realists' metaphysical theories.

Connected with names such as Graham Harman, Levi Bryant, and Timothy Morton, object-oriented ontology (OOO)—with speculative realism as its close associate—is a brand of metaphysical realism that brings together "a set of positions that refuse to privilege the human-world relationship as the only one."[71] This basic idea is also shared by some of the various "new materialisms" developed in recent decades and associated with names such as Karen Barad, Jane Bennett, Manuel DeLanda, Quentin Meillassoux, and others. It is beyond the scope of this book to discuss the differences and points of convergence amongst the thinkers aligned with these movements.[72] I will also not rehearse here the many astute critiques of these movements, which I for the most part support.[73] In what follows, I will raise only a few points of critique that directly connect with this book's argument.

In *Alien Phenomenology*, Bogost confesses that he was "fortunate" to have "arrived at the metaphysics of things by way of inanimacy rather than life—from the vantage point of a critic and creator of computational media in general and videogames in particular."[74] The prompt for thinking up this metaphysics was the intimate encounter with the computer, which Bogost sees as "composed of molded plastic keys and controllers, motor-driven disc drives, silicon wafers, plastic ribbons, and bits of data."[75] As a pile of parts (made out of a lot of plastics), the computer appears indeed to be conspicuously *in*animate. Yet, as I showed in Chapter 2, there are many layers of animacy to the computer, especially when it is considered—as hardware *and* software—in the social contexts in which it functions. A perspective that takes this into consideration will reveal software "as a material object, as a means of production, as a human-technical hybrid, as medium of communication, as terrain of political-economic contestation—in short as sociality."[76]

Being narrowly "object-oriented" and obsessed to eliminate all trace of the human from his account (which ultimately amounts to an erasure), Bogost evacuates sociality—and also historicity—from his metaphysics. This evacuation is, as I discussed in Chapter 1, very much in the spirit of Cartesian metaphysics that presents a world that is "purified" (voided) of social interaction and history.

In the spirit of Cartesian metaphysics (and of metaphysics more broadly), which traditionally employs an abstract framework that renders all things equivalent (same), Bogost too evacuates difference from his metaphysics (at one level, this evacuation is but a logical consequence of the evacuation of any considerations of sociality and history). From his perspective, the "secret universe" of the computer described as a pile of inanimate stuff exists on the same (flat) plane with "the disappearing worlds of the African elephant or the Acropora coral."[77] Bogost in fact declares that he views all these things with the *same* kind of "wonder."[78] But apolitical and asocial "wonder" is not terribly useful when encountering the dying elephants and corals, nor is it in any way responsible, it seems to me. Disaster tourists, who pay significant amounts of money to *see* sites struck by disaster (including ecological catastrophe), I imagine, must often view (or consume) the sites this way. Unsurprisingly perhaps, elephant tourism is a booming industry, in which elephants are put to work to entertain tourists—often in places whose histories are intimately tied to colonialism, such as South Africa, Botswana, or Zimbabwe. Some of the works that elephants are made to do are "are exploitative and mask cruel realities."[79] But there is no place for considering these kinds of complex realities in Bogost's "tiny," "flat ontology."

Admittedly, in one place in his book Bogost declares: "The funeral pyre is not the same as the aardvark; the porceletta shell is not equivalent to the rugby ball. Not only is neither pair reducible to human encounter, but also neither is reducible to the other."[80] But how can he— and the metaphysics he proposes—account for differences when he insists that the "power of flat ontology" comes "from its indiscretion. It **refuses distinction** and welcomes all into the temple of being"?[81] This universal welcoming, which is not all that different from other universalist discourses that have been around for centuries and have legitimated persistent and violent exclusions, glosses over the fact that all things and beings are *not* equal, and their inequalities are produced by powerful social systems.[82] Bogost's utopian asocial, ahistorical, and apolitical metaphysics leaves the socio-economic systems that (re)produce inequalities intact. Flat ontology's refusal of distinction amongst vastly different things also resembles the way in which "[d]ata regimes do not distinguish between bodies and novels, nature and culture; they rely on a process of recording and manufacturing data about everything,"[83] rendering everything equivalent through the reduction to data, just as commodity exchange renders everything equivalent through its reduction to money.

One of the mantras repeated enthusiastically by some of the thinkers affiliated with object-oriented ontology and speculative realism, including Bogost, is: "The world does not exist."[84] *The LEGO Movie's* world-saving promise notwithstanding, plastics—as a variety of hyperobjects "massively distributed in space and time relative to humans"— are amongst the "strange strangers" that "have brought about the end of the world," writes Timothy Morton, another speculative realist.[85] This is true in the sense that plastics, as they are being used and discarded in a consumerist-capitalist system of disposable redundancy, have contributed to the transformation of the world into a world picture and are persistently destroying the habitats and lives of numerous species. But this is not what Morton means. Rather, for Morton the end of the world is something to be celebrated. In pushing forth his argument for an ecology without world, *"without matter"* and *"without the present,"*[86] Morton shifts scales—from "the subatomic realm of the extremely small to the cosmological realm of the extremely large"—without shifting frameworks.[87] He concludes that "[i]n a strange way, every object is a hyperobject."[88] But then, as Ursula K. Heise asks in her review of Morton's book, "[i]f scale makes no difference, and global warming is not as a matter of principle different from 'pencils, penguins, and plastic explosives' . . . , what useful work does the concept of the hyperobject do?"[89]

The notion of "world" that these thinkers denounce and whose end they celebrate is that of a "container in which objectified things float or stand" and of a totalizing principle of coherence.[90] "Coherence" here is an effect of aesthetics—or, more precisely, of aestheticization. For this reason, Morton calls "world" an "aesthetic phenomenon" and gives *The Lord of the Rings* as an example to illustrate this idea. In his words:

> The idea of *world* depends on all kinds of mood lighting and mood music, aesthetic effects that by definition contain a kernel of sheer ridiculous meaninglessness. It's the job of serious Wagnerian worlding to erase the trace of this meaninglessness.[91]

As Morton describes it, the "idea of world" depends on the technology "backstage" and the aesthetic effects it produces. In this respect, this idea may remind us of Fontanelle and Descartes's conception of the world as machine discussed in Chapter 1. It also bears noting that the Wagnerian *Gesamtkunstwerk* (total work of art)—a form of synthetic art-making—is not all there is to aesthetics, nor is a principle of totalizing all there is to "world." In fact, rendering the world into a totality, as globalization arguably does, is the end of the world and the beginning of the world picture. The idea of world the speculative realists are attacking is but an effect of globalizing, capitalist modernity. Such an idea indeed deserves to be condemned. It is a reduction of the world. But so is the alternative that the speculative realists propose in its place.

Borrowing the term from Manuel DeLanda, Levi Bryant calls the alternative "flat ontology," and so does Bogost following Bryant. The plane of flat ontology is two-dimensional. Bogost goes one step further with the reduction, proposing a one-dimensional "tiny ontology":

> If any one being exists no less than any other, then instead of scattering such beings all across the two-dimensional surface of flat ontology, we might also collapse them into the infinite density of the dot. Instead of the *plane* of flat ontology, I suggest the *point* of tiny ontology.[92]

The reduction to zero-dimension, to a point, is Cartesian in spirit: it is a function of computing with clear and distinct elements, as I showed in the first chapter of this book. As Flusser reminds us, in computation "[t]hose elements are taken to be symbols which mean points of the extended world."[93]

The sense of the world is broader and much more nuanced than the picture of the world that has come to dominate in globalizing modernity. It is also broader and more nuanced than what the "flat" or "tiny ontology" allows for. It is indeed a matter of aesthetics, for it concerns the sensible: what can be sensed, and how things can come to be sensed and made sense of. It is a matter of a thoughtful practice, and not so much of conception (which is not to say that the practice is not at some level conceptual). To be more precise, a practice of the sense of the world is not a matter of coming up with another conception of the world. As Jean-Luc Nancy expressed it, "[i]t is no longer a matter of lending or giving the world one more sense, but of entering into this sense, into this gift of sense the world itself is."[94] And if the space of the political is the "space of the 'there is,' "[95] of being together in spite of—and against—separations and divisions ("divide and conquer" being the principle and *modus operandi* of imperial power), then practicing the sense of the world is a crucial political task. Countering the voiding, the reduction of dimensions involved in Cartesian metaphysics and in the "flat," "tiny ontology," the practice of the sense of the world involves an opening up of dimensions—and a play with dimensions. Theatricality can arguably enable such play.

Working with theatricality and with plastics as her primary material, Turkish-American transdisciplinary artist Pinar Yoldas engages in a labor-intensive practice of world/sense-making in her multimedia project *An Ecosystem of Excess* (2014). Yoldas's practice is not utopian; rather, it involves the inhabitation of the existing world through a performance of theatricalized forms of life generated—or programmed—in reaction to the forces that structure the ("real") world in our time. The capitalist system of disposable redundancy constitutes one of these forces. Pushing the idea of plastics as the substrate of all matter to its limit, Yoldas asks: "What if life started now in today's oceans, in our contemporary primordial soup of plastics?"[96] To answer this question, Yoldas creates a kind of 3D *Synthetica* with a twist: her *Ecosystem of Excess* consists of alien entities made of plastics that are capable of sensing and metabolizing plastics. Following Bernhard Waldenfels, I use "alien" here to refer to the (seeming) "inaccessibility of a particular region of experience and sense."[97] As "hyperobjects" that break down into microplastics, synthetic plastics are widely inaccessible to many biological systems of perception, digestion, and metabolism. If we take this seriously, a key (and very difficult) question that arises is: "How to begin to form a viable relationship to alien entities such as plastics?"

Ian Bogost proposes "alien phenomenology" as a suitable practice for dealing with alien entities. Bogost articulates what this philosophical practice amounts to thus:

> As philosophers, our job is to amplify the black noise of objects to make the resonant frequencies of the stuffs inside them hum in credibly satisfying ways. Our job is to write the speculative fictions of their processes, of their unit operations. Our job is to get our hands dirty with grease, juice, gunpowder, and gypsum.[98]

As articulated here, this practice may sound compelling (or, at least, not terribly problematic), although it is unclear what the humming in "satisfying ways" may mean and why we might want to seek satisfaction in these matters. One may wonder: Satisfying to whom? To us who "get our hands dirty" with "gunpowder"? And why does it need to be "satisfying"? And how might getting "our hands dirty" help, especially when some of the stuff is toxic and we are exposed to it anyway?

A key presupposition undergirding Bogost's alien phenomenology is that all things that exist are "fundamentally alien," which is not unlike Morton's saying that all things are "hyperobjects." In Bogost's words, referring back to Thomas Nagel's essay "What It's Like to Be a Bat": "Bats are both ordinary and weird, but so is everything else: toilet seats, absinthe louches, seagulls, trampolines."[99] This totalizing statement is motivated by Bogost's desire "to release objects like ghosts from the prison of human experience."[100] I am not in principle opposed to releasing objects "from the prison of human experience," but, as mentioned earlier, it seems to me crucial to begin to discern the differences between the wide variety of existing alien things and beings—including documented and undocumented "aliens," rendered "alien" by immigration policies, and "alien" species threatened with extinction, which are quite different from the various "alien" consumer products. It seems important to me to recognize that some of these "alien" objects (including plastics) are products of a capitalist, consumerist system that (re)produces disposable redundancy in pursuit of incessant profit-making—profit at the expense of everything and anything. When carelessly discarded, such objects can exert what Rob Nixon has called "slow violence."[101] We might of course find it convenient to think their existence and effects independently of humans and of human experience, but I fear that doing so might also inadvertently or purposefully remove the demand for humans' (taking) responsibility for these effects.

Concerned about the violent effects of plastics, Pinar Yoldas engages in a hands-on form of alien phenomenology that is quite different from Bogost's. This is a transdisciplinary practice that brings together speculative biology, design, philosophy, installation art, and theatre in a piece that engages plastics with all their metaphysical subtleties. To create *An Ecosystem of Excess*, Yoldas works with her hands in plastics, touching the materials, working with their resistance. She also works with the intellectual tools of scientific knowledge (as a collection of facts established by the scientific community), intervening in the game of (re)programming genetic information. One of Yoldas's forms of engagement with science bears the name of "speculative biology." Speculative biology is an art practice that couples synthetic biology ("a field of science that involves redesigning organisms for useful purposes by engineering them to have new abilities")[102] with speculative design and cultural criticism.[103] "Speculative biology simulates futurities," writes Yoldas.[104]

Both with her hands and with conceptual tools, Yoldas works speculatively. Speculation belongs traditionally to the realm of metaphysics as well as to the realm of commerce, where it means "to engage in risky commercial ventures."[105] Traditionally, metaphysical speculation goes beyond the realm of the senses.[106] In a sense, Yoldas's speculative practice also concerns itself with the suprasensible. More specifically, it concerns itself with rendering that which functions as the suprasensible in our times into a matter of experience. Yoldas describes herself as being engaged in designing an experience that would convey to the audience troubling information, real facts.[107] These are facts that are often ignored or denied, facts that most people are often insensitive to, such as that "1,000,000 seabirds die per year due to plastic pollution," as stated on a screen that displays the "primordial soup of plastics" in *An Ecosystem of Excess*.[108] In addition to cultivating sensitivity to known but often ignored or denied facts, Yoldas also goes beyond scientific facts and beyond the realm of what at the moment constitutes possible experience—and existence, for that matter. In *An Ecosystem of Excess*, she stages a form of trans-sensitivity: sensing beyond the sensible. Her *Ecosystem of Excess*, all made of plastic materials, has the capacity to sense (detect and digest) and metabolize plastics. Yoldas terms this capacity "plastoception."[109] With plastoception, as a mode of trans-sensitivity, metaphysics meets alien phenomenology.

The mode of Yoldas's design process is future past: it touches on a resistance from a possibly impossible future, developed in the image of a past that we are currently living, all in hopes of creating a future resistance. It enacts a step not beyond, still in time, where there is still place to inhabit. The designed ecosystem arises at an extreme of adaptation/plasticity: adaptation to the extreme conditions generated by (micro)plastics, which were in turn generated by humans feeding the consumerist-capitalist system of disposable redundancy. This alien ecosystem is staged theatrically (Figure 6), in an installation that inhabits the structure of the natural history museum as well as the structure of biological classification called Linnaean taxonomy. It includes the following alien forms of life: "Plastisphere bacteria";[110] "Stomaximus" ("digestive organ for the plastivore"); "Petrogestative System" ("digestive

FIGURE 6. The theatrical setup of *An Ecosystem of Excess*, by Pinar Yoldas, 2014.

Photo credit Pinar Yoldas. Courtesy of the artist.

system for metabolizing plastics"); "Petronephros" ("kidneys for the plastivore"); "P-plastoceptors" (organs "for sensing plastics"; Figure 7); "Plastisphere insects";[111] "Pacific Balloon Turtle"; "PV Sea Worm and Sea Snake Symbiosis"; and "transchromatic eggs" from "a Benthic Reptile."[112]

The real existence of the life form first listed, the Plastisphere microorganisms endowed with the (super)capacity to metabolize plastics, has been inferred through sophisticated scientific procedures. These procedures rely on various kinds of data, microscopic and molecular.[113] The Plastisphere microorganisms were an inspiration for *An Ecosystem of Excess.* Shifting scales, Yoldas plays with the logic of scientific fact

FIGURE 7. P-plastoceptors in *An Ecosystem of Excess,* by Pinar Yoldas, 2014.

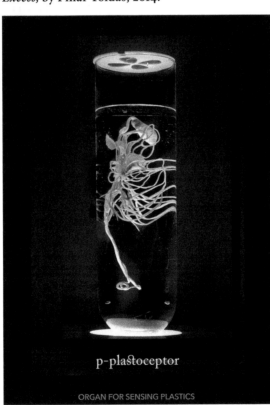

Photo credit Pinar Yoldas. Courtesy of the artist.

production, producing multidimensional and multisensory data for a science yet to come. This is data about plastic nature.

Products of an embodied speculative practice that brings together imagination with observation and conception, the things that constitute *An Ecosystem of Excess* are both theatrical and performative. They both enact a desired reality (organisms that can actually detect, digest, and metabolize plastics) and mediate a relationship to an existing reality (the presence of plastics in the environment today) that is both too obvious and often imperceptible to humans (microplastics). Viewed from the perspective of J. L. Austin's conception of the performative, the alien entities that constitute Yoldas's *Ecosystem of Excess* might be called failed ("void," "hollow"), like all performatives that take place in a theatrical setting.[114] But this is a rather simplistic view. In fact, the objects that comprise Yoldas's *Ecosystem of Excess* do what their names say they do, at the perceptual level. At the ontological level, like all theatrical things, they both are and are not what their names say they are. They are not, yet . . .

Yoldas's *Ecosystem of Excess* is a plastic nature, both literally (they are made of industrial plastic materials) and figuratively. The notion of plastic nature actually goes back to seventeenth-century philosophy. For the Cambridge Platonist Ralph Cudworth, for instance, "plastic nature" is incontestably "incorporeal, all life being essentially such."[115] Incorporeal substances, by contrast to "passive" matter, are "essentially active."[116] They have "internal energy and self-activity," which Cudworth takes to be the equivalent of "life."[117] "Plastic nature," for Cudworth, is an incorporeal substance of a lower kind; it is, he writes, "an inferior and subordinate instrument."[118] Seventeenth-century philosopher, playwright, and early science fiction writer Margaret Cavendish disagrees with this view, arguing that "plastic power" is the "power of the corporeal, figurative motions of nature," and that "nature" is "entirely wise and knowing."[119] If humans deny this and treat other, non-human beings as "ignorant, dull, stupid, senseless and irrational," then this is a sign either of their conceit or of their ignorance.[120] For, all parts of nature have "sense and reason, which is life and knowledge."[121] All parts of nature, which are widely varied, are "self-moving"; they are thus also "self-knowing and perceptive."[122] Cavendish defines perception and self-knowledge as follows:

[A]s all sensitive perception is a kind of touch, so all rational perception is a kind of thoughtfulness . . . all self-knowledge is a
kind of thoughtfulness and . . . thought is a rational touch, as
touch is a sensitive thought.[123]

Unlike Cudworth's plastic nature, the specimens of Yoldas's ecosystem of excess are not passive and incorporeal. On the contrary,
like Cavendish's plastic nature, they are corporeal, self-moving, self-
knowing, and perceptive. As both sensing and metabolism, the kind
of perception they perform, which Yoldas terms "plastoception," can
be said to be "a kind of thoughtfulness," where "thought is a rational
touch," and "touch is a sensitive thought" (as Cavendish wrote). An encounter with a plastic nature of this kind constitutes an invitation to
practice thoughtfulness, towards transforming one's habits of perception and action. But substantial transformation necessarily takes time
and an enduring practice. And it is often hard work. Certain kinds of
artistic practices may provide a starting point for such transformation.

ON GATHERING: THEATRICAL LABORS

In the face of the voracious consumerist-capitalist economic system
of disposable redundancy, American photographer, filmmaker, and
activist Chris Jordan creates not maps of plastics but, rather, depictions—or "portraits," as he calls them—of the widespread habit of rendering things disposable. An acknowledged influence on Yoldas's own
work with plastics, Jordan's practice is a labor-intensive performance of
concern, a mode of engagement with the world that involves repeating
with difference certain states of affairs so as to open the possibility for
transformation (of behavior, first and foremost). Jordan is concerned to
counteract behaviors that are harmful and persistent precisely because
they are collective, habits that are harmful because they are widespread.
These habits are sustained by industries and corporations that drive the
economic system of disposable redundancy.

    In some of his works, Jordan is a collector of things, and his art
practice relies on a kind of synthesis that is radically different from the
one used in chemical/industrial plastic production. He gathers objects
that have been disposed after single (or, in best-case scenarios, short-

term) use; for the most part, these are serial objects, repeatable "units" (to channel Bogost's term). Jordan photographs each one of the collected items in different positions. He then prints a number of these photos equal to the number featured in select statistics related to certain contemporary collective behaviors. For example, Jordan's 2007 piece *Plastic Bags* "depicts 60,000 plastic bags, the number used in the US every five seconds."[124] In the final stage, through painstaking digital manipulation, Jordan combines the numerous printed photos in a large photomosaic that sometimes looks like a somewhat abstract landscape, especially in the collection *Running the Numbers: An American Self-Portrait* (2006–current), and, at other times, like an iconic image, especially in the collection *Running the Numbers II: Portraits of Global Mass Culture* (2009–current). In both forms, these photomosaics are attempts at rendering very large finitude tangible, so that it no longer seems to be something "out there" removed from "me," something that does not concern "me." In *Return of the Dinosaurs* (2011), for instance, if we step back (or zoom out online), we come to realize that the 240,000 plastic bags take the form of a dinosaur.[125] The humorous (or tragicomic?) logic of the choice of this figure is that plastic bags are "made of oil, and oil is made of dinosaurs."[126]

Jordan's work aims to enable an embodied experience and understanding of the problem at hand. He thus turns abstract data regarding countable (disposable) objects, which in fact hides collective behaviors, into portrait-like visual composites that one can begin to sense and make sense of. This opens up the possibility of responding by taking action. As Jordan states in an interview:

> These issues that are so important in the real world, exist only in our mind as an abstract figure. . . . If we can't comprehend the issue then we don't feel anything, therefore we don't act. I'm trying to create these images that point toward comprehension of the issues so we begin to feel something, so it's not just an intellectual exercise. If we feel angry, or sad, or frightened, that is when we act decisively.[127]

The numbers in the statistics are enormous, so the visual composites feature a large number of photographs, and the final images are over-

sized (*Return of the Dinosaurs*, for instance, is 44" x 57" and 60" x 77").
From a distance, Jordan's pieces may look like other artworks we have
seen before, even iconic ones, such as Botticelli's *The Birth of Venus*.
Jordan's 2011 *Venus*, birthed from the sea—60" x 103" in one panel and
8' x 13' in three panels—looks exactly like Botticelli's, from a distance.
However, if we get closer to it or zoom in online, we catch a glimpse of
what ultimately amounts to reproducible sameness as we begin to discern piles and piles of plastic bags—multiplied and manipulated images
of plastic bags that Jordan collected from stores in downtown Seattle,
where they were given away for "free" (Figures 8 and 9).[128] And then we
read the panel on the wall or under the digital image in the online gallery, which says that the piece "[d]epicts 240,000 plastic bags, equal to
the estimated number of plastic bags consumed around the world every
ten seconds," and maybe we begin to feel startled, even horrified.[129] Syn-
thesized as they are in this iconic image, the otherwise disposable and
valueless plastic bags come to matter. They too are things that need to
be taken care of.

From a distance, at first sight, Jordan's *Venus* may be judged to be

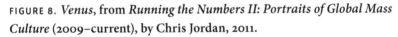

FIGURE 8. *Venus*, from *Running the Numbers II: Portraits of Global Mass
Culture* (2009–current), by Chris Jordan, 2011.

Courtesy of the artist.

FIGURE 9. *Venus* detail, from *Running the Numbers II: Portraits of Global Mass Culture* (2009–current), by Chris Jordan, 2011.

Courtesy of the artist.

beautiful. Venus, after all, is the goddess of beauty in the Western imaginary. The figure of Venus is particularly intriguing in relation to plastic, in several ways. The "Plastics in 1940" article featured—in addition to the *Synthetica* map discussed earlier—a two-page illustration of *An American Dream of Venus* consisting of a "surrealist derangement" of various plastic objects.[130] The "derangement" of objects includes a transparent, mannequin-like figure that looks more like Venus de Milo than like Botticelli's Venus. Notably, all the plastic products that compose the *American Dream of Venus* are said to "rise up from the plastic sea."[131] Since 1940, this metaphor has become fact: the oceans have literally become "plastic seas"; the dream has turned out to be a nightmare.

The caption that accompanies the *American Dream of Venus* emphasizes the metaphysical subtleties of plastic, its seemingly endless capacity to morph into anything and to produce "endless products of this new world in the process of becoming."[132] It also subtly suggests the connection between the development of plastics and (world) war, which may explain the need for plastics' durability: Venus, the "transparent lady," also "serves as the nonshatterable windshield on bombing planes," we are told.[133] A cliché of femininity and a "poster girl of sticky male fantasies,"[134] Venus, in its transparency, becomes a cover for the (world) destruction and division on which war thrives.

Revealing beauty in pollution and destruction could be read as a form of aestheticization, involving the voiding of content whereby intellectual perception is meant to attend only to the form of what is being presented. In Jordan's work, however, beauty is used strategically, to "trick the viewer."[135] Beauty is for Jordan like a "sugarcoating" that is meant to attract the viewer and enable engagement.[136] The spectators who engage with his work closely attend not only to form but also to what gives the form. They attend to pattern and to the individual bits and pieces that form the pattern. From a distance, this pattern displays a form of beauty that is supposedly timeless, such as Botticelli's painting, in the case of the *Venus* piece. Yet, as Jonathan Jones remarked, "[t]he world's most beautiful and timeless works of art are also its biggest clichés and most absurd cultural phenomena."[137] It is the image of this cliché that Jordan's *Venus* inhabits. Composed as it is of nonbiodegradable plastic bags (even if only in images), it ironically literalizes timelessness and, at the same time, registers a kind of urgent time of the planet, in this way challenging the very cliché of the timelessness it re-performs. When the cliché breaks open, horror pierces through the beauty, and the two coexist, blended, inseparable from each other: horror and beauty, beauty and horror.

Eugene Thacker conceptualizes "horror" not "as dealing with human fear in a human world (the world-for-us)"; instead, he proposes that "horror be understood as being about the limits of the human as it confronts a world that is not just a World, and not just the Earth, but also a Planet (the world-without-us)."[138] Speaking about my personal experience of Jordan's "portraits," I would say that the sense of horror I felt was indeed not fear. In some sense, what I felt had something to do with "the limits of the human as it confronts a world that is not just a World, and not just the Earth, but also a Planet," though this world—at least in my experience—was not "the world-without-us" but rather, "the world-*because*-of-us." What I felt was an intense sense of frustration and concern in the face of the massive violence and exploitation hidden

behind the plastic bags that composed the *Venus* nightmare, in which I
was (and am) complicit, whether I want it or not.

Jordan's work does not perform an aestheticization of the reality of
pollution and environmental destruction. Rather, it engages in multisensory, haptic practices of inhabiting—to the point of absurdity and
beyond—structures and mechanisms that shape reality in a given historical context. The point of these practices of inhabiting is to make
aware and, hopefully, to open the way for the transformation of widespread habits of thinking and living. These practices involve repetition
with a difference. In the case of Jordan's "portraits," we may think about
postmodern citationality, and indeed, Jordan's practice is citational, but
his work does not share the parodic, ironic, or cynical sensibilities of
postmodernism. On the contrary. The works that comprise Jordan's
Running the Numbers series inhabit the structure of beauty, and of an
aestheticized reality, theatrically. They render these structures problematic through the mode of engagement that they invite: zooming in and
zooming out, stepping closer and stepping back, lingering on plastic bag
as a unit of thought, multiplied. This mode of engagement replicates the
mode of thinking that Descartes recommends as part of his method for
training the mind in metaphysics: guided movements from the complex to the simple (breakdown of the complex into its simplest parts),
and from the simple to the complex (assembling the simplest units into
varied patterns). As I discussed in Chapter 2, such movements (call them
analysis and synthesis, if you will) undergird the mode of thinking called
computation. Jordan's works make this mode of thinking sensible, even
tangible: in the encounter with his works from the *Running the Numbers*
series, thought potentially becomes "a rational touch" and "touch . . . a
sensitive thought" (to repeat Cavendish's words).[139]

The mode of production of Jordan's works too counters the aestheticization of reality. Jordan's art practice is labor-intensive, produced on
low (or no) budgets, and not at all profitable. The labor it involves takes
a lot of effort and time, and it is often "obsessive" and "tedious."[140] As
Jordan elaborates:

> There is not a lot of artistic input in the process. For example,
> walking down a commercial street in Seattle and collecting 600
> plastic bags and then photographing every single one of them

and then in 10 different positions and then cutting all of those bags out from their different backgrounds and then comparing them to be built into a giant image of hundreds of thousands of plastic bags.[141]

The labor of gathering, rearranging, and organizing that Jordan performs is not a form of the "immaterial labor" that has become a dominant model of labor in neoliberal, post-Fordist times. As discussed in Chapter 2, through Maurizio Lazzarato, immaterial labor is in the business of (re)producing a certain model of subjectivity.[142] This model is defined by flexibility, adaptability, and the embracing of (ever-)new lifestyles, packaged and sold on the market as disposable things and the experiences they are designed to afford. Jordan's work is not in the business of the (re)production of the neoliberal model of subjectivity. Instead, it invites those who encounter it to occupy a position from which to face the reality of a very large finitude in which they are participants, and to engage with it across shifting scales, thoughtfully. And to relate to it as a consequence of consumerist behaviors in which everyone participates to some extent. Neoliberal (prepackaged) subjectivity manifests through such consumerist behaviors. The labor that Jordan performs—which ranges from the laborious conceptualization of a project, to the physical gathering of plastics, to various social interactions, to tedious digital manipulation, to the affective labor of attending to the violent effects of plastic pollution—blurs the boundaries between material and immaterial, intellectual and manual labor. In fact, I suggest, these different modes of labor are inseparable from each other as all labor is necessarily embodied. Also embodied is the labor of the viewer attending to Jordan's photomosaics: the conceptual work she/he/they perform (zooming in and zooming out) is tied to physical movement (moving closer and further away) and to affective labor (from a sense of beauty to horror and frustration, even sadness or grief). All of this is related to the materiality collected in the "portraits" and to the concept of the collection.

—Stop, breathe, feel something—[143]

Now consider this: the plastic, the ocean, the plastic that the ocean carries, the plastic that it brings ashore, the plastic washed up on the

shores of, for instance, Sian Ka'an, one of Mexico's largest federally pro-
tected biosphere reserves. This is a UNESCO World Heritage Site, with
more than twenty pre-Columbian archeological sites and a temporary
(but, when dispersed, likely more persistent than even the ancient ruins
nearby) Garbage Museum/Museo de la Basura. The artworks installed
in the museum, and on the coast of Sian Ka'an, are by Mexico City-
born, Brooklyn-based artist Alejandro Durán and his fellow plastic
gatherers. "By" here is not meant to indicate ownership but labor, and a
collective performance of concern. In this case, it is labor that is inextricably bound up with the place where it happens. It can be called site-
specific, but it is more than that. It gives place and puts into place things
that most often have no proper place to take. In this way, it participates
in the sense of the world, in the world's making sense, where "world"
is, following Nancy, "precisely that in which there is room for everyone:
but a genuine place, one in which things can genuinely *take place*."[144]

The labor of gathering bits and pieces of plastic washed ashore of
Sian Ka'an takes time and effort. The gathered pieces are sorted by types
and colors and arranged into site-specific installations, which make up
the *Washed Up* project. At times, the installations imitate the distri-
bution of the objects that the waves could potentially create; at other
times, "the plastic mimics algae, roots, rivers, or fruit."[145] Durán's work
repeats what is already the case. Engaging in a form of bio-mimesis, it
is a faithful imitation, but with a difference.

In plain sight on the shore, the collected plastics create what Durán
calls a "surreal" landscape, ironically in keeping with the caption accompanying *Fortune*'s plastic *Venus* illustration.[146] Except that *Washed
Up* is not a matter of "derangement" but, on the contrary, of arrangement and design: white bottles of various detergents, shampoos, oils,
and so forth lie on the rocky beach like oversized pebbles; green PET
bottles stretch over the rocks washed by the sea like algae; multicolored
striped plastic balls mix with coconuts at the foot of a coconut tree.[147]
At stake here is not really a matter of bringing order where there was
disorder; what may appear as disorder to unaided human perception
is highly ordered at the molecular level anyway. Instead, Durán's work
gathers rather than disposes of things, in a gesture of resistance to what
Durán calls "a new form of colonization by consumerism":[148] coloniza-

tion of the totality of the world by the relentless productions of capital and the habits and behaviors fueling the system of disposable redundancy. In the course of the *Washed Up* project, Durán has documented products made in "sixty different countries and territories."[149] This flow of multinational products pertains to globalization.

In this way, Durán's practice of plastic collection also doubles as a practice of data gathering: of building evidence for the obvious, for the commonplace. This evidence concerns the plastics that (re)surface stubbornly, as if they were looking for their makers, like Plastic Bag in Bahrani's film. The evidence gathered is meant to counter ignorance, denial, disinterest, indifference—all the "mental gymnastics" that keeps us from facing reality, as psychologist David Kidner put it.[150] Yet, the obvious comprises not only the plastics that are hyper-visible, which can be taken in hand, photographed, and (at least partly) recycled, but also the plastics that exist beyond the limits of unaided human perception (and, often, also of human knowledge): microplastics, or bits of plastic "that are less than five millimeters in length."[151] This is how plastics often exist in the oceans: obvious, all too obvious, but oftentimes imperceptible—and always (dis)simulating.

MIDWAY: DRIFTING/REFUGE

Floating, drifting, disintegrating plastics wash up on the shores of Midway, an island in the middle of the Pacific Ocean, "more than 2,000 miles away from the nearest continent," in the middle of nowhere and everywhere.[152] It is one of the many islands in the Pacific that has been bombed, dumped on, bulldozed, and parceled. Historically, Midway has also been a medium—a point of connection and portal of communication:

> In 1903, the Commercial Pacific Cable Company laid cables on Midway that carried the first around-the-world telegraph. . . . Midway later served as a key stopover for flights connecting North America and Asia.[153]

And for many long decades, Midway was a U.S. military base. During World War II, the United States defeated the Japanese Imperial Navy in the Battle of Midway, which marked "the turning point of the war in the Pacific."[154] Since the end of the Cold War, the military base has fallen into ruin, in the midst of which a national wildlife refuge has grown as a "monument" of nature: the Papahānaumokuākea Marine National Monument.[155] The refuge is the site of the world's largest albatross nesting colony, for there are no predators (except, recently, mice).[156]

Midway is a literal metaphor and a local symptom for a global problem. "With the birds on Midway, you don't have to see the quantity to understand the global problem," says Chris Jordan.[157] Jordan traveled to Midway repeatedly over the past decade. He had heard from an environmental scientist that the Pacific gyre was in the bellies of baby albatrosses on Midway, and he went to document it. When he traveled there the first time in 2009, he witnessed it in large quantities in the stomachs of disintegrating birds after all the surviving albatrosses had left the island. Upon his subsequent returns, the surviving birds were back on the island, with their stunning courting and hatching rituals, with their long expeditions that involve flying even 10,000 miles on one trip to collect food to bring back to their babies on the island. "An albatross is the grandest living flying machine on Earth. An albatross is bone, feathers, muscle, and the wind," writes Carl Safina poetically . . . but later adds: "But let's not burden albatrosses with our metaphors. Doing so, we fail to see the real birds, which connect us to what's happening in the seas in ways many of us can scarcely imagine."[158]

Albatrosses are scavengers, natural collectors. They collect food from the midst of the ocean, with all the visible and invisible stuff that floats in and on it, as "their instinct is to trust what the ocean provides, as they and their ancestors have done for millions of years."[159] Deceptive plastic tricks them; they take it to be nourishing food. A malicious deceiver intimately tied to capitalism and Cartesian metaphysics, synthetic plastic is not only an agent of simulation but also of dissimulation. It dissimulates as, and infiltrates in, food and water. Ingested by albatrosses, it sometimes gets caught in cavities or folds of bodies. Toothbrushes, cigarette lighters, red bottle caps, blue bottle caps, green bottle caps, straws, forks, syringes, round things, deformed things, pointed things, things with sharp edges . . . the refuse that refuses to go away . . . Sometimes, the plastics fill up bodies to the point of bursting, while the bodies feel (themselves) empty: after all, totalizing presence can be an equivalent of emptiness. "Some die from stomach punctures. Others slowly starve, weak and weighted down, their bellies full but empty of anything to nourish them."[160]

Jordan spent his time on Midway filming and photographing the albatrosses, all day long, without any script or agenda in mind:[161] filming them singing and dancing their tender dance of love (albatrosses only come to land to mate and raise their babies), hatching, learning to fly, preparing for their long first journey, and—many of them—dying before they even learn to fly or just as they are trying to take off. The photographs constitute a project titled *Midway: Message from the Gyre* (2009–current), and the footage forms the material for a film titled *Albatross* (2017).[162] The film is "offered as a free public artwork" that can be downloaded and watched by anyone, for doing otherwise and treating it "as a commercial product" would mean to "tacitly endorse the same destructive machine of mass consumption that filled our beloved birds with plastic in the first place."[163]

At one point in Jordan's film, the narrator reveals that all of the birds have plastics in them (Figure 10). This is known for a fact because, after the 2011 tsunami washed over Midway, killing many of the birds, the scientists and environmentalists working on the island opened up the corpses: they all had plastics in them. "The good news is that they are not all dying from it," the narrator's voice says. Some of their bodies can endure the plastics they bear inside them; they adapt. The adult albatrosses can regurgitate some of the ingested plastics. But the babies do not have the ability to regurgitate until they are six months old. They do so before they fly away from the island for the first time; they empty themselves before they fly out. Some have so much plastic inside them, plastic that their parents had fed them, that they cannot regurgitate it. Plastic does not crunch. Some perish because the plastics are sharp, poking holes inside their stomachs. And there is also the accumulating toxicity. Which albatrosses live, and which die . . . is "a lottery of horrors," Jordan tells me.

Jordan thinks Midway's message is about needing to heal something in us, such as the widespread habit of being in denial of death, which makes us kill indiscriminately, often from a distance, or let die,

FIGURE 10. *Midway: Message from the Gyre* (2009–current),
by Chris Jordan, 2009.

Courtesy of the artist.

even from close up. In some sense, synthetic plastics that seemingly
last forever literally embody the denial of death. Jordan stood with the
albatrosses as they were dying, complicit in their death, as I am, as you
are, in our different ways. As I write this, I am put in mind of Kim Tall-
Bear's articulation of "standing with" as a mode of being and research.
Substantially different from "setting before" (Heidegger's formula for
"representation"), "standing with" involves, in TallBear's words, being
"willing to be altered" as part of the research process, where research
is not so much—or not only—about "data gathering" but also about
"relationship-building."[164] In this light, *Midway: Message from the Gyre*
and *Albatross* can be seen as part of an artistic research project, one that
is both personal and collective (and collectively shared).

As participant observer and archivist of the lives and deaths of the
island, Jordan often stands very close to the ground, at the level of the

birds, coming closer and moving back in an ongoing improvised dance, sensing their presence and resistance. The work of filming, the dance of holding the camera following the birds, is physically demanding; it requires endurance, just as standing with the albatrosses as they die requires endurance. For Jordan, this way of standing with is also a practice of thoughtfulness and a ritual of grieving. He seeks to reenact the ritual together with the audience in *Albatross,* the film. The film starts with a still photograph of a dead albatross filled with plastics and the accompanying sound of a clicking camera. Cut. Five dying scenes follow, building incrementally in beauty and horror, towards the most intense and unbearable horror. At one point in the film, the narrator's voice speaks about summoning the courage to face the hard truths of our times, and not look away. "In the act of witnessing," the narrator says, "a doorway opens" that may even lead "home," which for Jordan refers to "our deepest connection with life."[165] This sounds poetic, but it need not be—or, need not be only poetic. "Home" is literally where the plastics come from, where the consumer habits are passed down, enacted, and (re)produced. But "home" is also that personal place that conjoins with the collective, the social and the political, through multiple mediations and ties: the place from where the undoing and remaking of habits can start.

Standing with the albatrosses as they are dying on Midway, the cameraman (played by Jordan for the most part) is crying, his whole body shaking, the image shaking. As I am watching it, the shaking image moves me in a way I have rarely experienced before, and my whole body starts to shake. Crying disarticulates something in me; something that was rigid and immovable softens. I begin to feel something for the birds, like (though *not* because) I feel for a friend whom I lost a few years ago—my dear friend who decades ago went into a store in Yugoslavia to ask for a free plastic bag, the same friend who shared with me the anecdote about the manipulated "automatic" arms narrated in the previous chapter. Now, after his too early passing, I feel his enduring absent presence, his present absence changes my way of being in the world. As I see them dying right before my eyes, I begin to care about the nameless albatrosses, not conceptually (which, as an ecologically minded researcher, I thought I always did), but in a different way, which I find hard to put down in words.

The albatrosses' dying as a result of the relentless workings and habits of the consumerist-capitalist system of disposable redundancy summons another scene of ongoing dying as a result of the relentless workings and habits of the *racial* consumerist-capitalist system of disposable redundancy, which I cannot help but think of. In a different part of the world, closer to my Romanian home, not only all kinds of plastics (synthetic fibers in clothes, Styrofoam objects, water bottles, rubber rafts, children's floaty devices, a small red whistle that says "OK") but also human bodies have been washing ashore lately, in these late late capitalist times.[166] Those who make it to the shore are wrapped in plastic (supposedly) "lifesaving" jackets, which are meant to help the bodies keep floating if the overcrowded boats capsize, as many boats have done—with several thousands dead and missing in recent years.[167] They are fleeing the "wars of global capital," in Afghanistan, Côte d'Ivoire, the Democratic Republic of Congo, Eritrea, Iraq, Palestine, Somalia, Syria, Tunisia, and elsewhere, wars that "Western Europe, the United States, and their global business partners are responsible for" and in

FIGURE 11. *Life Vest Landscape*, Lesvos, by Pam Longobardi, 2017.

Courtesy of the artist and Front Room Gallery, Hudson, New York.

which they are implicated through military presence and resource exploitation.[168]

"Europe's largest refugee camp"—"[w]ith more than 12,000 people living in squalid living conditions in a bleak tent camp designed for 3,000"—was in Lesvos (or Lesbos), until it was largely destroyed by a fire that Human Rights Watch researcher Eva Cossé has called "a testament to the European Union's negligence and Greece's negligence."[169] Unlike Midway, Lesvos, the refuge, is not a monument—unless we take its "lifejacket memorial," alternatively referred to as the "lifejacket graveyard" or the "mountain of misery," to be a monument (Figure 11).[170] Made of non-biodegradable plastics, like the Garbage Museum assembled by Durán and his co-workers, the "lifejacket memorial" will last (in some shape or form) close to forever; like any monument, it may—or may not—prevent forgetting, even if it keeps getting bigger. Perhaps the "lifejacket memorial" will also remain in a different way, as a monument in constant circulation, in the form of the bags that refugees and some locals living in Mytilene, Lesvos's capital, were at one point making out of the reusable nylon fabric from the lifejackets, as part of a project supported by the Lesvos Solidarity organization.[171] Maybe this too, the making of bags out of the discarded lifejackets, is a grieving ritual, and labor is very much part of it. It is a ritual performed under conditions of extreme precarity and increasing hostility from the Greek islanders. Many complications and complicated histories of violence, exploitation, and (neo)colonialism are woven within the fabrics that make up the bags. Can Plastic Bag carry all this weight?

CODA: THE WEIGHT OF PLASTIC BAG

In the opening scene of this chapter, Plastic Bag remained trapped amidst the continent of plastics floating in the Pacific, for a long time. Let us now return to it, by way of a conclusion. Eventually, the waves set Plastic Bag free again. Eventually, the currents carry it towards the shore. As it approaches the shoreline, it catches water, trapped as it is in the regular back and forth of the breaking waves. Filled with water, Plastic Bag entraps a performer's face, turning it into a distorted mask. The performer is Chicana interdisciplinary artist Nao Bustamante, and we are now watching *Sans Gravity* (1993–2003), performed in a theatrical space filled with plastic bags that stay put on the stage, kept in place by the weight of the water they contain.[172]

Head inside Plastic Bag, Bustamante seals her face, wrapping tape around the bag that surrounds her face and neck. "Beautiful" is floating on a large screen behind her, as her face gets distorted, running out of air inside the plastic bag filled with water. This image is deeply resonant, in manifold ways. Regarding *Sans Gravity*, Argelys Samuel Oriach notes that, "for a reader engaged in the discourse of blackness within a historical moment bent on perpetuating anti-black racism and reconfigurations of racialized slavery," the plastic bag filled with water suffocating the performer "is also symbolic of the trans-Atlantic slave trade and those slave ships that carried the unknown bodies of the African Diaspora across the expansive sea"—and of the bodies drowned in the wake of the slave ships.[173] In the current historical context, the image might also remind us of the thousands of refugees drowned after overcrowded boats capsized while crossing the Mediterranean. And it may put us in mind of the many living organisms inhabiting the oceans, earth, and sky that routinely get suffocated, choking on plastics. In all these readings, Plastic Bag filled with water becomes a remainder of the past that is not past, a past that is ongoing, "unfolding still."[174]

After Bustamante's temporary release from Plastic Bag's suffocating grasp, water-filled plastic bags begin to multiply on the performer's body. Following Bustamante's directions, audience members (acting as stagehands) attach more and more plastic bags to her body. They tape plastic bags all over Bustamante's body. The ongoing taping, seemingly increasingly furious, sounds like cutting. Burdened with plastic bags, the performer's body now carries the environment quite literally attached to her skin; she is in a sense composed by what surrounded her. The performer's body is now fully covered in plastic bags, and she looks like an alien creature. All the weight that burdens her makes it hard for Bustamante to move. Some of the stagehands/audience members give her support, aiding the difficult movement, without however removing the weight.

In an essay about Bustamante's work titled "The Vulnerability Artist," José Esteban Muñoz reads the burden attached to the performer's body as "the weight of affect" projected by others, making the body "vulnerable to the point of duress."[175] This reading draws on an understanding of "the force of cultural logics like racism or homophobia" as, "at an essential level, affective constructs, which is to say feelings projected outwards and inwards."[176] These kinds of projections, driven by the force of habit, shape the (social) space in which the body moves and affect its plasticity—its flexibility and potential for change. The body bears weight, the weight of histories of dispossession, violence, and injustice. In a white supremacist patriarchal system, gender, sexual orientation, race, ethnicity, class, and perceived ability play a significant role in shaping the kinds of burdens a body is forced to carry in different social spaces.

In *Sans Gravity*, the overburdening of the performer's body by taping water-filled plastic bags onto it is a manner of sculpting the body, in some sense. Bustamante in fact uses the language of sculpting in describing her work: "I think of my 'props' and gestures as a sculptor may think of materials—clay, plastics, shag carpet, etc."[177] In *Sans Gravity*, it is not Bustamante who does the sculpting but rather the audience members become stagehands, following her directions (in part). This kind of sculpting goes counter to the ideal, or fantasy, of plasticity as the potential for infinite changeability and flexibility: it is a manner of deforming and distorting that makes it hard to move and even breathe. This kind of sculpting turns the performer into a theatrical subject-object that resembles "a creature of social reality as well as a creature of fiction."[178] Through her insistent endurance of the growing weight to the point of duress, which makes the performance hard to watch but also hard to look away from, this theatrical subject-object performs a kind of "material objection" to the violent burdening of the body.[179]

According to Bustamante's description of the performance: "The weight and the movement of the water develop into extensions of the gesture and another layer of the distorted self. The audience becomes a mechanism of relief."[180] After having acted as a mechanism of burdening and entrapment, audience members/stagehands now act as a mechanism of relief. Muñoz reads this relief as a reparative moment, an "act of liberation or extraction of self from the affective burden of ugly feelings."[181] But the relief is not without violence. The audience members have been offered plastic forks, needles, and other sharp instruments. Sharp instruments in hand, they pierce Bustamante's burdened body. Plastic bags pop, water runs out of them. The reparation, theatrically actualized in the live moment of the performance, is but a gesture, an open possibility. For just like the (now pierced) plastic bags remain attached to the performer's body, the past—just like plastic—doesn't go away, only elsewhere, dragging into the future, carried in and by the body. The past—like plastic, and the Plastic Bag with which I started—accumulates layers of histories and of stories. It is a refuse that refuses to go away.

4

ON CIRCULATION

Virality and Internet Performances

••• Synthetic plastic is tied to histories of accumulation and the accumulation of layers of history undergirded by violence and the extraction of labor and resources in the pursuit of profit. Its stubborn persistence depends on the multiplication—and/through circulation—not only of the material called plastic but also of the habits of thinking and living that keep consumerism, capitalism's double, going. "Virality" may be another name for this mode of circulation: one that intensifies (the force of) what is being reproduced through the voiding of history and context. This chapter continues to explore the circulation of ideas, images, habits, and objects, and the virality that characterizes it, as it connects with the internet, the (dis)simulation machine—or, more accurately, networking of (dis)simulating thinking machines and the infrastructure that underlies them—that is central to the present-day capitalist attention economy.

Personally, since I left Romania fifteen years ago, I have spent a lot of my time on the internet, which—among other things—has enabled me to stay in touch with home. With the COVID-19 pandemic, the time spent online has only increased as many activities moved online by necessity; making live theatre was one of them. But life online is hard. (Hyper)connectivity comes at a price: information overload, fatigue and confusion, an increase in one's digital footprint, an expansion of the "minable social."[1] As many hours and lives get spent online globally (even as there is undoubtedly a digital divide that cuts across geographic as well as class and racial lines),[2] being on the internet emerges as a present-day condition that approximates *The Matrix* or the "brain in a vat" scenario, or Nozick's experience machine discussed in Chapter 1. The internet is an experience machine that is in the business of programming daily life, as well as its financialization.[3] Like the plastic card, it is a site (in fact, myriad sites) for data collection. And like plastic, it is a malicious deceiver intimately tied to capitalism and Cartesian metaphysics, one that has featured prominently in common understandings of the notion of post-truth. This chapter highlights how this malicious deceiver embodies the logic of (dis)simulation and looks to performance and theatricality for ways of countering, refusing, and displacing this logic and the virality associated with it. Specifically, I will engage with an online theatre performance that I co-created and directed—an experiment presented with findings. I will also engage with works by American Artist, an interdisciplinary artist who "makes thought experiments that mine the history of technology, race, and knowledge production,"[4] and by British-born Egyptian multimedia artist, musician, and writer Hassan Khan.

THE INTERNET AS (DIS)SIMULATION MACHINE

The internet—"the wider network that allows computer networks around the world run by companies, governments, universities, and other organisations to talk to one another," or the "computer as medium"—has become the main medium for social exchange.[5] At a basic level, what is being exchanged (circulated) is information. Oftentimes used interchangeably with "data," in a certain usage "information" is distinguished from the latter as follows: information is data that has been processed and thus has utility.[6] In this chapter, "information" is used with both of these meanings (as data, and as processed data that has utility). The distinction between data and information supposedly marks the difference between humans and machines: "Computers need data. Humans need information."[7] This distinction, however, needs to be complicated, for information is computational through and through; calculation undergirds it.

Drawing on the thought of Alfred Sohn-Rethel, Jonathan Beller argues that information is real abstraction, *"a capitalizing way of knowing and doing"* that emerges out of capitalistic commodity exchange, "specifically from price as a number that when attached to a denomination quantifies the value of anything whatever."[8] What information enables and sustains is "an instrumental approach to life by collapsing its dimensions."[9] As shown in Chapter 1 of the present book, the core elements of abstraction are shared between capitalism and the Cartesian metaphysics established through the experiment of radical doubt and the scenario of the malicious deceiver. These core elements are: the voiding of sensory material and history; the reliance on and reduction of the world to mathematics (calculation, quantification); the mind/body divide; and what Sohn-Rethel termed "the postulate of automatism."[10] Recall that, through the experiment of radical doubt, Descartes secured the existence of a thinking "I" and of a world construed as the subject matter of mathematics. I have argued that the kind of thinking that thus secures a hollowed out, impoverished "I" and world (picture) is performative: it is a matter of force, of producing a desired effect, which relies on the voiding of semantic content, sensory material, and history. This mode of thinking acts on and changes reality, rendering things equivalent as units of reproducible sameness within a mechanism ("the world as machine"). Building on that argument, I propose that information (and its exchange) is performative in this sense.

In his articulation of "The Mathematical Theory of Communication," Claude Shannon wrote:

> The fundamental problem of communication is that of reproducing at one point either exactly or approximately a message selected at another point. Frequently the messages have *meaning*; that is they refer to or are correlated according to some system with certain physical or conceptual entities. **These semantic aspects of communication are irrelevant to the engineering problem.**[11]

From the mathematical point of view, within the framework of engineering, what matters in the exchange of information is the production of the desired effect (effectiveness) rather than the semantic content transmitted, although information is commonly referred to as "content."[12] Performativity (simulation) is at play here, even as the information dissimulates—and may be perceived at the human end—as a statement of fact, a matter of truth and falsity. In light of this, rather than being an aberration, "information disorders"[13] such as mis- and disinformation, fake news, and so on—the whole range of phenomena associated with the notion of post-truth—are part and parcel of the logic of information, as well as of (dis)simulation. After all, to be dis- or misinformed is still a way of being informed.

Referring to "the political economy of post-truth," Evgeny Morozov noted that "post-truth is to digital capitalism what pollution is to fossil capitalism—a by-product of operations."[14] In this book I have shown that it is in fact a product of the logic of (dis)simulation, which is the structuring logic not only of *digital* capitalism but of *all* capitalistic exchange. In capitalism, the ultimate desired effect is profit generation; in the capitalist attention economy—which in its latest phase coincides with the monetization of the web and, relatedly, with big data—a key way of making profit is by re-selling attention, for paying attention online enables the collection of data as traces of one's online behavior. It is through the production and consumption of "content" (information, dis/misinformation, fake news, etc.) that attention is harvested and data captured—hence, Bill Gates's "Content Is King."[15] What Gates called "content," Guy Debord termed "the spectacle," which—taking the form of "information or propaganda, . . . advertisement or direct entertainment consumption"—is in fact "the other side of money: . . . the general abstract equivalent of all commodities."[16] In this, it resembles synthetic plastics, the substrate for modern payment systems, which in fact are the precursor to "the internet and its mobile appendages."[17] Like plastics, information has planned obsolescence built into it. Like plastics, as it disintegrates, it memetically becomes more of itself, remaining as an "enduring ephemeral."[18] Like plastics, information is ubiquitous and ever-proliferating. Its ubiquity, the sense of being "always there," serves the function (or impression) of "keeping you *in touch*,"[19] while its overabundance produces a scarcity of what it consumes: namely, attention.[20]

Virality names the quantifiable measure of the success (effectiveness) of the "content" in drawing and keeping users' attention; it is a measure of the spread (circulation) of a piece of information and the reaction it generates. Since its earliest conceptualization and practice, virality has been inextricably tied to fakeness, dissimulation, trickery, drama(tization), which more effectively draw attention, elicit emotions, and garner reactions. The conceptualization and practice of virality can be traced back to Jonah Peretti, co-founder of BuzzFeed and *The Huffington Post*, which "pioneered what would become known as clickbait."[21] In his "Notes on Contagious Media," Peretti defines "contagious media" as "the kind of media you immediately want to share with all your friends."[22] Being "contagious," or what we now call virality, refers to a certain media item's quality of being shareable—thus not only catching the attention of a media consumer but multiplying the attention through circulation. Peretti gives the following examples of media items characterized by "this sort of viral propagation": "[h]umorous emails, joke websites, web-based games, silly video clips, and political calls to action."[23]

As Peretti's own experiments with "contagious media" demonstrate, virality is from its inception tied to deception (dissimulation). Such an experiment is *Black People Love Us!*, a fake website that Peretti created in 2002 together with his sister Chelsea Peretti. The website presents a white couple, Sally and Johnny, "psyched" because they are "well-liked by Black people."[24] It features images of the said couple surrounded by their Black friends, as well as testimonials from the said "friends." In these testimonials, the supposed Black friends present Sally and Johnny's racist statements and behaviors couched in the form of praise for the white couple, such as: "Johnny is generous enough to remark how 'articulate' I am! That makes me feel good."[25]

The fact that one of the earliest experiments in online virality is tied to racism is significant. As Cedric Robinson showed, capitalism is *racial* capitalism; building on Robinson, Beller notes that the central role of what Robinson termed "civilizational racism"—and of racial abstraction—in the development of capitalism "extends to and deeply into capitalist calculation and machinery during the entire period in which the world economic system seems to have moved from the paradigm of the commodity to a paradigm of information."[26] Racism is embedded into the spectacle, as Safiya Umoja Noble has pointed out. Racism is profitable, and the spectacle serves not only as a means to generate profit but also a means to cover up the racism and to hamper social changes towards racial justice.[27] The hyped notion of post-truth, which has gained prominence and media attention since 2016, far precedes the internet and is intimately tied into racial politics and racial capitalism.[28]

The Perettis' *Black People Love Us!* was intended by its creators "as a form of social activism, a way of examining the infinitely complex subject of race relations."[29] But, these intentions notwithstanding, the website lacks sufficient framing—or theatricality, understood as an embodied, *"problematic process of placing, framing, situating"*[30] that gestures towards its own staged nature—to ensure that the replay of racist statements and behaviors is read critically and called into question, as opposed to being taken at face value (which some of the website visitors did). According to Chelsea Peretti, "[t]he site should come with a warning. This is a satirical Web site. Think critically while browsing."[31] But this warning is missing, and any critical framing gets easily lost with/in online circulation. Even if not taken at face value, the website is more likely to be read as fun (or done "for fun") as opposed to critical (or done for critique).

The distinction between something meant seriously and something intended as a critique through satire and parody, or simply as done "for fun," arguably collapses on the internet. Poe's law, invoked by danah boyd in a 2018 talk on the limitations of media literacy and the weaponization of critical thinking, states: "Without a clear indicator of the author's intent, it is impossible" to "tell the difference between an extreme view and the parody of an extreme view on the Internet."[32] Just as on the backend everything is rendered equivalent through the reduction to data, so on the frontend everything is rendered equivalent—as circulating information onto which a multiplicity of divergent meanings can be projected—through the voiding of context and history. Any differentiation that emerges occurs in terms of quantifiable effects (number of likes, shares, comments, etc.) rather than semantic content. To be clear, I understand semantic content to be intimately tied with use; on the internet, as noted in Poe's law, how something is used is unclear unless it is accompanied by a clear specification, solid framing (which, even if provided in the initial posting, may nevertheless be easily removed through subsequent circulation). That said, individual consumers of information *do* derive their own meanings out of what they consume (some took *Black People Love Us!* at face value, others took it in jest, and yet others perhaps took it as a form of critique), which depends in large part on the "deep memetic frames" and habits of thought through which they process the information, on the kinds of platforms on which they encounter it, and the kinds of content brought before their view by algorithms (in conjunction with which they viewed *Black People Love Us!*).[33] But there is something else, in addition to the meaning derived, that matters as much or perhaps more when it comes to the consumption of online content: the entertainment effect. One meaning of "entertainment" is directly tied to the capture of attention, which is in fact what is being monetized in the attention economy: "Entertainment is a form of activity that holds the attention and interest of an audience."[34]

The feeling of realness (authenticity) arguably plays an important role in the ability of content to hold the attention and interest of an audience. Miles Beckett, one of the creators of another early—and widely successful—experiment in virality, thus states: "Somebody was going to create a scripted show on YouTube that uses the vlogger format and if they were marketing savvy they **would make it feel real so there would be talk about it**."[35] Beckett and his collaborator, Mesh Flinders, did just that, and the result was Lonelygirl15. Launched in 2006, Lonelygirl15 seemed to be (about) "an innocent, home-schooled 16-year-old, pouring her heart out for her video camera in the privacy of her bedroom"[36]— until it was revealed to be a fake, a hoax, a scripted performance enacted by actors.

The feeling of realness as an important ingredient of online virality connects with television's ideological promise (and selling point) to offer unmediated access to a "real" that escapes the programmed flow of information, that breaks the script.[37] But, as discussed in this book's Interlude in relation to television, it is also about the content creating its own reality through the specific mode of both its production and circulation. This involves performing (which implies repetition) for the camera as well as, in the case of the YouTube performance that Lonelygirl15 was, for the YouTube algorithm. Beckett and Flinders worked hard to figure out how the YouTube algorithm functioned and adjusted the script based on that. For instance, to get the video up on the most viewed section on YouTube, "[w]hen they realised YouTube counted every single comment including the ones you made yourself, they would make it their mission to reply to every single one—so they appeared in the most commented section constantly, boosting their profile, adding more views."[38] As they adjusted the performance for the algorithm, the algorithm in turn aided the circulation of the video performance, enabling it to reach more viewers and generate greater reaction. The viewers in turn themselves created more content around it, for instance by posting on Lonelygirl15.com's forum or in chats and blog posts outside of this forum, aiding in the construction of the real that is inescapably fake (synthetic). Lonelygirl15 thus became (more) viral—and more profitable.

Lonelygirl15 was the first web series on YouTube and the first to prove that "you could actually make money on YouTube."[39] It was also the first to feature product placement,[40] a capitalistic form of dissimulation of the real intent behind the production and spread of content: namely, the promotion (selling) of products or ideas and reinforcement of consumerist habits. Tellingly, the reveal of its fakeness did not reduce Lonelygirl15's effectiveness; on the contrary, it boosted the show's popularity.[41] Virality, the measure of effectiveness of online content, does not depend in any way on something being true (as opposed to false). Rather, it is intimately connected with performativity. As a reminder, performatives were introduced by philosopher J. L. Austin as a class of statements that are "the doing of an action."[42] As such, they are *not* "either true or false," even as they may "masquerade" as statements of fact and even as they may nonetheless serve to "inform you" (or dis/misinform you).[43] Thus, given that the operative logic here is not that of truth/falsity but of performativity, there should be no surprise that the revelation of something as fake does not undermine its spread; in fact, it may aid it by generating further reactions. As with *Black People Love Us!*, in the case of Lonelygirl15, performativity was conjoined with deception (dissimulation), even as outright deception might not have necessarily been the ultimate intention of the creators. Beckett thus states:

> We just wanted them to see it for what it was. We never lied, we just put it out there. When people asked us if it was real or not, we never responded, we just let it ride.[44]

They put it out there without a framing; in fact, they actively concealed its theatricality, its staged nature. And the internet took care of the rest.

Since these early experiments in virality, there has been an explosion in content created in order to go viral. Afterall, virality is the measure of the effectiveness (success) of anything posted online. The internet optimizes for—and rewards—virality; (dis)simulation, the conjoining of deception and performativity, is imbricated with it. As shown in this book, the pursuit of profit at all costs leads to (dis)simulation. Consider the phenomenon known as "fake news," which has been seen as a distinguishing phenomenon of the so-called "post-truth era." Encompassing computational propaganda, dis- and misinformation, lies, rumors, hoaxes, conspiracies, and other forms of deception masquerading as facts, "fake news"—recently reworded as "junk news" or "viral news" by some scholars[45]—can be traced back to these early experiments in virality. In fact, virality is at the very core of fake news. As Alexandra Juhasz has written in her collaborative *#100hardtruths* primer, "#fakenews . . . reveals the logic and cycles of virality, a mad explosion of attention that flattens and simplifies whatever is under scrutiny by having to bear the weight of mass attention and production."[46] Fake news production is profit-driven and profitable: for advertisers, for sponsored content companies, for the junk news writers whose stories draw views and clicks, and for social media platforms. For instance, the men behind the fake news site *Liberty Writers News* "said they made up to $40,000 per month in the runup to the 2016 presidential election."[47] As for social media platforms, as a report found, their "business models rely on revenue coming from the sale of adverts and, because the bottom line is profit, any form of content that increases profit will always be prioritised," regardless of its truth or facticity.[48]

Fake news is highly performative. It is performative communication disguising as statements of fact. Fake news excellently embodies Austin's definition of the performative as statements that do things in the world. It is information, or rather dis- and misinformation, that is written for effect: to get views, to generate emotion, to incite reaction and re-posting—in other words, to go viral. Like plastics, fake news is deceptive. Like plastics, it seems to be spreading everywhere in the online world. And, like plastics, it persists. Fake news spreads by being re-posted, rediscovered on the web, and even by being debunked.[49] Fake news stories get picked up by other sites, sometimes by legitimate ones that get fooled and often by other fake news sites, as well as by individual users, who re-post them to social media. As a form of dis-/misinformation that is produced in order to be spread, fake news is performative in a sense of this term that is closer to Jacques Derrida's conceptualization of performativity engaged in Chapter 1. Derrida builds on (or rather, deconstructs) Austin and argues that the "force" of the performative—"force" as opposed to "truth value"—is the performative's defining characteristic.[50] The force of fake news lies to a large extent in its spreadability and the "viral pollution" that it generates.[51] This is one of the reasons why Tommaso Venturini proposes "junk news" as a more useful concept than "fake news," which he calls a "misleading label."[52] The force of viral news lies primarily in its "spread" rather than its falsity (fakeness).[53] This force is a matter of performativity, of simulation: it changes reality, it constructs the synthetic real.

The persistent effect of fake news, which is another aspect of its force, has to do with the "enduring ephemeral"[54] nature of the online circulation of information, as well as with the mind's automatisms. The programmed proliferation machine that is the internet taps into the reinforcement (thinking) machine that is the human mind. In a report titled *Lies, Damn Lies, and Viral Content*, Craig Silverman identifies several phenomena that make debunking dis- and misinformation very challenging. These phenomena concern how "our stubborn brains" process information and how repetition breeds and reinforces belief and believability.[55] They include cognitive habits such as confirmation bias, defined as cherry-picking data to reinforce what one already believes, and group polarization, which refers to the reinforcement and radicalization of beliefs when in conversation with a like-minded group of people.[56] Social media algorithms automate these phenomena through the creation of echo chambers. Consider, for instance, how Facebook's and Twitter's algorithms focus on "likes," "retweets," and "reshares," thus profiting off of and reinforcing confirmation bias,[57] or how You-

Tube's recommendation algorithm has been found to steer viewers to increasingly extremist content in an attempt to keep them glued to their screens.[58] Francis Haugen's revelations regarding Facebook (now Meta) also show how its algorithm optimizes for "engagement, reaction"; this optimization is guided by Meta's own research, which shows "that content that is hateful, that is divisive, that is polarizing" garners more engagement.[59]

Driven by algorithms and the imperative of profit maximization, the performativity of fake news thus feeds off and amplifies the performativity of thinking. It does so by tracking online behavior, which matters for predictive systems "not in isolation but in relation to others" who are deemed to be like us.[60] Undergirding this is homophily, "the idea that similarity breeds connection."[61] By virtue of the homophily that grounds recommendation systems and social media networks, the action of liking a curly fries page on Facebook comes to mean high intelligence. Computer scientist Jennifer Golbeck explains: "by the end, the action of liking the curly fries page is indicative of high intelligence not because of the content, but because the actual action of liking reflects back the common attributes of other people who have done it."[62] Liking a curly fries page is thus performative in the Derridean sense highlighted above: it is not the actual semantic content that matters but rather the communication of a "force" within a system of "conventions" grounded in "iterability."[63] Based on such an action and on the homophily programmed into networks, a user will be shown content that users deemed to have the attribute of high intelligence have liked or should like.

Behind the automatisms of "our stubborn brains" that algorithms automate and reinforce lie what Whitney Phillips and Ryan Milner have termed "deep memetic frames," socially shared epistemological-affective frameworks through which one "viscerally" experiences and understands the world.[64] To these frameworks pertain stubbornly persistent myths and habits of thought, which viral content often reproduces. Consider, for instance, the meme called "red-pilling" or "taking the red pill," whose name is obviously derived from *The Matrix*. Also referencing the name of a Reddit community ("The Red Pill") described by Reddit as being "dedicated to shocking or highly offensive content,"[65] red-pilling purports to expose hidden truths about present-day society. Such "truths" turn what red-pillers claim to be the dominant, mainstream belief system on its head. Red-pilling can be read as a version of the Cartesian experiment of radical doubt, where the invented malicious deceiver is supposedly the dominant, mainstream belief system. In fact, doubt plays an important role in red-pilling: danah boyd identifies the seeding of doubt as the initial moment in the process of red-pilling, which thrives on the weaponization of critical thinking and on the act of casting doubt by throwing things into question.[66] As in the case of Descartes, making doubt (or what supposedly lies beyond any doubt) the sole arbiter of truth leaves one with little to fall back on, except for the "deep memetic frames" that shape understanding and experience, either individually or socially (or both). And while red-pilling is often described by its proponents as a rejection of the dominant belief system, it in fact often amounts to reinforcing a system of belief (and action) that has dominated the world for centuries, forged through racial capitalism and colonialism.

Describing a movement from initial doubt (of what one has purportedly been taught or told) to faith, red-pilling effectively amounts to the conversion to conservative, white nationalist, and far-right beliefs, associated with the creation of a "digital alternate reality" that fuels and sustains such beliefs.[67] In a sense, this is an inversion of how the red pill is used in *The Matrix* in that the online world and (some of) what circulates there is deemed to be the true reality. In her analysis of the "Alternative Influence Network" comprising YouTube content creators promoting "a range of political positions, from mainstream versions of libertarianism and conservatism, all the way to overt white nationalism," Rebecca Lewis notes that:

> White nationalists often describe this [taking the red pill] as a stepwise process. For example, in one possible pathway, they may start by rejecting the mainstream media and "PC culture"; then embrace anti-feminist ideas; then embrace scientific racism or the idea that racial oppression is not real; and then finally, the idea that Jewish people wield positions of influence and harbor malicious intents against white people.[68]

Such a stepwise process is described in a red-pilling narrative titled "My Red Pill Journey" by a YouTuber who goes by "Blonde in the Belly of the Beast." In this video, Blonde defines taking the red pill in more general terms that, she says, go beyond being simply anti-feminism:

> [Y]ou've begun to see through narratives you've been told your whole life about gender, race, culture, globalism, sex, society, relationships. You begin to develop an intellectual curiosity that you apply to your life to find your own answers, to find the truth.[69]

Blonde recounts her journey of coming to "see through narratives you've been told your whole life" by listing some experiences that she says shaped her worldview, starting with growing up in an upper middle class, homogeneous community. She says that an important moment in her red-pilling journey was when she began to notice that the Black students at her high school "self-segregated" and had different "demeanors," despite being given "equality of opportunity."[70] The "demeanors" Blonde mentions—"more dropouts, teen pregnancies, and physical fighting"—are, as Lewis notes, "three tropes that are common among white supremacist depictions of black people."[71] Blonde goes on to claim that this self-segregation was "not institutional, because the administration had been incredibly accommodating," and "it wasn't white racism, because none of the white people I knew were racist."[72] This denial of white racism is also a common white supremacist frame, as is the assertion of pride in being "Western" that Blonde makes. She thus proclaims that an outcome of her "red-pilling journey" is her "deep, lasting reverence and loyalty to Western civilization" and her "sense of pride for being descended of Western people, who I had never really been taught have had an unparalleled positive effect on civilization."[73] This is the myth that lies behind the imperative to "catch up" with the West discussed in this book's Interlude.

Blonde frames her red pill journey in terms of "personal growth and self-betterment."[74] She emphasizes "personal responsibility" and her "own self-authoring program," which has created what Blonde says is a lot of positive change in her life, including becoming "more feminine" and smoothing out relationship issues she previously had because she was "too dominant."[75] When Blonde discusses the costs of corporate success for women who desire to have children and a family, she implies—pointing to her own story—that it is a matter of individual choice and personal responsibility whether a woman chooses to be in that world or not. (Blonde says she decided to leave it and take a lower-paying job instead.) For Blonde, just as per the neoliberal dictum, the source of the problem is the individual who needs to take responsibility for her/his/their problem.

Blonde also frames her red pill journey in terms of individual discovery by applying one's "intellectual curiosity."[76] Thus framed, the "journey" appears to be not all that different from the Cartesian thought experiment of radical doubt, as its mode of inquiry seems to be that of doubting everything one has been taught. Only, Blonde does not doubt everything; on the contrary, she doubts only what serves her agenda to doubt (even as she claims otherwise). In fact, what Blonde presents as an individual journey of discovery of a radical, new, and suppressed worldview is in fact just a repetition of stubbornly persistent white supremacist and patriarchal habits of thought that have been the dominant worldview for centuries. Such habits of thought have been used to keep in place a system that creates and sustains inequality and dispossession and to justify ongoing violence against Black, Indigenous, and people of color as well as against queer and trans people: the myth of the grandeur and superiority of "Western civilization"; of "the white man's (or woman's) burden"; of the submissive and feminine woman; of gender binarism and heteronormativity; and of the individual (especially the poor, racialized individual) as the root cause for systemic social problems. Blonde voids the history and present of these myths and the violence they have helped and continue to help perpetrate and justify.

The mode of Blonde's argumentation is that of paranoid reading, which, as Wendy Chun has argued (writing about cyberspace), is both performative and reparative. Specifically, it has the force to "repair" a world (a white supremacist world, in this case) of its problems "by erasing the source of these problems—by blinding oneself to them, by identifying as them and by doing so 'pass' as the oppressed but now liberated hero."[77] This is a twisted form of repair that reasserts supremacy in the face of a supposed fear of being "displaced" and "silenced" (along with "hundreds of millions of dejected and downtrodden Westerners," says Blonde).[78] That this twisted form of repair is performed on and through the internet is no surprise, for, as Chun shows, when it emerged in the early 1990s as "cyberspace," the internet "was sold as reparative: a technological solution to our political problems" that would "free individuals from oppression and national sovereignty because it was 'the new home of the Mind'"—a "Mind" separated from the body.[79] This "rewriting of the Internet as emancipatory, as 'freeing' oneself from one's body"—a kind of Cartesian utopian space—"naturalized racism."[80]

Engaged in this form of paranoid reading, Blonde forecloses any possibility for the examination and critique of the cause of the problems she mentions; namely, the exploitative racial capitalist system, the ultimate malicious deceiver that has for centuries sustained and profited off of racism, white supremacy, and patriarchy. Notably, videos such as "My Red Pill Journey" are produced with the intention to promote a white supremacist ideology as well as make money: the video description includes a list of "ways to donate."[81] YouTube, owned by Google, also incentivizes and rewards this kind of audience-driven content.[82] As Kevin Roose notes, even as it has been "outwardly liberal in its corporate politics,"

> YouTube has inadvertently created a dangerous on-ramp to extremism by combining two things: a business model that rewards provocative videos with exposure and advertising dollars, and an algorithm that guides users down personalized paths meant to keep them glued to their screens.[83]

YouTube's recommendation system incorporated a type of AI called "reinforcement learning" (or "Reinforce"), which would feed viewers increasingly more extreme content.[84] Recall the "stepwise process" that Lewis described, from rejection of "the mainstream media and 'PC culture,'" to the embrace of anti-feminism and "scientific racism," to anti-Semitic conspiracist theories.[85] This stepwise process of radicalization occurs not only on and through YouTube, but across the different internet platforms, and profitably so. It works by exploiting and intensifying feelings of dissatisfaction, frustration, fear, and anger; sowing doubt; engendering deception (and self-deception); spinning narratives that are sexist, anti-feminist, racist, white supremacist, anti-immigrant, homophobic and transphobic; and sustaining them through repetition and reinforcement.[86] At play here is repetition with sameness, repetition of the same that virally perpetuates itself—with the aid of racial capitalism's mechanisms in which the logic of (dis)simulation is congealed. In what follows, I turn to performance and theatricality for ways of countering, refusing, and displacing this logic and the virality with which it is associated.

PERFORMING LIVE ONLINE

In Chapter 2, I argued that theatre can be a suitable medium for critically engaging the (dis)simulative performance of algorithmic thinking machines. Following that line of thought, in the present investigation of ways to counter online virality and (dis)simulation, I again turn to the theatre, specifically to a form of live theatre performance that takes the internet as its stage—out of necessity. Media artist, composer, and programmer Mark Coniglio, of Troika Ranch fame, calls this form of performance "remote theatre"—"a new form that is facilitated by technology but fueled by the pandemic," different from both TV and theatre as commonly understood.[87] A kind of digital performance, which encompasses "performance works where computer technologies play a *key* role rather than a subsidiary one in content, techniques, aesthetics, or delivery forms,"[88] remote theatre is distinctive in that its conditions of production and viewership are dictated primarily by the COVID-19 pandemic situation rather than other considerations. Out of necessity, theatre artists turned to the internet as both a tool to interrogate and a space to explore and treat as a stage. They asked: "As artists, how are we performing the internet? . . . Can we reconceptualize our relationship to the internet by dismantling, questioning, and addressing the internet in our creative work?"[89] In the words of theatre director and multimedia designer Jared Mezzocchi, this situation "is a really great opportunity to hone our craft, to tell stories no matter what condition, as site-specific performance."[90] My impulse was similar, and I found fellow artists and researchers—based in Brazil, Canada, Romania, and the United States—who shared the feeling.[91] In collaboration with an interdisciplinary team based out of the Digital Democracies Institute at Simon Fraser University, we created a site-specific performance: an online piece about being online in times of pandemic. Titled *Left and Right, Or Being Who/Where You Are*, the performance was presented by the Brown Arts Institute as part of their *REMAKING the Real* series of programs and by Re-Fest,[92] an art and technology festival organized by CultureHub (2021). It was a devised, interactive, online performance that took place on the virtual event platform ohyay and could only be experienced live, where liveness is understood in terms of the spatial and temporal co-presence of the actors and audience—even as, it turns out, the time and space will not be exactly the same.[93] As I show below, in the struggle to achieve this kind of theatrical co-presence, a possibility of countering (dis)simulation and virality may open up.

Left and Right took the reality of the COVID-19 pandemic and of lives shifted even more fully online as its given circumstances. The COVID-19 pandemic accelerated the adoption of the networked digital and its expansion into different areas of life and activity, further actualizing what performance theorist Jon McKenzie calls "the age of global performance"—where performance defines "a stratum of power/ knowledge that emerges in the United States after the Second World War."[94] The performance stratum is notably structured and sustained by information technology: "hypermediating media" such as "digital media and the Internet."[95] As physical proximity became dangerous, lives moved even more fully online, from interactions with friends and family, to education, business, and many forms of work and cultural production. At the same time, electronic connections became necessary in order to keep in touch and maintain a semblance of a "new normal" life. An article from April 2020 on how "The Virus Changed the Way We Internet" describes a rise in the use of video chat as a mode of connecting.[96] This mode of connecting facilitates co-presence in time and (virtual) space—which is one definition of liveness.[97]

In the context of the COVID-19 pandemic, video conferencing became one of the common modes of conducting synchronous classes and work meetings and of hanging out with friends and family. But, as it has been widely experienced, video chat can be exhausting, especially when done for extended periods of time. Studies of the phenomenon that has come to be termed "Zoom fatigue" have shown that part of the reason for the exhausting nature of video conferencing is that it requires us to perform (communication) to a much greater extent than in-person exchanges. In the words of psychology scholar Jeremy Bailenson:

> On Zoom, one source of load relates to *sending* extra cues. Users are forced to consciously monitor nonverbal behavior and to send cues to others that are intentionally generated. Examples include centering oneself in the camera's field of view, nodding in an exaggerated way for a few extra seconds to signal agreement, or looking directly into the camera (as opposed to the faces on the screen) to try and make direct eye contact when speaking. This constant monitoring of behavior adds up. Even the way we vocalize on video takes effort.[98]

Being present on video chat with the camera on is a matter of performing, which takes effort. This performance is exhausting also because the performer is simultaneously a spectator to her/his/their own performance. According to Bailenson, this condition of self-spectating, and its frequency and duration, are unprecedented in history, with perhaps the exception of "people who work in dance studios and other places that are full of mirrors."[99]

Being online carries with it the imperative to perform in a different way as well: that of constantly checking for the latest updates and of "acting" through the use of "social buttons" such as "like" and "share."[100] During the pandemic, the internet became the source and site of ongoing, live updates on an evolving situation riddled with uncertainty and unknowns, a go-to for making meaning in the midst of crisis. "Doomscrolling"—"trawling through feeds without pause, no matter how bad the news is or how many trolls' comments" one reads—became so common and widespread that Oxford Languages included it in its "Words of an Unprecedented Year."[101] The compulsion to always check for the latest update, built into social media's programming of behavior, thus became intensified. Along with it, so did the need (or compulsion) to be digitally present—or live, understood in the "sense of always being connected to other people, of continuous, technologically mediated temporal co-presence with others known and unknown."[102]

During the COVID-19 pandemic, mediation and media saturation (the two being linked, as McKenzie's term "hypermediating media" suggests) have arguably increased. The pandemic has been intensely and incessantly covered, both by the established news outlets and on social media. According to recent studies, the coverage of the COVID-19 pandemic in U.S. newspapers and televised network news has been highly politicized and polarized from the onset and may thus "have contributed to polarization in U.S. COVID-19 attitudes."[103] In addition to polarization, certain kinds of coverage, of mediatization of the pandemic, have brought about what some have called "an information apocalypse"—a notion that has also been used in reference to deepfakes.[104] In an article from May 2020, for instance, Craig Silverman writes about *The Plandemic*, a short film that in the first few days since its release "racked up more than 8 million views across YouTube, Facebook, Instagram, and Twitter, peddling outright falsehoods and conspiratorial claims about the origins of the current pandemic."[105] Silverman argues that *The Plandemic*, and the wealth of mis- and disinformation proliferated around the pandemic, have ushered in "an information apocalypse"; in his words, referencing disinformation expert Renée DiResta, "there's little need for deepfakes when you have a pandemic to exploit."[106] Sophisticated technology is not necessary for an information dystopia; the internet—with the virality for which it optimizes and which it rewards—is enough. In order to underscore their reality-making effects, Ganaele Langlois has called the dis- and misinformation that have abounded in the context of the COVID-19 pandemic "real fakes."[107] If anything, such "real fakes" have only amplified the so-called "post-truth world" we have been living in.

This internet of "real fakes" and polarization is what *Left and Right* took as its stage and site of investigation. The performance featured both human and machinic actors (bots), engaging in dialogue about topics related to the COVID-19 pandemic.[108] As the mediatization of the pandemic has been highly politicized and polarized from the onset, engaging in topics related to the pandemic has involved reproducing archetypical political beliefs and identities. As defined by media theorist and *Left and Right* dramaturg Melody Devries, the notion of the archetype refers to "scripted ways-of-being-(political) that limit our ability to express political life beyond mainstream or hegemonic notions of capital and power."[109] The scripts underlying archetypes involve processes of abstraction. Recently, the use of political archetypes—constructed from "Facebook data harvested from a personality quiz app and purchased from a third party"[110]—came to public attention through the Cambridge Analytica scandal, in which their use ostensibly enabled "psychographic microtargeting."[111]

To dispel the "essentializing logics" undergirding the deployment of archetypes and to show how the scripts and patterns underlying them are not natural but rather maintained through "a process of homophilic performativity that solidifies" a user's "identity and its political features," Devries introduced the concept of the "homophilic avatar."[112] The "homophilic avatar" is a character aggregated via homophilic (online and offline) networks. It comprises patterns that reinforce archetypical political beliefs and identities, which online users reproduce and embody in various ways and to varying degrees.[113] *Left and Right* repurposed the homophilic avatar towards an artistic end. It took as its data different kinds of coverage of the COVID-19 pandemic across the political spectrum, including the kinds of "real fakes" that raised alarms about an ensuing "information apocalypse" mentioned earlier,[114] as well as scripts for homophilic avatars discerned through research and analysis. The performance aimed to undo these scripts so as to imagine more capacious ways of being (online) and being political. It sought to arrest the circulation of "real fakes" and counter the twinned logics of performativity and virality that sustain the production and spread of "information disorders" in two ways: (i) through theatricality understood as "a *problematic process of placing, framing, situating*" that gestures towards its own staged nature; and (ii) through liveness understood as the co-presence in space and time of all the participants in the performance, both actors and spectators—albeit a co-presence that is mediated, multilayered, syncopated.[115]

We worked with the concept of the homophilic avatar in order to develop both the conceptual framework and the characters for our performance, which evolved based on research and improvisation. As introduced by the actors in the beginning of the performance, the human actors and characters were:

MARCELA: My name is Marcela Mancino. I am a Brazilian multimedia artist and creative technologist currently living in
Brazil. Tonight, I will be performing Maitê Stédile. She's 22
years old, Brazilian, and was studying acting in the US until
the pandemic hit. She is a white, cisgender woman, proudly
bisexual, feminist, antiracist, vegan, and zero waste. She is
a big fan of Djamila Ribeiro, Sabrina Fernandes, and Grada
Kilomba. . . .

PATRICK: Hi everyone, my name is Patrick Elizalde. I am a recent
college grad who studied theatre arts and economics and was
born and raised in New York. I will be playing Sean Lin, who
became friends with Maitê through their mutual involvement
in college theatre. He is 24 years old, Christian, a 2nd generation Taiwanese-American from Flushing, NY, and is now
working at a top consulting firm in Boston. . . .

FABIOLA: My name is Fabiola Petri. I am a Romanian actress. To-
night, I will play Mara Stan. Mara is a 29-year-old Romanian
woman, secretly bisexual, Eastern Orthodox by birth. She is a
psychiatrist, but wants to become an actor. She doesn't believe
in political identity. She sometimes follows popular people
without thinking of their political orientation, just by default.
She prefers to research more about theatre. She loves nature
and supports recycling. Mara represents the Exhausted Majority. In this show, I am many. . . .

ANDRA: Hi everyone. My name is Andra Jurj. I am also a Romanian actor and a trained physician. I also play Mara Stan.
Another version of Mara Stan than the version portrayed by
Fabiola. My version of Mara is disillusioned, detached, ironic,
empathetic and poetic. But we are both the same character
representing the Exhausted Majority.[116]

In the world of the play, Mara met Maitê and Sean at the theatre festival in their Romanian hometown (which also happens to be my hometown) the year prior. The three characters reconnect online after the
outbreak of the COVID-19 pandemic and share their lived experiences
and media-informed opinions on politicized topics, such as the rele-
vance of the lockdowns. Throughout the ninety-minute performance,

the actors step in and out of their characters as they interact with each other, the bots (on which more later), and the audience.

The figure of the archetype lay at the center of *Left and Right*'s "lecture machine."[117] It did so both conceptually and quite literally: the eighth scene of the performance, titled "Profile of . . . an Archetype," was an extended lecture on the archetype and its (de)construction in the performance given by the two actors playing Mara (Andra Jurj and Fabiola Petri). The archetypes we worked with in *Left and Right* were drawn from a recent study of the U.S.'s polarized political landscape, titled *Hidden Tribes*.[118] This study identified seven homophilic groups, or "tribes," based on "commonalities in aspects of their psychology, beliefs and behaviors."[119] These groups, or archetypes, are: "Progressive Activists," "Traditional Conservatives," "Devoted Conservatives," and what the study calls "the Exhausted Majority"—"Traditional Liberals," "Passive Liberals," "Politically Disengaged," and "Moderates."[120] More in Common, the organization that produced the study, also developed a quiz meant to help a quiz taker determine which "tribe" he/she/they belong to.[121] This is the quiz that the audience members of *Left and Right* took prior to the beginning of the performance. During the first scene, based on the label they had been assigned from the quiz, they were invited to position themselves on the digital stage through an avatar in the form of a colored dot and to comment through the live chat on whether they found that label to be suitable. This kind of placing of archetypes from across the political spectrum on the same digital stage was meant to theatrically push against the algorithmic construction of echo chambers online. Through audience interaction, it also aimed to begin to problematize the construction of political archetypes.

Over the course of the performance, the human actors, and the characters they performed, played with and against the *Hidden Tribes* archetypes: Maitê as the Progressive Activist, Sean as the Devoted Conservative, and Mara as the Exhausted Majority. The performance also featured two machinic actors created by media artist, computer programmer, and researcher Roopa Vasudevan, with media scholar Anthony Burton serving as consultant. These were chatbots trained on news articles about the pandemic, immigration, and climate change from the beginning of the pandemic to the end of the year 2020. One of the bots, Nick, was trained on articles that a Progressive Activist would read, while the other, Kimberly, was trained on a dataset consisting of articles that would appeal to a Devoted Conservative.[122] The machinic actors, Nick and Kimberly, were intended to perform a sort of over-identification with the respective archetypes they represented, to the point of absurdity. However, it took our team a lot of work and active manipulation of the datasets to arrive at some semblance of the polarized positions that the bots were meant to (over)represent. We originally started with a dataset comprising nearly a thousand articles (per bot), collected based on "algorithmic sorting and categorization of Twitter users into different locations on a horizontal political spectrum," using the online media-tracking database Media Cloud.[123] The result, however, was a high degree of "randomness and factual-sounding statements" that reproduced the "objective" (sounding) tone of journalistic writing in the bots' output, rather than the polarizing exchange we intended.[124] Thus, we shifted our approach to the careful curation of the dataset, consisting in the selection of fifty handpicked articles (per each bot) based on the profiles of the archetypes that the bots were designed to represent. These profiles were drawn from the *Hidden Tribes* study.

While this careful curation helped give some sense of the different, polarized archetypes that the bots were designed to embody, the overall effect was—as media scholar and *Left and Right* collaborator Anthony Burton put it—that the bots "in a sense talk past each other, they share the space, but they're not necessarily listening, and that's what ultimately the question on political dialogic spaces is about: it's about the production of utterances versus the question of listening" (Figure 12).[125] Circulated online, such utterances are performative: they are speech acts produced for effect, to elicit a reaction. In *Left and Right,* we aimed to counter performativity through theatricality, by staging these speech acts through live interactions between the machinic actors and the human actors as well as between the bots and the audience members in ways that aimed to counteract their force (their intended emotionally charged, divisive effects). Especially in the case of the audience's interaction with the bots, the sense of liveness that usually emerges through the bots' responsiveness to the audience's input was troubled by their oftentimes random/nonsensical output, which betrayed their programmed nature and the fact that they were not really "listening."[126] As with the chatbots in Annie Dorsen's algorithmic theatre piece *Hello Hi There* discussed in Chapter 2, the bots in our performance did not dissimulate their machinic nature in order to pass for human, and the interaction with them did not create the powerful "mimetic illusion" that Brenda Laurel called for.[127] Rather than optimizing for engagement and immersion, our performance optimized for disengagement and (critical) distance.

The characters played by human actors too sometimes talked past each other, especially when they rehearsed ideas about the lockdowns or immigration that had been so often repeated on the internet that they became a sort of ideological ready-mades. One spectator to a performance of *Left and Right* described the effect achieved as follows:

> [F]or me the spoken lines appeared like talking points, like intentional clichés. It made me think of the way public discourse often sounds like acting roles, as if we are all bots spewing out ideas we read elsewhere. We all have a little algorithm in our head that enables us to synthesize what was already said into our own "opinion," in order to appear to others credible, enlightened, woke, or what have you. It is a political Turing machine that makes us pass

FIGURE 12. Nick and Kimberly conversing with Maitê (played by Marcela Mancino) and Sean (played by Patrick Elizalde) in *Left and Right, Or Being Who/Where You Are*, directed by Ioana B. Jucan, 2021.

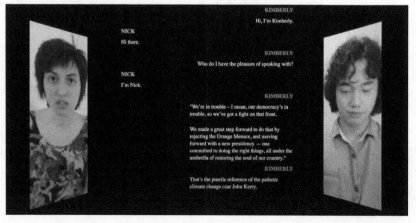

Courtesy of the author.

as informed, where in fact we're all just rehearsing lines we only pretend to believe in, like good or not-so-good actors who end up getting type-cast into those ideological boxes from the survey the audience completed before the performance even began.[128]

Rather than simply reproducing these ideological ready-mades, our ultimate goal was to push against archetypes by theatrically replaying them through both the human and the machinic actors. We thus aimed to point to the performative processes undergirding the archetypes and to the broader information ecosystem surrounding them, as well as to interrupt the interplay between the programmed proliferation machine that is the internet and the reinforcement machine that is the human mind, however momentarily.

We employed several strategies to this end, such as having the actors step in and out of their roles to expose the construction of the archetypes. Thus, in the scene "Profile of . . . an Archetype" mentioned earlier, the two actors playing Mara gave an extended lecture on the concept of the archetype and showed how the *Left and Right* characters replayed specific archetypes. Another strategy we used was that of displacing the archetypes through a transnational perspective that drew on the actors' own national contexts: for instance, a communist or a liberal within the Romanian or Brazilian context is quite different than in the U.S. context. In a scene titled "Liberal/Communist," Sean, played by Patrick Elizalde, calls Maitê, played by Marcela Mancino, a "communist" when she argues that meritocracy is a myth; she in turn accuses him of being a "liberal" for believing that the market is the force that will solve society's problems. This prompts a discussion of these two labels among the four characters, from their different perspectives, locations, and frames of reference. Even if in this particular scene Maitê ends up tentatively embracing the label "communist" to refer to her own anti-capitalist stance, in the final scene of the performance the actors—pushing against the limits of their roles—create their own self-descriptions and poetic articulations of their characters' political identities and invite the audience to do the same for themselves. Regarding the latter, Figure 13 shows some of the audience members' responses to the question posed in the end of the performance: "If you were to label yourself, what would you be?"

FIGURE 13. Some of the audience members' responses to the question, "If you were to label yourself, what would you be?," in *Left and Right, Or Being Who/Where You Are*, directed by Ioana B. Jucan, 2021.

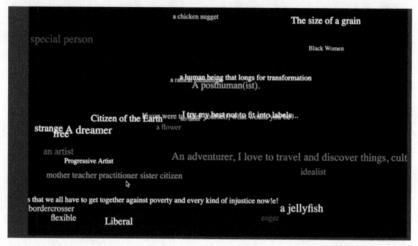

Courtesy of the author.

Another strategy that we used in order to push against archetypes and the performative processes undergirding them was that of inhabiting the space(time) between what McKenzie terms "discursive performatives" and "embodied performances" as well as the possibilities opened up by liveness and embodied gestures in the context of online performance. According to McKenzie, "[d]iscursive performatives and embodied performances" form "the building blocks of the performance stratum."[129] McKenzie theorizes performances as "territorializations of flows and unformed matters into sensible bodies" and performatives as "encodings of these bodies into articulable subjects and objects."[130] This distinction is not meant as an absolute separation, for the two are intimately imbricated in practice. In the space(time) between them, the possibility for displacement or destratification arguably opens up. McKenzie calls one such possibility the "catastoration of behavior" understood in terms of seizing an "arrangement of forces and processes," putting it "'between quotation marks,'" and reinscribing it "elsewhere and elsewhen."[131] In *Left and Right,* we aimed to enact a sort of catastoration of political belief and the habitual actions that sustain it.

In *Left and Right,* the space(time) between discursive performatives and embodied performances was inhabited by the actors' bodies through choreographed movement developed in collaboration with choreographer Adriana Bârză-Cârstea and with the aid of the digital design by creative technologists, interaction designers, and new media artists Tong Wu, Yuguang Zhang, and Nuntinee Tansrisakul. In one scene early on in the performance, for instance, Sean is shown scrolling through YouTube. The video recommendations on display suggest the beginnings of what may turn out to be a rabbit hole of alt-right content, becoming ever more extreme the further down one goes. While Sean makes an effort to maintain attention, his body gets in the way, falling asleep and pulling him away from the screen (this is enacted through choreographed movement). Fatigue sets in. The fall down the rabbit hole is interrupted, for the moment. It will be enacted later, towards the end of *Left and Right,* both aurally—through a sound piece featuring a collage of soundtracks from YouTube videos of prominent alt-right figures—and through choreographed movement that suggests both the fall down the rabbit hole and resistance to it. Here, the actor's body resists its encoding into an articulable subject within the alt-right ideological matrix. By theatrically arresting the circulation of the videos, this (virtually) embodied (re)enactment also aims to counter the logic of virality that drives YouTube and other social media platforms.

In another scene, titled "Who Are You?," Mancino, playing Maitê, and Elizalde, playing Sean, are shown taking the *Hidden Tribes* quiz that the audience members had also taken prior to the performance. This quiz reproduces archetypical beliefs—or, "core beliefs driving polarization," according to the *Hidden Tribes* study.[132] Maitê and Sean take it in an embodied manner, physically and verbally pushing against it as they interrogate the assumptions embedded into its questions and reductive response choices. The latter are theatrically displayed on the virtual stage as "tangible blocks" encroaching upon the performance space of the actors (Figure 14).[133]

The archetypical beliefs reproduced by the quiz are further contested and nuanced in the next scene of *Left and Right,* titled "What I Believe." Here, the separation between the actors' live feeds is eliminated by overlaying them, thus creating an impression of being in the

FIGURE 14. Maitê (played by Marcela Mancino) and Sean (played by Patrick Elizalde) take the *Hidden Tribes* quiz in an embodied way in *Left and Right, Or Being Who/Where You Are*, directed by Ioana B. Jucan, 2021.

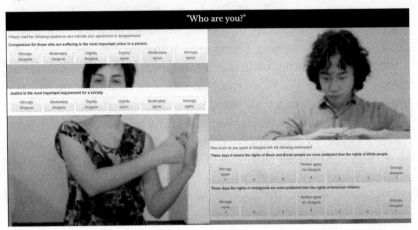

Courtesy of the author.

same (physical) space and expanding the possibilities of relating to each other in a more (fully) embodied way despite the ideological differences they are given to enact (Figure 15). One such belief stated by Sean, drawn from the *Hidden Tribes* profile for the Devoted Conservative archetype, is: "Being of my religion is important to me."[134] In *Left and Right,* this belief is displaced and reinscribed elsewhere: R.E.M.'s "Losing My Religion," sung by the actors who also dance to its tune. The singing is then taken over by a sound composition (by sound artist Peter Bussigel) suggestive of the universe of social media platforms. The actors' camera feeds are again separated, and, as they become immersed in the aural universe, their bodies gesturally enact the programming behind these beliefs through "nonconscious or habitual" actions, which, as Wendy Chun has argued, "count more than our words" in the drama "drama 'Big Data'" (Figure 16).[135] As the sound becomes more intense, the ensuing disorientation and distortion are made palpable through the live manipulation of the image with the aid of HSV (hue, saturation, value) filters, which enabled our digital designers to dynamically adjust the colors and vibes of the actors' webcam feeds.

FIGURE 15. "What I Believe," in *Left and Right, Or Being Who/Where You Are*, directed by Ioana B. Jucan, 2021.

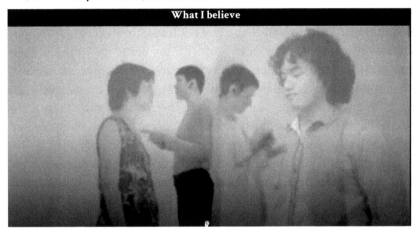

Courtesy of the author.

FIGURE 16. Gesturally enacting the programmability of belief in *Left and Right, Or Being Who/Where You Are*, directed by Ioana B. Jucan, 2021.

Photo credit Yuguang Zhang.

Staging embodied movement on a digital stage in *live* online performance is a challenging task. It is challenging primarily due to the
limitations imposed by technology, to the condition of being physically
remote, and to the time difference that comes with being located in different parts of the world. These limitations have to do with the confines
of the frames within which the camera feeds are displayed, manipulatable only to a certain extent, and with the delay, the time lag, built
into networked communication. Liveness understood as co-presence in
time and space, troubled by "the advent of broadcast technologies" such
as radio and television,[136] undergoes another modification in the context of "hypermediating," networked media. In this case, the space and
time of the live performance both are and are *not* the same.

In *Left and Right,* the actors, the members of the production team,
and the audience members, located in different physical spaces, gathered in the same digital space that we staged on the design platform
ohyay. But within this space, the audience members were visually present on the screen only at the start of the performance, if they chose
to "step on the stage" by selecting a prearranged box and turning on
their cameras. Due to technological limitations (having to do with how
many camera feeds could be displayed simultaneously without crashing
the platform), we restricted the number of boxes available to audience
members to sixteen. The audience members had the option of making
their presence known at different points in the performance: in the first
scene, through an avatar in the form of a colored dot to be placed on
the digital stage; in scene four, by interacting with the bots; and in the
last scene, through their anonymous responses to a quiz asking them
to reflect on their own sense of identity and share a formulation that
best describes it. Apart from this, throughout the performance, the
audience members had the option to make their presence known/felt
by using the chat function. The audience members' co-presence in the
same space thus spanned a range of options, from simply logging into
the performance space and "silently" watching (or perhaps doing something else on the computer at the same time), to actively interacting
with the actors through the chat function. As for the actors' spatial co-
presence with one another, the actors for the most part remained con-
fined within the separate box-like frames within which their camera

feeds were displayed. To push against these restrictions, we altered the actors' presence "by applying live visual manipulation to their feeds" (see Figure 16).[137] In this way, we were able to imbue the performers with a "digital performative existence" that was "not subject to their physical restrictions."[138] It was also not subject to the actors' immediate control. In a sense, this is a form of alienated presence.[139] At play here is "the embodiment of digital virtualities" that trouble the "live bodies/mediatized bodies" opposition.[140]

As for the temporal co-presence, all the *Left and Right* team members gathered at the same time to rehearse and perform, but the time was not same: there was a seven-hour time difference between the East Coast of the United States and Romania (six between Romania and the region of Brazil in which our Brazilian performer was located). In addition, our audience members were located in different parts of the world with their own time zones, such as Brazil, Canada, Germany, Portugal, Romania, South Korea, Turkey, and the United States. Co-presence, in the same time and virtual space, across geographic distance, has time difference built into it, from the usually small, often imperceptible delay to a difference between night and day. While we were able to organize our schedules and find rehearsal times that worked for everyone without having to rehearse what would be very late nights or very early mornings for some of our team members, the performance time was less flexible. In order to have a larger U.S. and Brazil-based audience, in addition to matinees (i.e., evenings for a European audience), it made sense to hold evening performances, which meant very late nights for the Romanian actors. While not necessarily visible to the naked eye, these actors' bodies carried into the performance the experience of a day already past and the tiredness that comes with it. The time—and sense of time—of the different actors, members of the production team, and audience members were thus not same by virtue of the different geographic locations in which they found themselves.

The time—and sense of time—of the different actors, members of the production team, and audience members were also not the same by virtue of the delay built into communication networks. Even as the internet capitalizes on instantaneity, it has the time lag built into it. While often small, during the run of *Left and Right* this lag was at times perceptible enough to interrupt and even disrupt the rhythm of the performance, at least for some audience members. In an article on XR (extended reality) experience, Thomas Vits writes that the delay, the "latency" built into communication networks "is driven by four factors: protocol latency, errors causing retransmission, congestion and distance."[141] In our own experience of performing *Left and Right*, we noticed that those of us who had older computers often experienced greater delays and glitches, so that is also a contributing factor. The delays that an actor or audience member experiences will be different from both those that another actor or audience member might experience and from the delays potentially experienced by the same person on different nights of the performance. In this way, the performance becomes a quite personal(ized) experience, not by choice or design but by virtue of taking place *live* online.

Vits emphasizes that reducing (and ideally eliminating) the latency is essential for "truly immersive XR experiences."[142] XR encompasses virtual reality, augmented reality, and mixed reality. Of the three, augmented reality—understood in the very basic sense of a "simple combination of real and virtual (computer-generated) worlds," the augmentation by technology of a "real-world image with extra layers of digital information"[143]—is the most relevant in the case of *Left and Right*. The "real-world image" of the actors' real-world performance spaces and bodies were at times augmented with extra layers of digital information, as shown above. But the intended effect in our case was not that of immersion. This is in fact one of the reasons we specifically decided not to create a gamified experience and not to use humanoid avatars for the actors and the audience. The manipulation of the actors' feeds and their overlay was not intended to create a more natural sense of being in the digital space—of feeling "like we're in the same place, even if we're in different states or hundreds of miles apart," something that Mark Zuckerberg has spoken about in connection with the "metaverse," his vision for an "embodied internet."[144] On the contrary: it was intended to keep open a space for critical thinking and feeling, to inhabit the different forms of spatial, temporal, and ideological distance and difference with attention and care in a shared present moment, an "interval by which one time is not another time even as the times coexist" (to borrow the words of Rebecca Schneider).[145]

One time is not another time even as they may coexist in another sense as well, one that Sarah Sharma has theorized in terms of "power-chronography."[146] This approach to time "is about the micropolitics of temporal coordination and social control between multiple temporalities," where temporality refers to "awareness of power relations as they play out in time."[147] These power relations, inscribed and reproduced through the different positioning "within a larger economy of temporal worth" and the labor performed within it, account for the differentials and unevenness in the lived experiences of time even as the times may coexist.[148] While it does not, just by virtue of being *live*, reveal the power relations at play in temporal coordination, live online performance does reveal synchronization as a matter of labor, albeit to different extents for different participants. For instance, audience members may have to occasionally refresh the page or to imagine the parts of the performance they may have missed due to glitches, or they may have to juggle multiple things going on in their physical and/or digital space while watching the performance. Given the default latency, the actors' labor to be in sync with one another involves continuous attention and effort, even when there are no major tech issues (for instance, the pause that naturally occurs in-between lines in face-to-face exchanges would have to be eliminated or drastically reduced to account for the default delay; the movement of one actor would have to be started faster for coordination with another actor to be able to occur). Being in sync also requires careful and sustained viewing of oneself on the screen throughout the performance. As discussed above, being a performer and simultaneously a spectator to one's own performance can be exhausting.

That "the present . . . is not primal, but rather, reconstituted, . . . that there is no purity of the living present" (in Derrida's words) is thus amply evident in live online performance, even as the different temporalities at play may not be.[149] This reconstituted present moment is filled with both complexity and possibility, and here is where another sense of liveness comes in: the sense that anything can happen.[150] This sense, I would argue, is intensified in the context of live online performance, in which the time lag is an inescapable condition and technological failure a constant possibility. This is something we experienced repeatedly both in rehearsals and during performances for *Left and Right*. While admittedly not desirable and potentially very frustrating, the time lag and the possibility of technological failure troubles the supposed smoothness of connectivity as well as technological effectiveness, organizational efficiency, and social efficacy. According to McKenzie, these three constitute the "performative valorimeters" in the name of which the world is challenged to perform in "the age of global performance," which is also the age of big data and neoliberal capitalism.[151] In the context of live theatre performance, the time lag may serve as a reminder of the many layers of mediated embodiment, distance, and difference, which are not to be smoothed over.

Gathering live online in the reconstituted present, punctuated by delays, as part of a theatre performance, can thus be an experience of both connection and disconnection, of feeling some sense of togetherness without immersion, across distance and difference. In my view, live online performance opens interesting possibilities for interrogating what it means to perform—and be performed (by and through algorithms/software)—online while performing online. As a form of site-specific performance, it has the potential to cast light on the connections between global performance, big data, and post-truth. It also has the potential to expand access, bringing together actors and audiences from different parts of the world, as well as to counter the logic of virality through theatricality, through the careful staging (framing) of the (dis/mis)information that circulates online and the performative processes that sustain its spread so as to counteract their effects. However, as a performance that takes the internet as its stage, it also risks replicating some of the problems inherent in the (dis)simulative "system of digital virality,"[152] or simply losing the audience, whose attention may turn to more engaging online offerings, especially if the latency and technical issues prevail during the performance. Whether this kind of remote theatre has a future beyond a pandemic context remains an open question. For now, I turn to performance pieces that step outside of the internet, moving to a different (offline) medium in order to interrogate, refuse, and displace the logic that drives the internet.

INTERRUPTING VIRAL CIRCULATION, REFUSING
AND DISPLACING (DIS)SIMULATION

Being online by default means participating in the social exchange of information through the consumption and production of content, which involves dissimulation and performativity. As argued throughout this book, the kind of performativity theorized here entails the voiding of context, lived experience and history, a reduction of dimensions of what is, an impoverishment of existence. As a way to counter online performativity, specifically the performativity enabled by social media "that impacts how individuals capture their experiences and what they subsequently share with the world," American Artist proposes a practice of refusal.[153] Tina Campt defines refusal as:

> a rejection of the status quo as livable and the creation of possibility in the face of negation i.e. a refusal to recognize a system that renders you fundamentally illegible and unintelligible; the decision to reject the terms of diminished subjecthood with which one is presented, using negation as a generative and creative source of disorderly power to embrace the possibility of living otherwise.[154]

An interdisciplinary artist who "makes thought experiments that mine the history of technology, race, and knowledge production,"[155] American Artist has created a body of work that centers refusal. This body of work revolves around the notion of the "dignity image," which Artist defines as an image "withheld from circulation on social media," as part of a practice of refusal where a user chooses not to "provide content for a platform."[156] By withholding the personal (or parts thereof) from online circulation, this practice enables one to reclaim a space for the personal that is free from capture, from surveillance in the service of "the capitalistic objectives of corporations," and to "gain some measure of control" over the circulation of one's images and one's "increasingly mediated" identity.[157] It is important to note here that technologies of surveillance are applied differentially and with differing impact across intersecting lines of race, gender, class, religion, nationality, and sexual orientation.[158] As Simone Browne has shown, "racism and antiblackness undergird and sustain the intersecting surveillances of our present order."[159] Artist's work is shaped by this understanding. In their words:

> It's important for Black people and people of color to be able to photograph themselves and also . . . be able to choose how their images are distributed. . . . What does it mean for people like me to think about how their images are being circulated and . . . be able to have some control over that?[160]

The exhibitions that American Artist developed around the concept of the dignity image address this question in relation to specific locations, such as Bayview-Hunters Point in San Francisco or Harlem in New York City.

In the *Dignity Images: Bayview-Hunters Point* exhibition at the Museum of African Diaspora in San Francisco (2019), different dignity images—printed out photographs of dignity images shown on phones held in hands (Figure 17)—can be viewed on the walls of the exhibition space, their presence together framed by the description of the exhibition.[161] Their physical placing within an exhibition that clearly specifies their context delineates the conditions of their viewership. This mode of presentation refuses the decontextualization, equivalation, and reproducibility of online circulation and calls for a different notion of value, one that lies outside of the capitalist spectacle for which images withheld from circulation are "worthless."[162] This value lies in enabling one to recover "one's dignity, or political autonomy, online" by rejecting "the terms of diminished subjecthood with which one is presented" (to go back to Campt's definition of "refusal").[163] One may argue that this kind of refusal is not ultimately a viable, effective solution as social connection increasingly depends on the sharing (circulation) of information online, or that an individual's refusal is too small a gesture to lead to any significant social change. In response to the latter objection, it is worth emphasizing that this kind of practice of refusal that occurs at the level of the individual does not in any way preclude or negate the importance of systemic change, nor does it disregard the fact that "surveillance capitalism" (in Shoshana Zuboff's phrasing) and its technologies, with their exploitative and harmful effects, are systemic issues.[164] Regarding the former, it is important to note that to engage in a practice

FIGURE 17. *Dignity Images: Bayview-Hunters Point*, by American Artist, 2019.

Courtesy of the artist.

of refusal requires disengaging from the logic of effectiveness, of (re) productivity.[165] Through this disengagement, the "possibility in the face of negation" that Campt wrote about may open up.

Another piece belonging to the body of work that American Artist has created around the dignity image is an online performance called *A Refusal* (2015–2016).[166] In this online performance of refusal, American Artist removed their online images from social media platforms such as Facebook, replaced them with a blank blue rectangle, and printed these images in a photo album. "In order for someone to see the photos they must actually meet me and see them first hand from my album," Artist stated.[167] These photos are Artist's own dignity images. Replacing the images with a blank blue rectangle both literalizes and counters the voiding of context and history performed by the (dis)simulating machine that is the internet. The choice of a particular shade of the color blue in this performance is significant. American Artist calls this shade "New Glory Blue," in contrast to the "Old Glory Blue" of the Confederate flag, which "carries a painful relationship to forced human labor and the ownership of slaves in the United States."[168] Primarily known "for its use in fatal computer error warnings" and "seen on television monitors when no signal is present," New Glory Blue connotes what Artist terms "an active void," "identifiable by the charge of electricity that brings minute changes with each refresh of the screen" and that "conveys discreetly the color's natural desire to act, and its potential to produce images."[169] Notably, New Glory Blue is inextricably tied to failures in technology, to moments of malfunction or non-function, in which the machinic nature of the technologies is revealed, and in which it becomes necessary to reset, to restart. Artist writes that, "[a]s a sign," New Glory Blue "represents a lack of information or a space of non-activity" within which lies potential and compares it to the way in which the American working class "are treated as a void while they are actually a constantly feeding entity" within which lies a revolutionary potential.[170]

American Artist also calls New Glory Blue "a color that cannot be captured," that defies physicality, and compares it to the hacktivist collective Anonymous. This links the performance of refusal to "anonymity and ephemerality," seen by Artist as "important tools to acquire liberty within a state of mass surveillance."[171] Yet the accompanying gesture of printing out the images in an album that can only be accessed by meeting Artist in person and seeing them "first hand in the album" interestingly balances and complicates the notions of "anonymity and ephemerality" and the voiding implied in New Glory Blue. It does so by recentering context, history, and accountability, all of which can be hollowed out through and by online anonymity and ephemerality, with violent and harmful effects. Consider, for instance, how anonymous message boards that have ephemerality built into them like 4chan, where Anonymous began, or 8kun (previously 8chan) have become breeding grounds for hate speech, conspiracy theories, and far-right radicalization.[172] Consider also the popular conspiracy theory, movement, and "collective delusion" known as QAnon, which is intimately tied to 4chan and 8chan and which thrives on (the performance of) anonymity.[173] The deciphering of the clues dropped by the anonymous "Q Clearance Patriot" by its internet followers reveals how the voiding of semantic content online enables anything that circulates on the internet to be read as anything one wants—within the "deep memetic frames" one is operating.[174] Ethan Zuckerman thus writes that "QAnon is an inevitable outgrowth of the Unreal, an approach to politics that forsakes interpretation of a common set of facts in favor of creating closed universes of mutually reinforcing facts and interpretations."[175] Yet, what Zuckerman calls the "Unreal" is in fact a synthetic real that is tied to real-life violence, including the pro-Trump 2021 riot and siege at the U.S. Capitol.[176] Thus, online anonymity and ephemerality on their own do not necessarily lead to liberatory outcomes; they may in fact enable the contrary.

Despite its refusal of the logic of online circulation, as a performance that takes place online, *A Refusal* can itself be read as "proof" within the "closed universes of mutually reinforcing facts and interpretations." This kind of conspiracist reading is staged in a YouTube video accompanying Artist's *A Refusal,* which bears a dramatic title that mimics the titles of clickbait content: "American Artist Refusal EXPOSED!!! Satanic Conspiracy DO NOT FOLLOW!!! THE VIGILANT NETWORKER 2016."[177] In the video, one Jake Wynters from the People's Sanctuary for Capitalist Networking Economies (PSCNE) denounces Artist's *Refusal* as satanic conspiracy, accusing Artist of being "a dark lord, a puppet of Satan," a "demon," "a practitioner of evil" who "sneaks around, implementing tricks of the devil, using his iconography, remaining anonymous, posting corrupt messages in order to take down the social network from within" by refusing to offer up personal content to the network "saviors" and by thus disrupting the "algorithms used by the network."[178] The satanic conspiracy narrative is a "deep memetic frame" connected with Evangelical Christian theology—a frame that "stems from a centuries-old belief that embedded within every rung of society are demonic elements whose sole, nefarious purpose is to undermine Christianity and, indeed, Western Civilization itself."[179] This is a version of Descartes's scenario of the malicious deceiver (which actually is better known as the "evil demon"). Recently, it has come to media attention in conjunction with QAnon and their accusations that various figures (Democratic politicians as well as performance artist Marina Abramović) are engaged in Satan-worshiping rituals.[180]

Presented on American Artist's website in conjunction with other artifacts connected with the performance of A Refusal (such as screen captures of Artist's "blued" out Facebook profile, or an e-mail from Artist to their mother that provides context to the project), the YouTube video "exposing" Artist's Refusal as a satanic conspiracy serves as a way to problematically frame the performance of Refusal within the broader context of the contemporary post-truth information ecosystem. Within this ecosystem, social media is often equated with social connection and community, which the practice of refusal arguably threatens. Thus, in the YouTube video, Jake, the "vigilant networker," stresses that Artist's refusal to offer up personal content to the network leads to "alienation," to a lack of community, to an inability to connect. This potential cost is in fact something that Artist points to in an e-mail to their mother that accompanies A Refusal, where they write: "I realize you are one of the few people who will be emotionally affected by my refusal of social media so let's make sure to keep in touch more often and Skype more often, and rely less on distant and removed images from my public feed."[181] Through such "distant and removed" images and other kinds of personal content offered freely in the name of connection, social relations get abstracted into data, with very high costs. Nick Couldry and Ulises Mejias have written about these "costs of connection" in relation to the legacies of colonialism and have described them in terms of "a more extreme degree of alienation than usually recognized within a traditional Marxist perspective, because subjects are estranged not only from the products of their labor but from their own personhood, their basic realities as living beings."[182] Artist's practice of refusal centered around dignity images is an attempt to counter this kind of alienation and make a claim for a more capacious way of being than that afforded by data-thirsty social media platforms and the logic of (dis)simulation that they embody.

To conclude this chapter's engagement with theatrical ways of countering the viral circulation of information and the logic of (dis) simulation embedded in the internet, I turn to another performance of refusal, one that foregrounds the colonial legacies of the viral circulation of information/commodities, including the stubbornly persistent white supremacist myths and habits of thought rehearsed by Blonde. The multimedia piece *The Keys to the Kingdom* (2019) by multimedia artist, musician, and writer Hassan Khan is a site-specific project that Khan created for the Palacio de Cristal (the Crystal Palace) in Parque del Retiro in Madrid, where I saw it in November 2019. Formerly belonging to the monarchy and now a prominent tourist attraction, Parque del Retiro and the Palacio de Cristal, "[a]n elegant airy building in glass and metal originally built in 1887 for the General Exposition of the Philippines Islands (then a Spanish colonial possession)," exude grandeur and imperial ambitions, markers of the so-called greatness of "Western civilization."[183] I happened upon it by chance on my tour of various tourist attractions of Madrid. This is perhaps the way in which this work is meant to be encountered: by a tourist or city resident strolling leisurely through the park, taken by its grandeur (and photographing it, as many people were doing when I was there, myself included), forgetful or unaware of the history behind it. *The Keys to the Kingdom* interrupts any forgetfulness and enacts a powerful reminder.

The Keys to the Kingdom is a theatrical performance that gathers and stages a collection of different things so as to open up thinking through an embodied *"problematic process of placing, framing, situating."*[184] The things *The Keys to the Kingdom* brings together and stages within the Palacio de Cristal include an algorithmic "Infinite Hip-Hop Song" (from which the line "timing time to raise the ghost" especially stood out to me), "illustrated flags, a ceramic mural of digitally printed computer generated images, glass columns produced by exerting direct pressure and a variety of other forms."[185] This coming together of different things crosses multiple—seemingly incongruent—temporalities and fills the Palacio de Cristal with multiple rhythms, such as the beats of *The Infinite Hip-Hop Song*; the interrupted circulation of the symbols represented on the flags; the suspended movement in the digitally printed computer-generated images; the different rhythms and movements of the exhibition visitors. Khan describes this process of coming together and taking place as follows:

> This is the story of how a chance encounter with a mid-nineteenth century pedestal table, that so accurately, and offensively, channeled and celebrated the racial politics that built what we call the modern world, became the starting point for an exhibition. This is also, and by necessity, a story of transformations and causes; why the tousled outline of Boris Johnson's hair ended up an emblem on a banner, or how an early noughties marketing tool for cellphone ringtones and an appropriated meme signaling hatred produced by the hysterical fear of losing white privilege met one day and became something else. This is a tale of surprises; how a dairy shop sign of two cows kissing on the streets of Abdeen becomes the gateway to collective projections, or a smiling ceramic pig on the buffet table of a cheap hotel a totem of collective fears.[186]

As I entered the Palacio, I was directly confronted by the illustrated flags, displayed in the center of the Palacio in a diamond shape. "Icons that relate to the metaphysics of possession and power relations,"[187] these flags seem to me to function both as keys and as memes—stubbornly persistent myths and habits of thought (re)packaged in different guises. The one that immediately caught my attention was the "appropriated meme signaling hatred produced by the hysterical fear of losing white privilege" mentioned above (Figure 18). Marked as a hate symbol by the Anti-Defamation League in 2016, Pepe the Frog started as a character in a 2005 comic by cartoonist Matt Furie and became popularized on 4chan, arguably the birthplace of memes and in recent years a "hub for Trump support and members of the alt-right."[188] The physical, embodied rendering of Pepe in *The Keys to the Kingdom* interrupts the meme's viral (decontextualized and instant) circulation through its problematic placing and framing within a context of other "keys." What makes this placing and framing problematic is, on the one hand, the meme's repetition (which holds the possibility of its amplification, especially if taken out of context), and, on the other hand, the very framing of it as a problem—a problem that needs to be carefully attended to and reckoned with.

FIGURE 18. *The Keys to the Kingdom,* detail of flags including the Pepe–Crazy Frog emblem, at Palacio de Cristal, Parque del Retiro, Madrid, by Hassan Khan, 2019.

Photo credit Ioana B. Jucan.

Inhabiting the very logic of memes, which involves circulation and transformation,[189] Khan transformed Pepe by hybridizing this emblem with that of the animated Crazy Frog, "the force behind a viral ring-tone that spawned a global chart-topping single in 2005," which also appeared in an ad for cell phone ringtones from the 2000s and which recently made a viral comeback inspired in part by TikTok trends.[190] This hybridization of Pepe, a racist symbol associated with white supremacy, and the Crazy Frog, which Khan sees as "the emblem of a certain high-speed consumer culture,"[191] points to the political economy of the present moment, the interlinking of the political and the economic, undergirded by performativity. The resulting Pepe–Crazy Frog emblem is placed and framed within a physical context of other keys that point to both the long history and the persistent present of the racial violence and white supremacy that undergird the *Happy Empire,* which names

FIGURE 19. *The Keys to the Kingdom,* detail of *Happy Empire,* at Palacio de Cristal, Parque del Retiro, Madrid, by Hassan Khan, 2019.

Photo credit Ioana B. Jucan.

another work in Khan's exhibition. This kind of framing opens up a space for thinking and feeling, for reckoning with the meme and what lies behind it as a problem that needs to be urgently attended to.

A component of the artwork titled *Happy Empire,* the central key of Khan's exhibition is a "mid-nineteenth century pedestal table, that so accurately, and offensively, channeled and celebrated the racial politics that built what we call the modern world" (Figure 19).[192] Once a luxury commodity, now a museum artifact on display at the Museum of Romanticism in Madrid, the table—a testimony to the so-called grandeur of "Western civilization"—is also a meme of sorts. Displayed at the Museum of Romanticism as a decontextualized aesthetic object, devoid of any critical framing, the table is an object that scripts thinking, reinforcing stubbornly persistent and long-institutionalized habits of thought and perpetuating the violence it represents. Reading the table as "a metonym that celebrates and . . . embodies the conditions of the real that it is a metonym of,"[193] Khan staged it—by reconstructing it through a different medium (the computer), thus tearing it out of its decontextualization and recontextualizing it—in a context of other keys, as part of artworks that "are interested in an overt formalization of power relations and their phantasmatic metaphysics."[194]

Khan writes about this central key in the exhibition pamphlet (where images of it are also included):

THE IMAGE ACCOMPANYING THIS TEXT IS A COMPUTER-GEN-ERATED 3D RENDER OF A TABLE I SAW IN THE MUSEUM OF RO-MANTICISM ON MY THIRD VISIT TO MADRID IN PREPARATION FOR THIS EXHIBITION. IT MADE ME VERY ANGRY AND FOR A MOMENT I WAS TEMPTED TO TAKE THE TABLE AND PLACE IT ALONE IN THE MIDDLE OF THE CRYSTAL PALACE. ALTHOUGH THIS DID NOT FEEL SUFFICIENT THE TABLE BECAME THE KEY TO THIS EXHIBITION ABOUT KEYS. LOOK AT ITS PRINTED DIGI-TAL REPLICA – IT IS BOTH GROTESQUE AND SUBLIME. LOOK AT HOW IT MAKES THE PERSON IT REPRESENTS MONSTROUS AND UNHUMAN. HOW IT EXERTS VIOLENCE BY TWISTING THEIR NECK AND EXAGGERATING THEIR FEATURES AND USING THEM AS SUPPORT FOR THE WOODEN TABLETOP. PLEASE LOOK AT

HOW IT MIXES BRUTAL INHUMAN CONTORTIONS WITH ELE-
GANCE AND REFINEMENT TO PRODUCE A GROTESQUE EFFECT.
LOOK AT THE WAY THE TABLETOP SEEMS STRANGELY SUS-
PENDED IT FEELS SUBLIME. IT FEELS LIKE IT IS FLOATING BE-
CAUSE THE SCULPTED FIGURE OF THE UPSIDE-DOWN SLAVE
SUPPORTING THE GOLD ENAMELLED MAHOGANY STRUCTURE
IS A TRUE MANIFESTATION OF REAL CONDITIONS. THE IMAGE
OF THE SLAVE IS REAL BECAUSE IT OFFERS A KEY TO UNDER-
STANDING HOW THE SYSTEM WORKS. THE VIOLENT DEHUMAN-
IZING PHYSICAL CONTORTIONS OF ENSLAVED PEOPLE FORCED
INTO LABOUR PRODUCED FOR SOME WEALTH AND POWER AND
WHAT THEY CALL BEAUTY. BUT POWERFUL EMOTIONS WERE
ALSO HARVESTED. THE HATRED YOU HAVE FOR THE DOMI-
NATED. A SENSE OF YOUR RACIAL ENTITLEMENT. AN INTENSE
RAGE REPLACING WHAT YOU DON'T HAVE. THE DESIRE TO
PROTECT WHAT YOU THINK IS PRECIOUS. THE FEAR OF LOSING
WHAT YOU OWN. ENVY OF THOSE WHO ALLOW YOU TO ACCU-
MULATE VALUE. I THE ARTIST USING THIS ELEMENT AS PART OF
THEIR WORK IN THIS EXHIBITION WROTE THIS TEXT.[195]

The last few lines of this statement, about the powerful emotions harvested by the white supremacist system of domination, describe the (concealed, unacknowledged) emotions that lie behind Blonde's tirade—emotions and habits of thought produced by racial capitalism.

I quote Khan's statement here in full because it places the artist in relation to the piece and frames the exhibition. Functioning as "an invisible work" that becomes part of the official discourse, this statement aids in the process of recontextualization and repoliticization of a commodity/art object/image that was intended to be consumed—both in its time and presently as an artifact displayed in the museum—as a purely aesthetic object voided of history, content, and context.[196] Khan's statement also holds a powerful call (note the repetition of "look") and reminder of a past that is ongoing, "unfolding still" (to borrow Christina Sharpe's words).[197] This is a past, and a history of relentless racism and racial capitalism, that has been long misrepresented and manipulated through the narratives of the grandeur of European/white "civilization" and its "great discoveries," the kind of history that I learned in school in the early days of "catching up" in post-communist Romania. This is the reminder that I would like to hold on to in the closing of this book, a reminder that points to what lies behind the (dis)simulation machines that this book has attended to.

Epilogue
NOTES TOWARD A LIVING PRACTICE

• • • In a theatre play that I wrote a few years ago, Descartes's malicious deceiver appears in the guise of a character referred to as "the entity." One of the characters, Clara, an ex-judge, enacts its deceptive performances together with Anka, a programmer, who plays the voice of "the people":

CLARA

This entity landed in our town apparently out of nowhere, like an extra-terrestrial creature. We never see it, but we always see on TV the same faces who govern us, who tell us that the entity brings us economic growth.

ANKA

"What's that?"

CLARA

We ask. The entity, however, speaks our language. It tells us that it will give us "a better quality of life."

ANKA

"That's what we want."

CLARA

In turn, it will cut down all our trees, it will take away all our
copper, iron, gold, oil, natural gases, all our land, water, and air.
We say:

ANKA

"Sure, take them, they're just lying there anyway."

CLARA

The entity immediately grabs them. And sells them. We buy
them from it, and think we have a better quality of life. Soon,
they become too expensive. We can't afford to buy them
anymore. The entity tells us that we're lazy and stupid. And
backward. That's why we don't have a good quality of life. That's
what those whom we have elected to represent us also tell us.
We believe them. Eventually, we realize that we're running out
of air.

ANKA

And everything is waste.

CLARA

Our town looks like it's from another planet.[1]

Clara, Anka, and their friend Roza, a philosopher, seek ways to resist
"the entity." They come up with two plans: A and B. Plan B involves
sending out a viral message to the whole world, through all possible
channels of communication, from television to the internet. Bearing
the code name "Prayer.Curse," Plan B capitalizes on the performativity
of language and on the hope that language can bring things into being,
which we know it can (though why only sometimes?). Here it is, the
message to be broadcast on all channels of communication worldwide,
to be incessantly reproduced as "breaking news," brought to you by an
Official:

They
    want the mountains, bleeding
    want the oil, pouring
    want the wood, chopped

want the water
to be sold to us, bottled
want us to be poor and dependent
and buying and buying and buying
business as usual
Redundant to the history of being
                    (nostalgia for the afterlife—in the off time)

The   factory
     country
is   rusting
from
tears
        trees
        trees   trees   trees
    trees   trees   trees
    trees   trees
    grow   trees
        trees   trees
    out of imperial houses.   trees
    Outgrow imperial houses.
I
   still
remember
fairytales
where trees start walking
            destroying destroyers
            yelling
This needs to stop.

I hope you masters of profit will be struck down by trees falling
with rage. The irony of this happening would make me laugh.
Catharsis.[2]

Plan A comes in two versions. The first version is modeled on the
"Baltic Way/Chain of Freedom," and it proposes the formation of an
embodied, uninterrupted chain of human connection, across the globe.

The inspiration for this version of Plan A was the peaceful protest that took place across the three Baltic states (Estonia, Latvia, and Lithuania) against the Soviet occupation. The protest occurred on August 23, 1989, the fiftieth anniversary of the German-Soviet Pact in which "the two totalitarian powers divided Finland, Estonia, Latvia, Lithuania, Poland and Romania—in violation of international law—into respective spheres of influence."[3] The Baltic Chain consisted of around two million people, standing together in the name of freedom from the USSR. The protest was also a global media event.[4] At the end of the play, the characters invite the audience to form this kind of chain and chant together: "We are the resistance."

FIGURE 20. *Resistance (Happening),* performed at the Sibiu International Theatre Festival, Romania, written and directed by Ioana B. Jucan, 2017.

Photo credit Mara Mărăcinescu.

Roza, the philosopher, thinks that this version of Plan A is "pure idealism" and proposes an alternative, based on the idea that global capitalism implies a global workforce. Thus, the second version of Plan A proposes a "General World Strike of All Workers Worldwide" (Figure 20). In Roza's words:

> In our times, in this . . . system of global exploitation, our only real chance—conceptually speaking—is to take seriously the hypothesis of a general world strike: a general strike which would take place simultaneously worldwide. Imagine it: We would all have solidarity with each other; we are all workers, after all, even if we don't want to admit it. We will stop working until all our governments will agree to properly tax those who have money, all those . . . multinational corporations. And our governments will finally support, as they should, our health and educational systems, so that health and education can become free and accessible to all. It's simple.[5]

Plans A and B may not be *the* solutions to the problems of the world. In fact, the plans are intensely questioned by the characters, as is eventually the very idea of a plan. Yet, articulated in the public space of a theatre, Plans A and B potentially function as gestures, as sensual and conceptual openings, as hypotheses submitted for thinking in common in a shared space, for a practice of sense-making. Self-critique—as a mode of putting oneself and the self's relation to the world in question, of problematically staging the embodied "I"—plays a role in this practice of sense-making. This is a kind of critique that is different from passing judgment, or from fault-finding,[6] or from throwing everything into doubt. For Roza/R, the philosopher and her double (played by two different actors in the staging of the play that I directed), it takes the following form, which also expresses their life philosophy:

ROZA	R
I'd like to be able to define my life. To analyze it, and change it where I don't like it.	I. Here. Zoom in, zoom out.
I'd start with the moment when I took up philosophy. No, actually, with the moment when I began to ask myself about the world. What's going on?	I have stopped seeking for a sense.
	I believe in concrete things, things that are real.
	Life must be lived, in a beautiful way.
Why are people so ignorant, so indifferent, so egoist?	Time fools us. The earth need not endure the effects of our illusions. Nature will beat us in the struggle for survival.
I'd like to help them change.	My little Roza will grow up.
But the first step towards change is to change myself. Not to judge anymore.	She will ask me questions. Like: "Why didn't you do anything?"
	Why didn't you do anything?[7]

The play described here is *Resistance (Happening)*, a theatrical thought experiment that I wrote and directed in 2016. The performance, produced by the Radu Stanca National Theatre and the Lucian Blaga University in Sibiu, my hometown, was presented both in the United States and in Romania. As part of an initiative of the Sibiu International Theatre Festival, one set of audiences for which *Resistance (Happening)* was performed in 2017 was comprised of NATO soldiers from a nearby NATO Training Area.[8] I share this because the call for a people-focused rather than a market-focused politics and for solidarity, as well as this theatrical moment in which actors and NATO soldiers chant together "We are the resistance" to global capitalism, are things I have often re-turned to as I try to make sense of the current world (picture), its contradictions and the relentless violence being perpetrated—especially in the recent months since Russia's ongoing invasion of Ukraine, sustained by profits from petro-capitalism, with the (dis)simulation machines that both accompany and preceded it and that harken back to the (dis)simulation machines presented in this book's Interlude.[9]

While not something I anticipated writing about when I set out on the present book project, Russia's invasion of our neighbor Ukraine and its implications and potential consequences have been very much on my mind and heart as I was working on finishing this book. How to make sense of it and what to do in the face of it? Seen by some as "a new Cold War,"[10] the invasion of Ukraine has also been seen by others as a consequence of a "global historical process . . . , a political project to remake the world in the image of, and for the benefit of, the USA after the end of the Cold War," as well as a continuation of imperial ambitions fueled by both nationalistic and capitalistic ends on the part of the world's nuclear-backed superpowers.[11] To hold in view these different perspectives and broader context is in no way to exonerate Russia of its atrocious actions in Ukraine or to shift the blame elsewhere; the invasion, the violence, and destruction are unjustifiable on any grounds whatsoever. Without brushing over the particularities of this specific situation, holding these different perspectives in view is rather to begin to engage in a problematic process of framing, placing, situating, understanding the invasion in the context of the other ongoing "wars of global capital" in Afghanistan, Côte d'Ivoire, the Democratic Republic of Congo, Iraq, Libya, Morocco, Somalia, Syria, Tunisia, Yemen, as well as "the urban and rural warfare that prevails in economically dispossessed places in Latin America, the Caribbean, and the United States,"[12] and in the context of a persistent colonial-imperial machine of dispossession and destruction with which global, racial capitalism has been tied for centuries. Russia's invasion is a movement of this capitalist-fueled *modern* colonial-imperial machine.

I am reminded here of a note that Adrienne Rich made in the context of the Cold War, where in the same paragraph she mentions "the news" (on TV at the time) as the medium through which abstractions are being fed: "we are not invited to consider the butcheries of Stalinism, the terrors of the Russian counterrevolution alongside the butcheries of white supremacism and Manifest Destiny."[13] Considering these two alongside each other does not by any means amount to equating them. There are significant differences between the two, just as there are significant differences between the ways in which white Ukrainian refugees have been largely welcomed by other European countries (at least so far) in comparison to the racialized refugees from the Global South, as well as between the ways in which white Ukrainians receive widely different treatment than racialized people within Ukraine.[14] As Denise Ferreira Da Silva has pointed out, "raciality accounts for why those displaced by wars of global capital do not really move out of . . . the zone of violence."[15]

For this kind of consideration—and more capacious way of thinking that takes into account coexisting and related, although seemingly disparate, realities and histories—to be possible, it is necessary to pick up "the long struggle against lofty and privileged abstraction," Rich suggests.[16] But how is one to do this practically, as a living practice rather than just a philosophy? How is one to engage in a living practice toward meaningful change, toward enacting what Vishwas Satgar has called "a politics of human and non-human solidarity"?[17] The answer to these global problems—which are problems produced by global racial capitalism, the preeminent malicious deceiver—lies at the systemic level; even so, the practice starts with oneself, or? As I ponder these questions and struggle to find an answer, I turn again and again to Rich's words from her "Notes toward a Politics of Location," which I would like to hold on to in the end of this book, as a beginning again, a continuation of a struggle to keep learning, and learning to think beyond and against abstraction, and to keep changing:

A movement for change lives in feelings, actions, and words. Whatever circumscribes or mutilates our feelings makes it more difficult to act, keeps our actions reactive, repetitive: abstract thinking, narrow tribal loyalties, every kind of self-righteousness, the arrogance of believing ourselves at the center. It's hard to look back on the limits of my understanding a year, five years ago—how did I look without seeing, hear without listening? It can be difficult to be generous to earlier selves . . . . Yet how, except through ourselves, do we discover what moves other people to change? Our old fears and denials—what helps us let go of them? What makes us decide we have to re-educate ourselves, even those of us with "good" educations? A politicized life ought to sharpen both the senses and the memory. . . .

The movement for change is a changing movement, changing itself, demasculinizing itself, de-Westernizing itself, becoming a critical mass that is saying in so many different voices, languages, gestures, actions: *It must change; we ourselves can change it.*

We who are not the same. We who are many and do not want to be the same.[18]

ACKNOWLEDGMENTS

This book took and changed shape over many years, and it would not have been possible without the many people who have supported and inspired it and enriched my life.

The seeds for this project were planted during my time at Brown University, where I found a second home after leaving Romania. I owe a deep gratitude to mentors, colleagues, and friends with whom I formed lasting connections going back to this precious time. A very special thank you goes to Wendy Hui Kyong Chun, whose mentorship, support, and scholarship have profoundly shaped my thinking and my trajectory in academia over the years. Spencer Golub has provided me with an ever-inspiring model of experimental creative scholarship and, with both kindness and rigor, encouraged and supported my own adventures as a writer, thinker, and theatre-maker. Rebecca Schneider's thinking about history and temporality in relation to performance has informed my own, and I could not be more grateful for her inspiring scholarship as well as her continued support. Adi Ophir kept my appreciation of philosophy alive at a time when I was intensely questioning the discipline, and his insightful thinking and openness to ideas that jump disciplinary fields helped clarify my own thinking in the early stages of this project. My artistic work has benefited from the mentorship of Kym Moore and Daniel Peltz. A resounding thanks to Justin Broackes for all his support and many rewarding conversations about philosophy and art and life.

In recent years, my thinking about fakeness and reality(-making) has been informed by my work with the Beyond Verification team out of the Digital Democracies Institute at Simon Fraser University. I would like to thank the team members with whom I had the privilege of working for very enriching conversations and collaborations: Wendy Chun, Alex Juhasz, Ganaele Langlois, Roopa Vasudevan, Melody Devries, Anthony Burton, Amy Harris, Carina Albrecht, and Esther Weltevrede.

I am grateful for the institutional support and the community of thought and practice I have found at Emerson College, and I would like to especially thank Dean Amy Ansell for supporting my scholarship and teaching, as well as my colleagues in the Marlboro Institute for Liberal Arts & Interdisciplinary Studies and the Business of Creative Enterprises program for their support and great conversations. My thanks to my students, who challenge me to keep pushing against abstraction and in conversation with whom I have had the opportunity to test, refine, and expand some of the ideas from the book.

The year I spent at the Center for Digital Cultures at Leuphana University Lüneburg as a postdoctoral researcher was an important incubation period for some of the ideas in the book. I would like to thank Timon Beyes, Boukje Cnossen, Randi Heinrichs, Lisa Conrad, Andreas Bernard, Daniela Wentz, Clara Wieghorst, Ina Dubberke, and Sophie Koester for their warm welcome and thought-provoking discussions.

I am grateful to my collaborators on *Left and Right* and *Resistance (Happening)*—you were amazing to work with, and I have learned so much from you all. For his support with these two projects, I thank Constantin Chiriac, the director of the Radu Stanca National Theatre and the president of the Sibiu International Theatre Festival in Romania. My deep thanks to Chira DelSesto, Sophia LaCava-Bohanan, and all the folks at the Brown Arts Institute, and to Billy Clark and Mattie Barber-Bockelman at CultureHub for all their support. I am also grateful to Wolfgang Ernst, Stefan Höltgen, and Florian Leitner for the invitation to share my early work on and performance of machine thinking in the Media Theatre at Humboldt University in Berlin and for the collaboration on a published essay that ensued from this.

I would like to express my deep gratitude to Annie Dorsen, American Artist, Chris Jordan, Milo Rau and the International Institute of Political Murder, and Pinar Yoldas for granting permission to include images of their work, as well as to Mara Mărăcinescu, Pam Longobardi, and Yuguang Zhang for allowing me to include their images in the book. My thanks to Chris Jordan and Pinar Yoldas for generously making time to be in conversation with me, and to Annie Dorsen for kindly making available videos of her work.

It is a joy and an honor to have this book appear in the Sensing Media series at Stanford University Press. I am profoundly thankful to the series editors, Wendy Hui Kyong Chun and Shane Denson, and to Executive Editor Erica Wetter, Associate Editor Caroline McKusick, and the entire team at SUP. My heartfelt thanks also to the two anonymous readers for engaging so carefully with the manuscript and for providing such valuable feedback.

I am grateful to Will Daddario for reading through the manuscript and offering helpful feedback. He has been a wonderful friend, collaborator, and fellow performance philosopher whose work never fails to inspire me. My thanks also to friends near and far on whom I know I can always count—you know who you are.

I owe an immeasurable debt of gratitude to Liviu Iftode, an extraordinary mentor and friend whose exceptional kindness, generosity, humor, and brilliance I will never forget. Our conversations—about pretty much everything from theatre, to computer science, to politics, to everyday life—nourished me since I left Romania for college, and some of them have even found their way into this book. My journey through academia would have not been the same without him. This book is dedicated to him and his forever enduring memory.

My family has been a vital source of love and care: my parents, Carmen and Cornel Jucan; my partner in life and conversation, Eze Onwugbenu; my sister, Ella Jucan; and my late Grandpa and Grandma, Ioan and Paraschiva Bogdan (or Bunicu și Buna). A special shoutout to my sweet Mama, Carmen Jucan, who has always been my biggest and unwavering support and supporter.

An early version of the section on Annie Dorsen's *A Piece of Work* from Chapter 2 appeared as "sys.begin to sys.exit: Software Performs *A Piece of Work"* in *TDR: The Drama Review* 59, no. 4 (Winter 2015): 149–168. An early version of my reflection on *How I Became a Thinking Machine* from the Interlude appeared in an essay titled "The Human Is the Problem: Scenes of Technology and Reason in Media Performance," co-authored with Florian Leitner, Anton Pohle, and Carolin Kipka, and published in *Hello, I'm ELIZA*, edited by Stefan Höltgen and Marianna Baranovska (Bochum/Freiburg: Projekt Verlag, 2018). Early versions of different sections of the discussion of *Left and Right* from Chapter 4 appeared under the title "Performing 'Left and Right'" in *Theatre Journal*, volume 73, issue 3 (September 2021): E9–E14, copyright @ 2021 Johns Hopkins University Press, published with permission by Johns Hopkins University Press, and under the title "Digitally Live: Performative Presence in Times of COVID-19" in *Performance Paradigm*, volume 17, 2022, republished here with thanks to the editors and the anonymous reviewers. I am grateful for the permission to include these materials here.

NOTES

Prologue

1. Thomas Nagel, *The View from Nowhere* (New York and Oxford: Oxford University Press, 1989), 11.

2. Richard Schechner, *Between Theatre and Anthropology* (Philadelphia: University of Pennsylvania Press, 1985), 36.

3. Samuel Weber, *Theatricality as Medium* (New York: Fordham University Press, 2004), 315; italics in original.

4. The idea also appears in Descartes's *Meditations*, but this exact formulation is from Descartes's earlier work, *Discourse on the Method*, in *The Philosophical Writings of Descartes, Volume 1*, trans. John Cottingham, Robert Stoothoff, and Dugald Murdoch (Cambridge and New York: Cambridge University Press, 1985), 127 (AT VI 32); italics in original. The abbreviation "AT" in the notes to Descartes refers to the standard Adam and Tannery edition of Descartes's works.

5. Lana and Lilly Wachowski (dirs.), *The Matrix*, 1999.

6. *Merriam-Webster*, s.v. "synthetic," accessed June 11, 2022, https://www.merriam-webster.com/dictionary/synthetic.

7. Naomi Scheman, *Engenderings: Constructions of Knowledge, Authority, and Privilege* (New York: Routledge, 1993), xii, xiv.

8. Walter Mignolo, *The Darker Side of Western Modernity: Global Futures, Decolonial Options* (Durham and London: Duke University Press, 2011), 80.

9. The notion of the "virtual window" is drawn from Anne Friedberg's book *The Virtual Window: From Alberti to Microsoft* (Cambridge: MIT Press, 2006).

10. I channel here Claire Colebrook's phrasing from *Gilles Deleuze* (London

and New York: Routledge, 2002), 46; italics in original. The expression "method in the madness" is adapted from Shakespeare's *Hamlet*.

11. I take the idea of "a new form of colonization by consumerism" from Alejandro Durán, in Anna Gragert, "Riveting Trash-Based Sculptures Mirror Significant Environmental Issues," *My Modern Met*, April 20, 2015, https://mymodernmet .com/trash-based-photo-series-mirrors-environment-issues/.

12. Wendy Hui Kyong Chun, "Big Data as Drama," *ELH* 83, no. 2 (Summer 2016): 368; Kevin Slavin, "How Algorithms Shape Our World," *TEDGlobal*, 2011, www.ted .com/talks/kevin_slavin_how_algorithms_shape_our_world?language=en; Christopher Steiner, *Automate This: How Algorithms Came to Rule Our World* (New York: Penguin Books, 2012).

13. Konrad Petrovszky and Ovidiu Țichindeleanu, "Sensuri ale Revoluției Române," in *Revoluția Română Televizată: Contribuții la Istoria Culturală a Mediilor*, eds. Konrad Petrovzsky and Ovidiu Țichindeleanu (Cluj: IDEA Design & Print, 2009), 30; my translation from Romanian; italics in original.

14. Vilém Flusser, "Television Image and Political Space in the Light of the Romanian Revolution," April 7, 1990, Kunsthalle Budapest, published on YouTube by Vasily Klenov on May 31, 2011, https://www.youtube.com/watch?v=QFTaY2u4NvI.

15. "Metaphysical subtleties" is borrowed from Karl Marx's analysis of the fetishism of the capitalist commodity from *Capital: A Critique of Political Economy, Volume 1*, trans. Ben Fowkes (Harmondsworth: Penguin Books, 1976), 163.

16. Durán in Gragert, "Riveting Trash-Based Sculptures."

17. See, for instance, Ian Bremmer, "The New Cold War Could Soon Heat Up," *Foreign Affairs*, May 5, 2022, https://www.foreignaffairs.com/articles/russia-fsu/ 2022-05-05/new-cold-war-could-soon-heat.

Chapter 1

1. "Word of the Year 2016," *Oxford Languages*, accessed June 11, 2022, https:// languages.oup.com/word-of-the-year/2016/. For the computer simulation hypothesis, see, for example: Jason Koebler, "Elon Musk Says There's a 'One in Billions' Chance Reality Is Not a Simulation," *Vice*, June 2, 2016, https://www.vice.com/en _us/article/8q854v/elon-musk-simulated-universe-hypothesis; Joshua Rothman, "What Are the Odds We Are Living in a Computer Simulation?," *New Yorker*, June 9, 2016, https://www.newyorker.com/books/joshua-rothman/what-are-the-odds -we-are-living-in-a-computer-simulation; Olivia Solon, "Is Our World a Simulation? Why Some Scientists Say It's More Likely Than Not," *The Guardian*, October 11, 2016, https://www.theguardian.com/technology/2016/oct/11/simulated-world -elon-musk-the-matrix.

2. René Descartes, *Early Writings*, in *The Philosophical Writings of Descartes, Volume 1*, trans. John Cottingham, Robert Stoothoff, and Dugald Murdoch (Cambridge and New York: Cambridge University Press, 1985), 2 (AT X 213).

3. René Descartes, *Rules for the Direction of the Mind*, in *The Philosophical*

Writings of Descartes, Volume 1, trans. John Cottingham, Robert Stoothoff, and Dugald Murdoch (Cambridge and New York: Cambridge University Press, 1985), 15 (AT X 371); italics in original.

4. René Descartes, *Discourse on the Method*, in *The Philosophical Writings of Descartes, Volume 1*, trans. John Cottingham, Robert Stoothoff, and Dugald Murdoch (Cambridge and New York: Cambridge University Press, 1985), 120 (AT VI 18).

5. Whitney Phillips and Ryan M. Milner, *You Are Here: A Field Guide for Navigating Polarized Speech, Conspiracy Theories, and Our Polluted Media Landscape* (Cambridge and London: MIT Press, 2021), 20.

6. Whitney Phillips, "Please, Please, Please Don't Mock Conspiracy Theories," *Wired*, February 27, 2020, https://www.wired.com/story/please-please-please-dont-mock-conspiracy-theories/.

7. René Descartes, *Meditations on First Philosophy*, in *Descartes: Selected Philosophical Writings*, trans. John Cottingham, Robert Stoothoff, and Dugald Murdoch (Cambridge and New York: Cambridge University Press, 1998), 76 (AT VII 17).

8. Ibid., 73 (AT VII 12).

9. René Descartes, *Optics*, in *Descartes: Selected Philosophical Writings*, trans. John Cottingham, Robert Stoothoff, and Dugald Murdoch (Cambridge and New York: Cambridge University Press, 1998), 57 (AT VI 81).

10. This proposal is inspired from Catherine Wilson's study of the effects of the discovery of the telescope and the microscope on both experimental philosophy and metaphysics in the seventeenth century, in *The Invisible World: Early Modern Philosophy and the Invention of the Microscope* (Princeton: Princeton University Press, 1995).

11. Daniel Tiffany, *Toy Medium: Materialism and the Modern Lyric* (Berkeley: University of California Press, 2000), 185. While beyond the scope of this book, it bears noting that the world revealed by these media was filled with speculation and imagination, even as it was supposed to be a product of objective, scientific observation. For an account of this, see Wilson's *The Invisible World*.

12. In fact, for philosopher and mathematician Gottfried Wilhelm Leibniz, Descartes's "optical theory and his designs for 'magnifying glasses with which we could see animals on the moon and all the finer parts of creatures' were that philosopher's greatest and most substantial achievements, by contrast with his absurd and imaginary metaphysics" (in Wilson, *The Invisible World*, 78).

13. Descartes, *Principles of Philosophy*, in *The Philosophical Writings of Descartes, Volume 1*, trans. John Cottingham, Robert Stoothoff, and Dugald Murdoch (Cambridge and New York: Cambridge University Press, 1985), 193 (AT VIIIA 5); italics in original.

14. Ibid.

15. Descartes, *Discourse*, 126 (AT VI 31).

16. Descartes, *Principles*, 193 (AT VIIIA 5).

17. Descartes, *Discourse,* 122 (AT VI 22).

18. Descartes, *Meditations,* 73 (AT VII 12).

19. Ibid., 76 (AT VII 18); also in *Discourse,* 127 (AT VI 32).

20. Descartes, *Meditations,* 81, 79 (AT VII 27, 22).

21. Ibid., 80 (AT VII 24).

22. Ibid.

23. Ibid.

24. This idea of surveillance may put us in mind of Michel Foucault/Jeremy Bentham's model of the panopticon; Michel Foucault, "Panopticism," in *Discipline and Punish: The Birth of the Prison,* trans. Alan Sheridan (New York: Pantheon, 1977).

25. Descartes, *Meditations,* 79 (AT VII 23).

26. Ibid.

27. Ibid. (AT VII 22); emphasis added.

28. Ibid., 82 (AT VII 27).

29. Descartes, *Discourse,* 127 (AT VI 32); italics in original.

30. Descartes, *Meditations,* 80 (AT VII 25); italics in original, emphasis added.

31. Ibid., 114 (AT VII 78).

32. Ibid., 80 (AT VII 24).

33. Ibid., 87 (AT VII 35).

34. This is so, says Descartes, because the idea of God as a "supremely intelligent, supremely powerful and supremely perfect being" can be clearly and distinctly perceived. What is more, perfection—which Descartes understands as total reality—precludes deception. This God ensures the persistence of finite things; the perceptible persistence of finite things is, in turn, proof of God's existence. Thus: "*The fact that our existence has duration is sufficient to demonstrate the existence of God*" (Descartes, *Principles,* 197, 200 [AT VIIIA 10, 13]; italics in original).

35. For instance, Thomas Paine in Georg Büchner's play *Danton's Death* argues the exact opposite, mobilizing the indubitable Cartesian piece of reasoning ("I think, therefore I am"), with a twist:

> There is no God; because either God made the world or He did not. If He did not, then the world contains its own origin and there is no God, because God is only God in that He embraces the origin of all being. However, God can *not* have created the world, because either the creation is eternal like God, or it has a beginning. If the latter is true, God must have created it at a specific point in time; in other words, having been quiescent for an eternity, He must have become active, that is He must have suffered a change in himself and become subject to the concept of time. But both concepts—change and time—are in conflict with the nature of God. Therefore God could not have created the world. Now since we know that the world, or at least our own consciousness, exists, and since we know from what I've just said that our

consciousness must have its origin either in itself or in something else that is not God, there can be no God. Q.E.D. (Georg Büchner, "Danton's Death," in *Georg Büchner: Danton's Death, Leonce and Lena, Woyzeck*, trans. Victor Price [Oxford and New York: Oxford University Press, 1971], 43)

Paine's argument for (a Christian) God's non-existence seems to me as good (or as bad) as Descartes's argument for God's existence. In fact, it is better, more logical, taking on the contradictions inherent in Descartes's view.

36. See, for instance, Swami Vivekananda, *Jnana Yoga: The Yoga of Knowledge* (Kolkata: Advaita Ashrama, 2009). In this framework, both the body and the mind—as ever-changing and impermanent—are a matter of deception, but they are pervaded by the presence of God, who is the unchanging, ever-perfect Self— the true nature of everything that exists, humans and nonhumans alike. This God is not in some heavens outside, but within each and every thing that exists, guaranteeing the radical equality of everything there is. What sustains the deception is the hyper-identification with body and mind, which Descartes in no way escapes: he simply swaps an investment in the body with an investment in the mind (a mind that concocts the malicious deceiver), problematically calling the mind immortal and making a certain way of (human) thinking the ground for existence.

37. I draw here from Hannah Arendt, *The Human Condition*, 2nd edition (Chicago and London: University of Chicago Press, 1958), 284.

38. Descartes, *Meditations*, 87 (AT VII 34–35).

39. Ibid., 83 (AT VII 29).

40. Ludwig Wittgenstein, *Tractatus Logico-Philosophicus,* trans. C. K. Ogden (Mineola: Dover Publications, 1999), §5.641.

41. Descartes, *Meditations*, 83 (AT VII 29).

42. Ibid., 110 (AT VII 71); emphasis added.

43. Descartes, *The World or Treatise on Light*, in *The Philosophical Writings of Descartes, Volume 1*, trans. John Cottingham, Robert Stoothoff, and Dugald Murdoch (Cambridge and New York: Cambridge University Press, 1985), 97 (AT XI 47); emphasis added.

44. I borrow this notion from Phillips and Milner, *You Are Here*, 19.

45. Descartes, *Meditations*, 116 (AT VII 80).

46. *Merriam-Webster,* s.v. "synthetic," accessed June 11, 2022, https://www.merriam-webster.com/dictionary/synthetic.

47. Vilém Flusser, *The Shape of Things: A Philosophy of Design* (London: Reaktion, 1999), 62.

48. Parts of *The World* were incorporated into Descartes's last work, *Principles of Philosophy* ("Translator's Preface" to *The World*, 177).

49. Descartes, *The World*, 90 (AT XI 31).

50. Ibid.

51. Ibid., 91 (AT XI 33).

52. Descartes, *Principles*, 279 (AT VIIIA 315). Notably, Descartes also regards the body as a machine—see, *Treatise on Man*, in *The Philosophical Writings of Descartes, Volume 1*, trans. John Cottingham, Robert Stoothoff, and Dugald Murdoch (Cambridge and New York: Cambridge University Press, 1985), 99 (AT XI 120).

53. I echo here the statement of legal scholar Antoinette Rouvroy, who wrote that the knowledge produced through the algorithmic processing of data is not "produced *about* the world anymore, but *from* the digital world." Antoinette Rouvroy, "The End(s) of Critique: Data Behaviourism Versus Due Process," in *Privacy, Due Process and the Computational Turn: The Philosophy of Law Meets the Philosophy of Technology*, eds. Mireille Hildebrandt and Katja De Vries (London: Routledge, 2013), 147; italics in original.

54. Bernard de Fontenelle, *Conversations on the Plurality of Worlds*, with notes by Jerome de la Lande, trans. Elizabeth Gunning (London: printed by J. Cundee, Ivy Lane; sold by T. Hurst, Paternoster-Row, 1803), 8.

55. Ibid., 9.

56. Ibid.

57. Ibid., 10.

58. Descartes, *Principles*, 288–289 (AT VIIIA 326).

59. Bernard le Bovier de Fontenelle, *Conversations on the Plurality of Worlds*, trans. H. A. Hargreaves (Berkeley, Los Angeles, and London: University of California Press, 1990), 35.

60. Ibid., 44; emphasis added.

61. Peter Szendy, *Kant in the Land of Extraterrestrials: Cosmopolitical Philosofictions*, trans. Will Bishop (New York: Fordham University Press, 2013), 54.

62. In fact, for Descartes, because of this sameness, "there cannot in fact be a plurality of worlds"; in Descartes, *Principles*, 232 (AT VIIIA 52).

63. J. L. Austin, *How to Do Things with Words* (London: Oxford University Press, 1962), 5, 6, 4.

64. Jacques Derrida, "Signature Event Context," in *Limited Inc* (Evanston: Northwestern University Press, 1977), 13; italics in original.

65. Ibid., 13–14.

66. "Word of the Year 2016."

67. Tommaso Venturini, "From Fake to Junk News, the Data Politics of Online Virality," in *Data Politics: Worlds, Subjects, Rights*, eds. Didier Bigo, Engin Isin, and Evelyn Ruppert (London: Routledge, 2019), 125.

68. Santiago Castro-Gómez, *Zero-Point Hubris: Science, Race, and Enlightenment in Eighteenth-Century Latin America*, trans. George Ciccariello-Maher and Don T. Deere (Lanham: Rowman & Littlefield, 2021), 12, 13; italics in original.

69. Ibid., 45, 46.

70. Ibid., 13.

71. See Castro-Gómez, *Zero-Point Hubris*, 7, 21, 31–32.

72. Martin Heidegger, "The Age of the World Picture," in *The Question Con-*

cerning Technology and Other Essays, trans. William Lovitt (New York: Harper & Row, 1977), 130.

73. Ibid., 149.

74. Ibid.

75. See Martin Heidegger, "The Age of the World Picture," "The Question Concerning Technology," and "Science and Reflection," in *The Question Concerning Technology and Other Essays*, trans. William Lovitt (New York: Harper & Row, 1977).

76. Heidegger, "The Question Concerning Technology," 12, 14.

77. Ibid., 17.

78. I here evoke Jon McKenzie, who, referencing Heidegger, speculated that "the age of the world picture is becoming *an age of global performance*"; in Jon McKenzie, *Perform or Else: From Discipline to Performance* (London and New York: Routledge, 2001), 171; italics in original.

79. Castro-Gómez, *Zero-Point Hubris*, 6.

80. Sylvia Wynter, "Unsettling the Coloniality of Being/Power/Truth/Freedom: Towards the Human, After Man, Its Overrepresentation—An Argument," *CR: The New Centennial Review* 3, no. 3 (Fall 2003): 260, 261, 264, 306.

81. According to the IMF: "The essential feature of capitalism is the motive to make a profit." Sarwat Jahan and Saber Mahmud, "What Is Capitalism?," *International Monetary Fund,* accessed June 10, 2022, https://www.imf.org/external/pubs/ft/fandd/basics/2_capitalism.htm.

82. On the inherently racial character of capitalism, see Cedric Robinson, *Black Marxism: The Making of the Black Radical Tradition* (Chapel Hill: University of North Carolina Press, 2000).

83. Guy Debord, *The Society of the Spectacle*, trans. Ken Knabb (Berkeley: Bureau of Public Secrets, 2014), thesis 2.

84. Ibid., theses 4, 6.

85. Robinson, *Black Marxism*; Angela Davis, "Angela Davis: We Can't Eradicate Racism Without Eradicating Racial Capitalism," *Democracy Now*, published on YouTube on June 14, 2020, https://www.youtube.com/watch?v=qhh3CMkngkY; Safiya Umoja Noble, "Teaching Trayvon: Race, Media, and the Politics of Spectacle," *The Black Scholar* 44, no. 1 (Spring 2014): 12–29.

86. On the connection between racial capitalism and the spectacle, see Noble, "Teaching Trayvon: Race, Media, and the Politics of Spectacle."

87. Debord, *The Society of the Spectacle*, thesis 5.

88. Notably, J. L. Austin makes direct reference to theatre in his theorization of the performative, specifically as an example of what he calls a "hollow" or "void" performative produced in "extra-ordinary" circumstances. In his words: "a performative utterance will, for example, be *in a peculiar way* hollow or void if said by an actor on the stage, or if introduced in a poem, or spoken in soliloquy" (Austin, *How to Do Things*, 22; italics in original). What enables the general equivalence

between a performative said by an actor on the stage and a poem is the voiding of theatricality, of the embodied nature of theatre and the particular mode of staging (framing) that defines it.

89. Samuel Weber, *Theatricality as Medium* (New York: Fordham University Press, 2004), 315; italics in original.

90. Ibid., 185; italics in original.

91. Ibid., 7.

92. Ibid., 109–110.

93. Ibid., 314, 315; italics in original.

94. See, for instance, Marvin Carlson, *The Haunted Stage: The Theatre as Memory Machine* (Ann Arbor: University of Michigan Press, 2001) and Rebecca Schneider, *Performing Remains: Art and War in Times of Theatrical Reenactment* (London and New York: Routledge, 2011).

95. Amélie Oksenberg Rorty, "The Structure of Descartes' *Meditations*," in *Essays on Descartes' Meditations*, ed. Amélie Oksenberg Rorty (Berkeley: University of California Press, 1986), 10.

96. Descartes, *Meditations*, 76–77 (AT VII 18).

97. Ibid., 81 (AT VII 26).

98. Ibid., 80 (AT VII 24).

99. Descartes, *Discourse*, 122, 116 (AT VI 22, 12).

100. Ibid., 125 (AT VI 28).

101. Descartes, *Early Writings*, 2 (AT X, 213).

102. William Shakespeare, *As You Like It*, eds. Barbara A. Mowat and Paul Werstine (New York: Washington Square Press, 1997), II.7.146–173.

103. Jean-Cristophe Agnew, *Worlds Apart: The Market and the Theatre in Anglo-American Thought, 1550–1750* (Cambridge and New York: Cambridge University Press, 1986), 16, 12.

104. Joseph de la Vega, *Confusión de Confusiones* [1688], in *Extraordinary Popular Delusions and the Madness of Crowds & Confusión de Confusiones, with a Current Perspective by Martin S. Fridson*, ed. Martin S. Fridson (New York: John Wiley & Sons/Marketplace Books, 1996), 169.

105. Ibid., 192.

106. Ibid., 178.

107. Ibid., 177.

108. Agnew, *Worlds Apart*, 56, 41.

109. Adam Smith, *An Inquiry into the Nature and Causes of the Wealth of Nations* (Edinburgh: Thomas Nelson, 1843), Book IV, 184; Wolfgang Ernst, "Digital Media Archaeology: Archive, Museum, and Sonicity," *CCAchannel*, published on YouTube on October 10, 2014, https://www.youtube.com/watch?v=f_GsDqKuOF8.

110. "Chronological Table of Descartes' Life and Work," in *The Philosophical Writings of Descartes, Volume 1*, xi.

111. Brandon Pepijn, "Marxism and the 'Dutch Miracle': The Dutch Republic and the Transition Debate," *Historical Materialism* 19, no. 3 (2011): 129.

112. Kerry Ward, *Networks of Empire: Forced Migration in the Dutch East India Company* (Cambridge: Cambridge University Press, 2009), 5, 15.

113. Karl Marx, *Capital: A Critique of Political Economy, Volume 1*, trans. Ben Fowkes (Harmondsworth: Penguin Books, 1976), 916.

114. Cited in Fernand Braudel, *Civilization and Capitalism, 15th–18th Century, Volume III: The Perspective of the World*, trans. Siân Reynolds (London: Williams Collins Sons; New York: Harper & Row, 1984), 30.

115. Cited in Marx, *Capital,* 916.

116. I quote here the words of Martin S. Fridson, former managing director at Merrill Lynch and author of the "Introduction" to the Marketplace Books edition of de La Vega's *Confusión de Confusiones,* 5, 7.

117. De la Vega, *Confusión de Confusiones,* 172, 194.

118. Ibid., 170.

119. Ibid., 167.

120. Ibid., 205.

121. Ibid., 204.

122. Ibid., 205.

123. Ibid.

124. Ibid., 174–175, 206.

125. Ibid., 211.

126. Ibid.

127. Martin S. Fridson, "Introduction," in *Extraordinary Popular Delusions and the Madness of Crowds & Confusión de Confusiones, with a Current Perspective by Martin S. Fridson,* ed. Martin S. Fridson (New York: John Wiley & Sons, Inc./ Marketplace Books, 1996), 1, 2.

128. Ibid., 1.

129. Peter Bernstein, "Preface," in *Extraordinary Popular Delusions and the Madness of Crowds & Confusión de Confusiones,* vii.

130. Charles Mackay, *Extraordinary Popular Delusions and the Madness of Crowds* [1841], in *Extraordinary Popular Delusions and the Madness of Crowds & Confusión de Confusiones,* 114–115. In *Tulipmania: Money, Honor, and Knowledge in the Dutch Golden Age* (Chicago and London: University of Chicago Press, 2007), historian Anne Goldgar has argued that the kinds of accounts offered in Mackay are based on "suspect" sources and involve exaggerations and stereotypes (6). While the proportions of the crisis and its supposed "madness" may have been less dramatic than in Mackay's descriptions, Goldgar nevertheless admits that tulipomania was a crisis, perhaps not a financial one, but "a social and cultural one" (7)—one that "rendered unstable the whole notion of how to assess value" and thus created a considerable "shock" in the society (17, 18).

131. Mackay, *Extraordinary Popular Delusions,* 119.

132. De la Vega, *Confusión de Confusiones,* 211.

133. Mackay, *Extraordinary Popular Delusions,* 119.

134. Goldgar, *Tulipmania,* 2.

135. Ibid., 225.

136. Goldgar highlights aesthetics as an important factor in tulipomania: "Tulipmania would probably not have happened in a society less commercially developed than the Netherlands. But in this case money intersected with aesthetics" (*Tulipmania*, 11).

137. The wording in German is *"ein sinnlich übersinnliches Ding"*; the translation into English is taken from Marc Redfield's *Phantom Formations: Aesthetic Ideology and the Bildungsroman* (Ithaca and London: Cornell University Press, 1996), 182, which seems to me more accurate than Ben Fowkes's "a thing that transcends sensuousness" (Marx, *Capital*, 163). Perhaps unsurprisingly, the tulip appears explicitly in Kant's *Critique of Judgment*, in the "Explanation of the Beautiful Inferred from the Third Moment" and in "§33 Second Peculiarity of a Judgment of Taste"; Immanuel Kant, *Critique of Judgment*, trans. Werner S. Pluhar (Indiana: Hackett Publishing, 1987), 84, 148.

138. Sam Marcy, " 'Tulip Mania' and Today's Speculation" [1982], in *Anatomy of the Economic Crisis*, published on *Workers.org*, accessed April 1, 2022, http://www .workers.org/marcy/cd/samecris/eccrisis/eccris01.htm.

139. Jean Baudrillard, "The Procession of Simulacra," in *Simulacra and Simulation*, trans. Sheila Faria Glaser (Ann Arbor: University of Michigan Press, 1994), 22.

140. Ibid., 3.

141. Friedrich Kittler, "Fiktion und Simulation," in *Philosophien der neuen Technologie*, ed. Ars Electronica (Berlin: Merve Verlag, 1989), 64; my translation from German.

142. Goldgar, *Tulipmania*, 225.

143. Alfred Sohn-Rethel, *Intellectual and Manual Labor: A Critique of Epistemology* (London and Basingstoke: Macmillan, 1978), 23, 58; see also 139.

144. Ibid., 33, 34, 57.

145. Ibid., 23, 34, 13–14. Sohn-Rethel uses "real" in contrast to "ideal" (mental) to emphasize that, while this kind of abstraction exists "nowhere other than in the human mind," it does not originate in the mind but in people's actions, "in the spatio-temporal sphere of human interrelations," having a social character (20). But this "real" abstraction has its mental equivalent *not* in the kinds of thinking that occur during the act of exchange itself, in which those involved in the exchange actually entertain ideas pertaining to the use value of the commodities they are selling or purchasing, but rather in "philosophical epistemology" (26, 27). The experiment of radical doubt—which Sohn-Rethel does not specifically engage, even as he mentions Descartes several times in his book—provides an exemplary illustration of this kind of abstraction.

146. Ibid., 180.

147. Ibid., 76.

148. Ibid., 119–122, 173–175.

149. Ibid., 27, 53, 57.

150. Ibid., 48–49.

151. Descartes, *Meditations*, 110 (AT VII 71).

152. Sohn-Rethel, *Intellectual and Manual Labor*, 112, 57.

153. Ibid., 112–113.

154. Ibid., 175.

155. Ibid., 122.

156. Ibid., 119, 121.

157. Jonathan Beller, *The World Computer: Derivative Conditions of Racial Capitalism* (Durham and London: Duke University Press, 2021), 16, 13.

158. Sohn-Rethel, *Intellectual and Manual Labor*, 123.

159. Vilém Flusser, "Time Reconsidered," Vilém Flusser Archiv: Manuscript No. 2797 [Encounters "Computer Culture," Villeneuve, July 12, 1983], 1. The link between computers and metaphysics (more broadly) has also been pointed out by Alexander Galloway, who noted that "the computer . . . remediates metaphysics itself (and hence should be more correctly labeled a metaphysical medium)," in *The Interface Effect* (Cambridge: Polity Press, 2012), 20.

160. See, for example, Koebler, "Elon Musk Says"; Matt Shore, "Constructed Reality: Are We Living in a Computer Simulation? —Tech Podcast," *The Guardian*, December 23, 2016, https://www.theguardian.com/technology/audio/2016/dec/23/constructed-consciousness-are-we-living-in-computer-simulation-tech-podcast.

161. Nick Bostrom, "Are You Living in a Computer Simulation?," *Philosophical Quarterly* 53, no. 211 (2003): 243–255; accessed through https://www.simulation-argument.com/simulation.html.

162. Shore, "Constructed Reality."

163. Ibid.

164. Bostrom, "Are You Living in a Computer Simulation?"

165. Ibid.

166. Ibid.

167. Elon Musk cited in Koebler, "Elon Musk Says."

168. Hilary Putnam, *Reason, Truth and History* (Cambridge and New York: Cambridge University Press, 1981), 5, 6.

169. Ibid., 6.

170. Putnam, *Reason, Truth and History*, 6; emphasis added.

171. Ibid.

172. Thomas E. Wartenberg, *Thinking on Screen: Film as Philosophy* (London: Routledge, 2007), 67.

173. See, for instance, Paul Ford, "Our Fear of Artificial Intelligence," *MIT Technology Review*, February 11, 2015, https://www.technologyreview.com/2015/02/11/169210/our-fear-of-artificial-intelligence/; Tad Friend, "How Frightened Should We Be of A.I.?," *New Yorker*, May 14, 2018, https://www.newyorker.com/magazine/2018/05/14/how-frightened-should-we-be-of-ai.

174. Christopher Steiner, *Automate This: How Algorithms Came to Rule Our World* (New York: Penguin Books, 2012).

175. Wartenberg, *Thinking on Screen*, 67.

176. Ibid.

177. Jean Baudrillard, *Simulacra and Simulation*, trans. Sheila Faria Glaser (Ann Arbor: University of Michigan Press, 1994). While a discussion of Baudrillard's view of the film lies beyond the scope of this book, I do want to mention that Baudrillard was actually critical of *The Matrix*, which he saw as "surely the kind of film about the matrix that the matrix would have been able to produce," one that contained "misinterpretations" of his theory; in "The Matrix Decoded: Le Nouvel Observateur Interview with Jean Baudrillard," trans. Gary Genosko and Adam Bryx, *International Journal of Baudrillard Studies* 1, no. 2 (July 2004), https://baudrillardstudies.ubishops.ca/the-matrix-decoded-le-nouvel-observateur-interview-with-jean-baudrillard/.

178. Debord, *The Society of the Spectacle*, theses 37, 6.

179. Robert Nozick, *Anarchy, State, and Utopia* (New York: Basic Books, 1974), 42.

180. Ibid.

181. Ibid.

182. Ibid.

183. Ibid., 43.

184. Ibid.

185. Wachowskis (dirs.), *The Matrix*.

186. This clear-cut distinction was in fact one of the points of Baudrillard's critique of *The Matrix*:

> The actors are in the matrix, that is, in the digitized system of things; or, they are radically outside it, such as in Zion, the city of resistors. But what would be interesting is to show what happens when these two worlds collide. The most embarrassing part of the film is that the new problem posed by simulation is confused with its classical, Platonic treatment. This is a serious flaw. ("The Matrix Decoded: Le Nouvel Observateur Interview with Jean Baudrillard")

187. Wendy Hui Kyong Chun, "Big Data as Drama," *ELH* 83, no. 2 (Summer 2016): 368.

188. See, for instance, Cathy O'Neil, *Weapons of Math Destruction: How Big Data Increases Inequality and Threatens Democracy* (New York: Crown Books, 2016) and Nick Couldry and Ulises A. Mejias, *The Costs of Connection: How Data Is Colonizing Human Life and Appropriating It for Capitalism* (Stanford: Stanford University Press, 2019).

Chapter 2

1. Bart Kosko, "2015: What Do You Think About Machines That Think?" *Edge*, 2015, https://www.edge.org/response-detail/26200; Kevin Slavin, "How Algorithms Shape Our World," *TEDGlobal*, 2011, www.ted.com/talks/kevin_slavin_ how_algorithms_shape_our_world?language=en; Christopher Steiner, *Automate This: How Algorithms Came to Rule Our World* (New York: Penguin Books, 2012).

2. "The World's Most Valuable Resource Is No Longer Oil, But Data," *Economist*, May 6, 2017, https://www.economist.com/leaders/2017/05/06/the-worlds -most-valuable-resource-is-no-longer-oil-but-data.

3. Cathy O'Neil, *Weapons of Math Destruction: How Big Data Increases Inequality and Threatens Democracy* (New York: Crown Books, 2016); Nick Couldry and Ulises A. Mejias, *The Costs of Connection: How Data Is Colonizing Human Life and Appropriating It for Capitalism* (Stanford: Stanford University Press, 2019).

4. For an account of both the supporters and the critics of the notion of the thinking machine, see John Haugeland, *Artificial Intelligence: The Very Idea* (Cambridge and London: MIT Press, 1985). Regarding businesses that contain "thinking machine" in their name, see for instance the now defunct Thinking Machines Corporation, https://www.computerhistory.org/brochures/t-z/thinking -machines-corporation-tmc/; Thinking Machine, https://thinkingmachine.co/; and Thinking Machines, https://thinkingmachin.es/.

5. Vilém Flusser, "Time Reconsidered," Vilém Flusser Archiv: Manuscript No. 2797 [Encounters "Computer Culture," Villeneuve, July 12, 1983], 1.

6. René Descartes, *Rules for the Direction of the Mind*, in *The Philosophical Writings of Descartes, Volume 1*, trans. John Cottingham, Robert Stoothoff, and Dugald Murdoch (Cambridge and New York: Cambridge University Press, 1985), 35 (AT X 404).

7. Manolis Kamvysselis, "Universal Turing Machine," *MIT.edu*, accessed June 1, 2022, http://web.mit.edu/manoli/turing/www/turing.html.

8. Charles Babbage, *Passages from the Life of a Philosopher* (London: Longman, Green, Longman, Roberts, & Green, 1864), 116–117, 128–129; italics in original.

9. Rob Kitchin, *The Data Revolution: Big Data, Open Data, Data Infrastructures & Their Consequences* (London: Sage Publications, 2014), 1.

10. Daniel Rosenberg, "Data Before the Fact," in *"Raw Data" Is an Oxymoron*, ed. Lisa Gitelman (Cambridge: MIT Press, 2013), 15.

11. Vilém Flusser, "Digitaler Schein," in *Digitaler Schein: Ästhetik der elektronischen Medien*, ed. Florian Rötzer (Frankfurt am Main: Edition Suhrkamp, 1991), 150; my translation from German. Another formulation of this idea appears in the chapter entitled "Vom Projizieren" from Flusser's posthumously published volume, *Vom Subjekt zum Projekt. Menschwerdung* (Bensheim und Düsseldorf: Bollman Verlag GmbH, 1994).

12. René Descartes, *Principles of Philosophy*, in *The Philosophical Writings of Descartes, Volume 1*, 279 (AT VIIIA 315).

13. A. M. Turing, "Computing Machinery and Intelligence," *Mind* 59, no. 236 (October 1950): 433; accessed through https://doi.org/10.1093/mind/LIX.236.433.

14. Alan Turing, "Can Automatic Calculating Machines Be Said to Think?" [1952], in *The Essential Turing: Seminal Writings in Computing, Logic, Philosophy, Artificial Intelligence, and Artificial Life, plus the Secrets of Enigma*, ed. B. Jack Copeland (Oxford: Clarendon Press; New York: Oxford University Press, 2004), 495.

15. Turing, "Computing Machinery," 433.

16. N. Katherine Hayles, *How We Became Posthuman: Virtual Bodies in Cybernetics, Literature, and Informatics* (Chicago: University of Chicago Press, 1999), xi.

17. Ibid.

18. Peter Steiner, "On the Internet, Nobody Knows You're a Dog," *New Yorker*, July 5, 1993; see https://en.wikipedia.org/wiki/On_the_Internet,_nobody_knows _you%27re_a_dog.

19. See, for instance, Ruha Benjamin, *Race After Technology: Abolitionist Tools for the New Jim Code* (Cambridge: Polity Press, 2019); Safiya Umoja Noble, *Algorithms of Oppression: How Search Engines Reinforce Racism* (New York: New York University Press, 2018); Rashida Richardson, Jason M. Schultz, and Kate Crawford, "Dirty Data, Bad Predictions: How Civil Rights Violations Impact Police Data, Predictive Policing Systems, and Justice," *New York University Law Review* 94 (2019): 192–233; Rebecca Heilweil, "Why Algorithms Can Be Racist and Sexist," *Vox*, February 18, 2020, https://www.vox.com/recode/2020/2/18/21121286/ algorithms-bias-discrimination-facial-recognition-transparency.

20. Santiago Castro-Gómez, *Zero-Point Hubris: Science, Race, and Enlightenment in Eighteenth-Century Latin America*, trans. George Ciccariello-Maher and Don T. Deere (Lanham: Rowman & Littlefield, 2021), 6.

21. See, for instance: Noble, *Algorithms of Oppression;* Jonathan Beller, *The World Computer: Derivative Conditions of Racial Capitalism* (Durham and London: Duke University Press, 2021); Yeshimabeit Milner and Amy Traub, *Data Capitalism and Algorithmic Racism* (Data for Black Lives and Demos, 2021), https:/ /www.demos.org/sites/default/files/2021-05/Demos_%20D4BL_Data_Capitalism _Algorithmic_Racism.pdf.

22. Turing, "Computing Machinery," 434.

23. For instance, Luigi Menabrea writes in his "Sketch of *The Analytical Engine* Invented by Charles Babbage" from October 1842:

> We know that numerical calculations are generally the stumbling-block to the solution of problems, since errors easily creep into them, and it is by no means always easy to detect these errors. Now the engine, by the very nature of its mode of acting, which requires no human intervention during the course of its operations, presents every species of security under the head of correctness.

Accessed April 2022, https://www.fourmilab.ch/babbage/sketch.html.

24. Alan Cooper, Robert Reimann, and Dave Cronin, *About Face 3: The Essentials of Interaction Design* (Indianapolis: Wiley Publishing, 2007), 249, 250.

25. Nicholas Negroponte, *Being Digital* (London: Hodder and Stoughton, 1995), 94, 101.

26. Donald Norman, "Foreword," in Brenda Laurel, *Computers as Theatre* (Reading: Addison-Wesley, 1991), xii.

27. Laurel, *Computers as Theatre*, 123, 115.

28. See Norman, "Foreword," xv.

29. Laurel, *Computers as Theatre*, 143.

30. Ibid., 115–116.

31. Wendy Hui Kyong Chun, *Programmed Visions: Software and Memory* (Cambridge and London: MIT Press, 2011), 59.

32. Robert Nozick, *Anarchy, State, and Utopia* (New York: Basic Books, 1974), 42.

33. B. Joseph Pine II and James H. Gilmore, *The Experience Economy: Work Is Theatre and Every Business a Stage* (Boston: Harvard Business School Press, 1999), ix, 13; italics in original.

34. See, for instance, "Are You Feeling It? Why Consumer Companies Must Master the Experience Economy," *World Economic Forum,* accessed June 17, 2022, https://reports.weforum.org/digital-transformation/moving-to-the-next-level -the-experience-economy/.

35. Julian Oliver, Gordan Savičić, and Danja Vasiliev, *The Critical Engineering Manifesto*, Criticalengineering.org (2011–2021), accessed March 29, 2022, https:// criticalengineering.org/en.

36. Laurel, *Computers as Theatre*, 32, 142.

37. Turing, "Computing Machinery," 450–451.

38. Chun, *Programmed Visions*, 59.

39. Adrian Mackenzie, *Cutting Code: Software and Sociality* (New York: Peter Lang, 2006), 24.

40. Michael Mahoney, "The History of Computing in the History of Technology," *Annals of the History of Computing* 10 (1988): 121; Friedrich Kittler, "There Is No Software," in *Literature, Media, Information Systems: Essays*, ed. John Johnston (Amsterdam: G + B Arts International, 1997), 148.

41. Mackenzie, *Cutting Code*, 24, 25.

42. Slavin, "How Algorithms Shape." This statement echoes a claim that Friedrich Kittler made in his provocatively titled essay, "There Is No Software": "We simply do not know what our writing [of code] does"; in Kittler, "There Is No Software," 148.

43. I do not by any means wish to suggest that this was also Laurel's intention. My point here is that the model of interface design that focuses on creating rich user experiences while concealing the computer's operations has turned out to be one that serves capitalist interests.

44. Wolfgang Ernst, "Digital Media Archaeology: Archive, Museum, and So-nicity," *CCAchannel,* published on YouTube on October 10, 2014, https://www.youtube.com/watch?v=f_GsDqKuOF8.

45. Ibid.

46. Wolfgang Ernst, *Digital Memory and the Archive,* ed. Jussi Parikka (Minne-apolis: University of Minnesota Press, 2013), 68; Ernst, "Digital Media Archeology."

47. Ernst, "Digital Media Archeology." The theorization of the computer as a "complex time machine" is cited from Wolfgang Ernst, *Chronopoetics: The Tem-poral Being and Operativity of Technological Media,* trans. Anthony Enns (London and New York: Rowman & Littlefield, 2016), 64.

48. Ernst, "Digital Media Archaeology."

49. Mackenzie, *Cutting Code,* 176.

50. Annie Dorsen, "On Algorithmic Theatre," originally published on the blog of *Theater Magazine* in conjunction with the "Digital Dramaturgies" edition (volume 42, issue 2, 2012), accessed June 15, 2022, https://www.onassis.org/cms/documents/103/on_algorithmic_theatre.pdf.

51. Mashinka Firunts, "Talking to Annie Dorsen," *Culturebot,* January 21, 2011, http://www.culturebot.org/2011/01/9285/talking-to-annie-dorsen/.

52. Annie Dorsen in Erik Piepenburg, "Coil Festival: 5 Questions About 'Hello Hi There,'" *ArtsBeat,* January 10, 2011, http://artsbeat.blogs.nytimes.com/2011/01/10/coil-festival-5-questions-about-hello-hi-there/?_r=0.

53. Joseph Weizenbaum, *Computer Power and Human Reason: From Judgment to Calculation* (New York and San Francisco: W. H. Freeman, 1976), 188; emphasis added.

54. Ibid., 3.

55. Ibid., 2.

56. Ibid., 7.

57. Ibid., 9.

58. Ibid., 8.

59. Annie Dorsen (dir.), *Hello Hi There,* performance presented at the Curtis R. Priem Experimental Media and Performing Arts Center (EMPAC) at Rensselaer Polytechnic Institute, Troy, NY, on February 18, 2012.

60. Marvin Carlson, "The Resistance to Theatricality," *SubStance* 31, no. 2/3, issue 98/99 (2002): 243.

61. Dorsen, *Hello Hi There.*

62. Ibid.

63. Dorsen in Piepenburg, "Coil Festival."

64. Laurel, *Computers as Theatre,* 114.

65. Dorsen, "On Algorithmic Theatre."

66. Ibid.

67. Andrew Russell and Annie Dorsen, "Interview," *A Piece of Work (Formerly False Peach), On the Boards* (2013), captured on the Internet Archive Wayback Ma-

chine on March 25, 2016, http://web.archive.org/web/20160325002648/http://www
.ontheboards.org/sites/default/files/dorsen_digital_NEW_title.pdf.

68. Initially titled *False Peach, A Piece of Work* was presented at On the Boards
in Seattle (February 2013), the Oslo International Theatre Festival (March 2013),
Bit Teatergarasjen in Bergen (March 2013), the brut in Vienna (April 2013), the De
Keuze Festival in Rotterdam (September 2013), La Villette in Paris (November
2013), and the Brooklyn Academy of Music in New York City (December 2013).

69. Gabriel, "A Piece of . . . Cake?" *On the Boards* (blog), February 22, 2013,
captured on the Internet Archive Wayback Machine on October 7, 2015, http://web
.archive.org/web/20171125193653/https://www.ontheboards.org/blog/piece-cake.

70. Regarding Hamlet's image as the paradigmatic intellectual of Western
modernity, see Paul Valéry's discussion of Hamlet in "La crise de l'esprit" / "The
Crisis of Spirit," cited in Jacques Derrida's *Specters of Marx*, trans. Peggy Kamuf
(London: Routledge, 1994), 5.

71. Wendy Hui Kyong Chun, "Big Data as Drama," *ELH* 83, no. 2 (Summer
2016): 368.

72. O'Neil, *Weapons of Math Destruction*, 163.

73. Andrea Gothing and Angela Muñoz-Kaphing, partners (at the time of the
writing of the article) at Robins-Kaplan LLP, "a national premier trial law firm,"
write that "big data's true importance comes from the exciting new business
solutions it enables." In "Protecting Big Data Systems in a Post-Alice World,"
Robins-Kaplan LLP, September 2014, captured on the Internet Archive Wayback
Machine on February 13, 2015, http://web.archive.org/web/20180830053156/http:
//www.robinskaplan.com/resources/articles/protecting-big-data-systems-in-a
-post-alice-world.

74. Timothy Morton, *Hyperobjects: Philosophy and Ecology After the End of the
World* (Minneapolis and London: University of Minnesota Press, 2013).

75. "*A Piece of Work*: Program Notes," *BAM.org*, 2013, https://www.bam.org/
media/3073100/a_piece_of_work.pdf.

76. Annie Dorsen, "*A Piece of Work*: Director's Note," *BAM.org*, 2013, www
.bam.org/media/3073100/a_piece_of_work.pdf.

77. Mackenzie, *Cutting Code*, 34.

78. "Computer Software in Plain English," *Commoncraft.com*, accessed May 25,
2022, www.commoncraft.com/video/computer-software.

79. N. Katherine Hayles, *My Mother Was a Computer: Digital Subjects and Literary Texts* (Chicago and London: University of Chicago Press, 2005), 50.

80. Ibid.

81. Ibid.

82. Alexander R. Galloway, *Protocol: How Control Exists After Decentralization*
(Cambridge and London: MIT Press, 2004), 165, 166; italics in original.

83. J. L. Austin, *How to Do Things with Words* (London: Oxford University
Press, 1962), 14; italics in original.

84. Chun, *Programmed Visions*, 24. Along similar lines, Adrian Mackenzie writes: "In saying something, code also does something, but never exactly what it says, despite all the intricate formality"; in *Cutting Code*, 177.

85. See, for example, Thomas H. Cormen, *Algorithms Unlocked* (Cambridge and London: MIT Press, 2013), 2.

86. Charles Duhigg, "Stock Traders Find Speed Pays, in Milliseconds," *New York Times*, July 23, 2009, www.nytimes.com/2009/07/24/business/24trading .html?_r=1&.

87. See, for instance, Carol Clark, "How to Keep Markets Safe in the Era of High-Speed Trading," *Federal Reserve Bank of Chicago* no. 303, October 2012, www .chicagofed.org/publications/chicago-fed-letter/2012/october-303; Tom Lauricella, Kara Scannell, and Jenny Strasburg, "How a Trading Algorithm Went Awry," *Wall Street Journal*, October 2, 2010, http://www.wsj.com/articles/SB1000142405274870 40293045755263901319167 92.

88. Scott Patterson, *Dark Pools: The Rise of the Machine Traders and the Rigging of the U.S. Stock Market* (New York: Crown Business, 2013), 338.

89. Nick Baumann, "Too Fast to Fail: Is High-Speed Trading the Next Wall Street Disaster?" *Mother Jones*, January–February 2013, www.motherjones.com/ politics/2013/02/high-frequency-trading-danger-risk-wall-street.

90. Ibid.

91. Steiner, *Automate This*, 1.

92. Ibid., 2.

93. Patterson, *Dark Pools*, 9.

94. I channel here Chun's phrasing from *Programmed Visions*, 24.

95. Regarding large-scale failed software programs, see for instance Rob Kitchin and Martin Dodge, *Code/Space: Software and Everyday Life* (Cambridge and London: MIT Press, 2011), 38.

96. Steiner, *Automate This*, 5.

97. Alexander Mordvintsev, Christopher Olah, and Mike Tyka, "Inceptionism: Going Deeper into Neural Networks," *Google AI Blog*, June 17, 2015, https://ai .googleblog.com/2015/06/inceptionism-going-deeper-into-neural.html.

98. Victor Riparbelli, "Our Vision for the Future of Synthetic Media," *Medium*, July 23, 2019, https://medium.com/@vriparbelli/our-vision-for-the-future-of -synthetic-media-8791059e8f3a.

99. Mike James, "Inceptionism: How Neural Networks See," *i-programmer*, June 20, 2015, https://www.i-programmer.info/news/105-artificial-intelligence/ 8709-inceptionism-how-neural-networks-see.html.

100. Turing, "Computing Machinery," 450–451.

101. Mordvintsev et al., "Inceptionism."

102. Clemens Apprich, "Data Paranoia: How to Make Sense of Pattern Discrimination," in *Pattern Discrimination,* eds. Clemens Apprich, Wendy Hui Kyong Chun, Florian Cramer, and Hito Steyerl (Minneapolis and London: University of Minnesota Press; Lüneburg: Meson Press, 2018), 109.

103. Mordvintsev et al., "Inceptionism." The specific images referred to here can be viewed at https://photos.google.com/share/AF1QipPXoSCl7OzWilt9LnuQ liattX4OUCj_8EP65_cTVnBmS1jnYgsGQAieQUc1VQWdgQ?key=aVBxWjhwSz g2RjJWLWRuVFBBZEN1d205bUdEMnhB.

104. Hito Steyerl, "A Sea of Data: Pattern Recognition and Corporate Animism (Forked Version)," in *Pattern Discrimination*, eds. Clemens Apprich, Wendy Hui Kyong Chun, Florian Cramer, and Hito Steyerl (Minneapolis and London: University of Minnesota Press; Lüneburg: Meson Press, 2018), 9, 10.

105. Ibid., 10, 9. For images produced by AI inceptionism containing proliferations of eyes, see Mary-Ann Russon, "Google DeepDream Robot: 10 Weirdest Images Produced by AI 'Inceptionism' and Users Online," *International Business Times*, July 6, 2015, https://www.ibtimes.co.uk/google-deepdream-robot-10 -weirdest-images-produced-by-ai-inceptionism-users-online-1509518.

106. Mordvintsev et al., "Inceptionism."

107. Immanuel Kant, *Critique of Judgment*, trans. Werner S. Pluhar (Indiana: Hackett Publishing, 1987), 52.

108. See, for instance, Samantha Cole, "AI-Assisted Fake Porn Is Here and We're All Fucked," *Motherboard*, December 11, 2017, https://motherboard.vice .com/en_us/article/gydydm/gal-gadotfake-ai-porn.

109. Joseph Foley, "14 Deepfake Examples That Terrified and Amused the Internet," *Creative Bloq.com*, April 13, 2022, https://www.creativebloq.com/features /deepfake-examples.

110. Joey Mach, "Deepfakes: The Ugly, and the Good," *Towards Data Science*, November 10, 2019, https://towardsdatascience.com/deepfakes-the-ugly-and-the -good-49115643d8dd.

111. Ibid.; emphasis in original.

112. Austin, *How to Do Things*, 22.

113. Sol LeWitt, "Paragraphs on Conceptual Art," in *Sol LeWitt: A Retrospective*, ed. Gary Garrels (New Haven: Yale University Press, 2000), 369.

114. Joseph Kosuth, "Art After Philosophy," in *Conceptual Art: A Critical Anthology*, eds. Alexander Alberro and Blake Stimson (Cambridge and London: MIT Press, 1999), 165.

115. Ibid., 170; italics in original.

116. Peter Goldie and Elisabeth Schellekens, "Introduction," in *Philosophy and Conceptual Art*, eds. Peter Goldie and Elisabeth Schellekens (Oxford and New York: Oxford University Press, 2007), x.

117. Hayles, *How We Became Posthuman*, 19. This notion of real abstraction harkens back to Sohn-Rethel. For a theorization of information as a form of real abstraction, which builds on the thought of Sohn-Rethel, see Beller, *The World Computer*.

118. Laurel, *Computers as Theatre*, 116.

119. Mackenzie, *Cutting Code*, 21.

120. Dorsen in Russell and Dorsen, "Interview."

121. It bears noting that the BAM audiences might not have experienced the same acute sense of frustration or confusion—or, experienced it in the same degree as the OtB audiences—given Dorsen and her team's significant tinkering with the system between the OtB and the BAM runs. My own experience of the BAM performance was less that of frustration and confusion than a sense of being excluded from the piece as a meaningful participant.

122. OtB, "What Did You Think of *A Piece of Work*," *On the Boards* (blog), 2013, captured on the Internet Archive Wayback Machine on October 7, 2015, http://web.archive.org/web/20151007045708/https://www.ontheboards.org/blog/what-did-you-think-piece-work.

123. This text and the other quotations from the performance cited in this chapter are transcribed from the BAM performance of *A Piece of Work* that took place on December 21, 2013, which I was able to (re)view on video, thanks to Annie Dorsen.

124. On the "alienness" of our software-based contemporary forms of communication, see, for instance, Finn Brunton, "Hello from Earth," in Paula Bialski, Finn Brunton, and Mercedes Bunz, *Communication* (Minneapolis and London: University of Minnesota Press; Lüneburg: Meson Press, 2019), https://meson.press/wp-content/uploads/2019/01/9783957961464-Communication.pdf.

125. Here are some audience responses to the OtB piece that suggest such an expectation: "I think the idea was experimental but it wasn't really enlightening or entertaining. Markov chains are kind of a crappy tool for navigating Hamlet"; "I didn't see the point. Experimental but not enriching for me" (see OtB, "What Did You Think").

126. Greg Beller in Annie Dorsen, "Talk About *A Piece of Work*: A Group Self-Interview," *TDR: The Drama Review* 59, no. 4 (2015): 141.

127. OtB, "What Did You Think."

128. In the words of an OtB audience member: "Someone behind me as I was exiting last night voiced my exact thoughts saying, 'if that was a visual installation in a museum that I could experience for five minutes and walk away, I would have liked it'" (OtB, "What Did You Think").

129. Dorsen, "Talk About *A Piece of Work*," 142; italics in original.

130. Ibid., 146.

131. Ibid., 139.

132. Ibid., 138.

133. Ibid., 141.

134. Spencer Golub, personal communication, 2017.

135. Vilém Flusser, "Curie's Children/Discovery," *ARTFORUM* 27, no. 7 (1989): 10, https://www.artforum.com/print/198903/discovery-34362.

136. Donna Haraway, "A Cyborg Manifesto: Science, Technology, and Socialist-Feminism in the Late Twentieth Century," in *Simians, Cyborgs, and Women: The Reinvention of Nature* (New York and Oxford: Routledge, 1991), 164.

137. Ibid.

138. See, for instance, Ted Schrecker and Clare Bambra, *How Politics Makes Us Sick: Neoliberal Epidemics* (Houndmills, Basingstoke, and New York: Palgrave Macmillan, 2015).

139. Ronald Howard, *Dynamic Probabilistic Systems, Volume 1: Markov Models* (Mineola: Dover Publications, 2007), 2.

140. William Stewart, *Probability, Markov Chains, Queues, and Simulation: The Mathematical Basis of Performance Modeling* (Princeton: Princeton University Press, 2009), 193.

141. Dorsen, "*A Piece of Work:* Director's Note."

142. Michael Fried, "Art and Objecthood," in *Art and Objecthood: Essays and Reviews* (Chicago and London: University of Chicago, 1998), 167.

143. Dorsen, "*A Piece of Work:* Director's Note."

144. Ibid.

145. See, for instance, Marvin Carlson, *The Haunted Stage: The Theatre as Memory Machine* (Ann Arbor: University of Michigan Press, 2001).

146. Herbert Blau, *Take Up the Bodies: Theater at the Vanishing Point* (Urbana: University of Illinois Press, 1982), 94; William Shakespeare, *Hamlet*, with an introduction by Burton Raffel (New Haven: Yale University Press, 2003), 5.

147. See, for example, Blau, *Take Up the Bodies*; Stephen Greenblatt, *Hamlet in Purgatory* (Princeton: Princeton University Press, 2001); Alice Rayner, *Ghosts: Death's Double and the Phenomena of Theatre* (Minneapolis and London: University of Minnesota Press, 2006).

148. Carlson, *The Haunted Stage*, 78.

149. Michal Kobialka, *Further On, Nothing: Tadeusz Kantor's Theatre* (Minneapolis and London: University of Minnesota Press, 2009), 104.

150. Ibid., 303.

151. Kantor cited in Kobialka, *Further On, Nothing*, 303.

152. When I write about laughter in connection to automatisms, I am thinking of philosopher Henri Bergson's extended philosophical essay on the meaning of the comic, *Laughter*, which links machinic behavior (witnessing automatisms) to laughter. Henri Bergson, *Laughter: An Essay on the Meaning of the Comic*, trans. Claudesley Brereton and Fred Rothwell (New York: Macmillan Company, 1914).

153. See Nick Couldry and Ulises A. Mejias, *The Costs of Connection: How Data Is Colonizing Human Life and Appropriating It for Capitalism* (Stanford: Stanford University Press, 2019), especially Chapter 4, "The Hollowing Out of the Social."

154. Heidi Biggs, "Algorithmic Theater—By and For the Non-programmer," *Annie Dorsen: A Piece of Work (Formerly False Peach), On the Boards*, 2013, captured on the Internet Archive Wayback Machine on March 25, 2016, https://web .archive.org/web/20160325002648/http://www.ontheboards.org/sites/default/files /dorsen_digital_NEW_title.pdf.

155. Chun, *Programmed Visions*, 161.

156. Ibid., 167; italics in original.

157. Ibid., 169; italics in original.

158. Ibid., 10, 172, 133.

159. Rebecca Schneider, "It Seems As If . . . I Am Dead: Zombie Capitalism and Theatrical Labor," *TDR: The Drama Review* 56, no. 4 (2012): 153.

160. Carlson, *The Haunted Stage*, 4.

161. Ibid., 1; italics in original.

162. Heiner Müller, *Hamletmachine*, in Hamletmachine *and Other Texts for the Stage*, ed. and trans. Carl Weber (New York: Performing Arts Journal Publications, 1984). For more information about The Wooster Group's *Hamlet*, see http://thewoostergroup.org/hamlet.

163. Chun, *Programmed Visions*, 167; italics in original.

164. Wendy Hui Kyong Chun, "Critical Data Studies or How to Desegregate Networks," Institute of the Humanities and Global Cultures, published on YouTube on July 31, 2018, https://www.youtube.com/watch?v=Qhp8oUXTvaQ.

165. Jacques Derrida, *Archive Fever: A Freudian Impression*, trans. Eric Prenowitz (Chicago and London: University of Chicago Press, 1996), 84; italics in original.

166. Jacques Derrida, *Specters of Marx*, trans. Peggy Kamuf (New York and London: Routledge, 1994), 7; italics in original.

167. Rebecca Schneider, *Performing Remains: Art and War in Times of Theatrical Reenactment* (London and New York: Routledge, 2011), 109; italics in original.

168. Dorsen, "Talk About *A Piece of Work*," 140.

169. Beller in Dorsen, "Talk About *A Piece of Work*," 140.

170. Dorsen in Russell and Dorsen, "Interview."

171. Shakespeare, *Hamlet*, 75.

172. In his preface to the 1924 edition of *On the Art of the Theatre*, Craig explains the function of the Über-marionette that is to replace the human actor: "I no more want to see the living actors replaced by things of wood than the great Italian actress of our day wants all the actors to die. . . . The Über-marionette is the actor plus fire, minus egoism: the fire of the gods and demons, without the smoke and steam of mortality." Edward Gordon Craig, *On the Art of the Theatre* (Boston: Small, Maynard & Company, 1924), vii, vii–viii.

173. Christopher Innes, *Edward Gordon Craig: A Vision of the Theatre* (Cambridge: Cambridge University Press, 1983).

174. Patrick Le Bœuf, "On the Nature of Edward Gordon Craig's Über-marionette," *New Theatre Quarterly* 26, no. 2 (2010): 102–114.

175. For an account along similar lines, see Paola Degli Esposti, "The Fire of Demons and the Steam of Mortality: Edward Gordon Craig and the Ideal Performer," *Theatre Survey* 56, no. 1 (January 2015): 4–27.

176. Ibid., 10.

177. Dorsen, "Talk About *A Piece of Work*," 148.

178. Dorsen in Piepenburg, "Coil Festival."

179. BAM, "*A Piece of Work*," accessed October 10, 2022, https://www.bam.org/theater/2013/pieceofwork.

180. Dorsen in Russell and Dorsen, "Interview."

181. Alfred Sohn-Rethel, *Intellectual and Manual Labor: A Critique of Epistemology* (London and Basingstoke: Macmillan, 1978), 173.

182. Maurizio Lazzarato, "Immaterial Labor," in *Radical Thought in Italy: A Potential Politics*, eds. Paolo Virno and Michael Hardt (Minneapolis: University of Minnesota Press, 1996), 143.

183. Paolo Virno, *A Grammar of the Multitude: For an Analysis of Contemporary Forms of Life*, trans. Isabella Bertoletti, James Cascaito, and Andrea Casson (Cambridge: Semiotext(e), 2004), 61.

184. Ibid., 61, 55.

185. Philip Agre, "Surveillance and Capture: Two Models of Privacy," in *The New Media Reader*, eds. Noah Wardrip-Fruin and Nick Montfort (Cambridge and London: MIT Press, 2003).

186. Ibid., 744.

187. Ibid., 749; emphasis added.

188. Virno, *Grammar of the Multitude*, 63.

189. Agre, "Surveillance and Capture," 743, 745.

190. Ibid., 753.

191. Lazzarato, "Immaterial Labor," 135.

192. Virno, *A Grammar of the Multitude*, 55.

193. This is the case, for example, in Pine and Gilmore's *The Experience Economy*.

194. Alexander Galloway, "The Poverty of Philosophy: Realism and Post-Fordism," *Critical Inquiry* 39, no. 2 (2012): 358.

195. The notion of "fugitive accumulation" is taken from Jordana Rosenberg, *Critical Enthusiasm: Capital Accumulation and the Transformation of Religious Passion* (Oxford and New York: Oxford University Press, 2011), 17.

196. Schneider, "It Seems As If . . . ," 157.

197. Paul Virilio, *Speed and Politics*, trans. Mark Polizzotti (New York: Semiotext(e), 1986), 119.

198. According to Scott Patterson:

At the end of World War II, the average holding period for a stock was four years. By 2000, it was eight months. By 2008, it was two months. And by 2011 it was *twenty-two seconds*, at least according to one's professor's estimates. One founder of a prominent high-frequency trading outfit once claimed his firm's average holding period was a mere *eleven seconds*. (*Dark Pools*, 46; italics in original)

199. Stephen Crocker, "Into the Interval: On Deleuze's Reversal of Time and Movement," *Continental Philosophy Review* 34 (2001): 64.

200. Baumann, "Too Fast to Fail."

201. Gertrude Stein, "Composition as Explanation," *A Stein Reader*, ed. Ulla E. Dydo (Evanston: Northwestern University Press, 1993), 501.

202. Schneider, *Performing Remains*, 158.

203. Gertrude Stein, "Plays," *Gertrude Stein: Writings and Lectures, 1911–1945*, ed. Patricia Meyerowitz (London: Peter Owen, 1967), 93.

204. Fried, "Art and Objecthood," 167.

205. I borrow these words from Mary Ann Doane's essay "Information, Crisis, Catastrophe," in *New Media, Old Media*, eds. Wendy Hui Kyong Chun and Thomas Keenan (New York and London: Routledge, 2005), 263.

Interlude

1. This performance took place in the media theatre of the Institute of Musicology and Media Studies at Humboldt University in Berlin (2016).

2. Regarding the human actor's challenge to play the machine's (supposed) lack of emotionality, see, for instance, Carolin Kipka's contribution on pages 219–221 in Florian Leitner, Ioana Jucan, Anton Pohle, and Carolin Kipka, "The Human Is the Problem: Scenes of Technology and Reason in Media Performance," in *Hello, I'm Eliza: Fünfzig Jahre Gespräche mit Computern*, eds. Marianna Baranovska and Stefan Höltgen (Bochum/Freiburg: Projektverlag, 2018).

3. René Descartes, *Meditations on First Philosophy*, in *Descartes: Selected Philosophical Writings*, trans. John Cottingham, Robert Stoothoff, and Dugald Murdoch (Cambridge and New York: Cambridge University Press, 1998), 83 (AT VII 29).

4. Elizabeth A. Wilson, *Affect and Artificial Intelligence* (Seattle: University of Washington Press, 2010), 10.

5. Ibid., 4.

6. René Descartes, *Early Writings*, in *The Philosophical Writings of Descartes, Volume 1*, trans. John Cottingham, Robert Stoothoff, and Dugald Murdoch (Cambridge and New York: Cambridge University Press, 1985), 2 (AT X 213).

7. I use the term "apparatus" rather than "machine" in relation to the Russian-influenced communist context in Romania because that is closer to that context, where it was used in reference to the Communist Party and its operations. Consider in this regard the Russian "*apparatchik*," which also stems from "apparat(us)."

8. Konrad Petrovszky and Ovidiu Țichindeleanu, "Sensuri ale Revoluției Române," in *Revoluția Română Televizată: Contribuții la Istoria Culturală a Mediilor*, eds. Konrad Petrovzsky and Ovidiu Țichindeleanu (Cluj: IDEA Design & Print, 2009), 30; my translation from Romanian; italics in original. All translations from Romanian in this chapter are mine unless otherwise indicated.

9. In this chapter I will only discuss the communist period in Romania under the dictator Nicolae Ceaușescu. The Communist Party came to power in Romania under Soviet occupation, at the end of the Second World War. Romania was never incorporated into the USSR but became a "satellite" state of the Soviet

Union. The Soviet troops withdrew from Romania in 1958. Romania began to distance itself from the Soviet Union in 1964, when the Romanian Labor Party, as the Communist Party called itself at the time, declared that it would not support the Soviet Union in its conflict with China. Nicolae Ceaușescu, who became the leader of the (now Romanian Communist) Party in 1965, continued to actively pursue independence from the Soviet Union, constructing a nationalist brand of totalitarian communism sustained by a strong personality cult ("Ceaușism") and, externally, developing relations with socialist and capitalist states. Despite the distancing from Russia, Romania remained a member of the Warsaw Pact and of its economic counterpart, CMEA/COMECON (the Council for Mutual Economic Assistance led by the USSR).

10. Traian Băsescu, "20 de Motive Pentru a Condamna Comunismul. Discursul lui Băsescu," *Ziare.com,* December 18, 2006, http://www.ziare.com/basescu/stiri-traian-basescu/20-de-motive-pentru-a-condamna-comunismul-discursul-lui-basescu-51208; Andreea Pora, "ÎCCJ: Traian Băsescu a Colaborat cu Securitatea și Pierde Privilegiile de Fost Președinte," *Europa Liberă România*, March 23, 2022, https://romania.europalibera.org/a/%C3%AEnalta-curte-decizie-definitiv%C4%83-traianb%C4%83sescu-este-colaborator-al-securit%C4%83%C8%9Bii-/31766339.html.

11. Băsescu, "20 de Motive Pentru a Condamna Comunismul."

12. Alexandru Polgár, "Restul Comunist," in *Genealogii ale Postcomunismului,* eds. Adrian T. Sârbu and Alexandru Polgár (Cluj: Idea Design & Print, 2009), 38.

13. Cornel Ban, "Sovereign Debt, Austerity, and Regime Change: The Case of Nicolae Ceausescu's Romania," *East European Politics & Societies* 26, no. 4 (November 2012): 744.

14. Satya Gabriel, Stephen A. Resnick, and Richard D. Wolff, "State Capitalism Versus Communism: What Happened in the USSR and the PRC?," *Critical Sociology* 34, no. 4 (July 1, 2008): 544. See also Polgár, "Restul Comunist," 37.

15. Ibid., 542.

16. Eva Hoffman, *Exit into History. A Journey Through the New Eastern Europe* (New York: Penguin Books, 1993), 292.

17. See, for instance, Julian Hale, *Ceaușescu's Romania: A Political Documentary* (London: George G. Harrap, 1971), 7; Lucian Boia, *Strania Istorie a Comunismului Românesc (Și Nefericitele Ei Consecințe)* (Bucharest: Humanitas, 2016), 6.

18. Paige DuBois, *Slavery: Antiquity and Its Legacy* (London and New York: I. B. Tauris, 2010), 123.

19. Karl Marx, Letter to Engels, London, February 27, 1861, in *Gesamtausgabe*, International Publishers, 1942; accessed through *Marxists.org*, March 27, 2022, https://www.marxists.org/archive/marx/works/1861/letters/61_02_27-abs.htm.

20. DuBois, *Slavery*, 123.

21. Narcis Anton, "Radiografia Economiei în Ultimii 30 de Ani: Inflație de Peste 250% și Recuperare Spectaculoasă a Decalajelor," *Hotnews.ro*, May 18, 2022, https:

//economie.hotnews.ro/stiri-fiscalitatea_la_zi-25563702-radiografia-economiei
-ultimii-30-ani-inflatie-peste-250-recuperare-spectaculoasa-decalajelor.htm.

22. Petrovszky and Țichindeleanu, "Sensuri," 30; italics in original.

23. It has been shown that "for every 1C of global warming lightning strikes will increase by about 12%, . . . but scientists don't yet know where increases will occur"; Suzanne Goldenberg, "Lightning Strikes Will Increase Due to Climate Change," *The Guardian*, November 13, 2014, https://www.theguardian.com/environment/2014/nov/13/lightning-strikes-will-increase-due-to-climate-change.

24. Petrovszky and Țichindeleanu, "Sensuri," 45.

25. Marian Alecu in Mihai Voinea and Cristian Delcea, "Interview: Povestea Venirii McDonald's în România: '16.000 de Oameni au Spart Geamurile la Deschidere,'" *Adevarul*, August 31, 2015, http://adevarul.ro/news/societate/interviu-povestea-venirii-mcdonalds-romania-16000-oameni-spart-geamurile-deschidere-1_55e33730f5eaafab2c131221/index.html.

26. Ibid.

27. Ibid.

28. Ibid.

29. Ibid.

30. Bogdan Murgescu, *România și Europa: Acumularea Decalajelor Economice (1500–2010)* (Bucharest: Polirom, 2010), 16.

31. Susan Buck-Morss, *Dreamworld and Catastrophe: The Passing of Mass Utopia in East and West* (Cambridge and London: MIT Press, 2000), xii.

32. Hoffman, *Exit into History*, 292.

33. Nicolae Ceaușescu, "Interview Granted to Selim El-Lozi, Editor-in-Chief of the Beirut 'Al-Hawadess' Review," in *Romania on the Way of Building Up the Multilaterally Developed Socialist Society, Volume 6* (Bucharest: Meridiane Publishing House: 1972), 425, 426; emphasis added.

34. Nicolae Ceaușescu, "Interview to French Daily 'Le Monde,'" in *Romania on the Way of Building Up the Multilaterally Developed Socialist Society, Volume 11* (Bucharest: Meridiane Publishing House, 1977), 879.

35. I channel here the words of Santiago Castro-Gómez from *Zero-Point Hubris: Science, Race, and Enlightenment in Eighteenth-Century Latin America*, trans. George Ciccariello-Maher and Don T. Deere (Lanham: Rowman & Littlefield, 2021), 12.

36. Mirela Oprea, "Development Discourse in Romania: From Socialism to EU Membership" (PhD dissertation, University of Bologna, 2009), 85, http://amsdottorato.unibo.it/2228/.

37. Ban, "Sovereign Debt," 749.

38. Digi24.ro, "Imagini Document. Anul 1953: Cincinalul în Patru Ani," March 14, 2014, http://www.digi24.ro/special/campanii-digi24/1989-anul-care-a-schimbat-lumea/imagini-document-anul-1953-cincinalul-in-patru-ani-214670.

39. Boris Souvarine, "The Five Year Plan," *Bulletin Communiste*, no. 31 (Feb-

ruary 1930), accessed through *Marxists.org,* April 25, 2022, https://www.marxists
.org/history/etol/writers/souvar/works/1930/02/fiveyearplan.htm#f36.

40. Vladimir Tismaneanu, *Raport Final* (Bucharest: Humanitas, 2007), 125, 414.

41. Ibid., 414.

42. Souvarine, "The Five Year Plan"; italics in original.

43. Ibid.

44. Ibid.

45. Ibid.

46. Ibid.

47. Tiberiu Cazacioc in *Comunism pe Burta Goală*: "Ep. 4 CINCINALU-n Patru
Ani si Jumatate," *Realitatea TV,* published on YouTube by Alexandru Eduard
Brinzea on July 17, 2009, https://www.youtube.com/watch?v=aKuP8clFHeQ.

48. Ștefan Doagă in *Comunism pe Burta Goală*.

49. On present-day "synthetic data," see Sara Castellanos, "Fake It to Make
It: Companies Beef Up AI Models with Synthetic Data," *Wall Street Journal,* July
23, 2021, https://www.wsj.com/articles/fake-it-to-make-it-companies-beef-up-ai
-models-with-synthetic-data-11627032601.

50. Toni Grecu in *Comunism pe Burta Goală*.

51. Boia, *Strania Istorie,* 143.

52. Ibid.

53. Petre Roman cited in Neculai Lupu, "Will Romania Be Capable in 2020 to
Keep the Pace with the European Union?" *Economy Transdisciplinarity Cognition*
(*ETC*) 19, no. 1 (2016): 10, http://www.ugb.ro/etc/etc2016no1/03_Lupu_Neculai.PDF.

54. Lupu, "Will Romania Be Capable," 10.

55. Petrovszky and Țichindeleanu, "Sensuri," 35.

56. Gabriel Liiceanu, *Dragul Meu Turnător* (Bucharest: Humanitas, 2013), 45, 237.

57. Josh Lauer, "Plastic Surveillance: Payment Cards and the History of Transactional Data, 1888 to Present," *Big Data & Society* 7, no. 1 (January–June 2020): 2;
see also Jathan Sadowski,"When Data Is Capital: Datafication, Accumulation, and
Extraction," *Big Data & Society* 6, no. 1 (January 7, 2019): 1–12.

58. This was the technical term used by the Securitate; in Romanian: *"penetra-
rea anturajului."*

59. Liiceanu, *Dragul Meu Turnător,* 237, 47, 48.

60. *Merriam-Webster,* s.v. "synthetic," accessed June 11, 2022, https://www
.merriam-webster.com/dictionary/synthetic.

61. Liiceanu, *Dragul Meu Turnător,* 53, 104.

62. Boia, *Strania Istorie,* 187.

63. Ana Blandiana cited in Milo Rau, "Die Letzten Tage der Ceausescus: The-
aterstück," in *Die Letzten Tage der Ceausescus* (Berlin: Verbrecher Verlag, 2010),
96; my translation from German.

64. Hannah Arendt, *The Origins of Totalitarianism* (Cleveland and New York:
Meridian Books, 1958), 475.

65. Nick Couldry and Ulises A. Mejias, *The Costs of Connection: How Data Is Colonizing Human Life and Appropriating It for Capitalism* (Stanford: Stanford University Press, 2019), 117.

66. Arendt, *The Origins of Totalitarianism*, 475.

67. Ibid., 474, 475.

68. Eli Pariser, *The Filter Bubble: How the New Personalized Web Is Changing What We Read and How We Think* (London: Penguin Books, 2011).

69. Couldry and Mejias, *The Costs of Connection*, 166.

70. See Michel Foucault, "Panopticism," in *Discipline and Punish: The Birth of the Prison*, trans. Alan Sheridan (New York: Pantheon, 1977).

71. Matei Vişniec, "*Richard al III-lea se Interzice sau Scene din Viaţa lui Meyerhold*," in *Procesul Comunismului Prin Teatru* (Bucharest: Humanitas, 2012), 90.

72. Liiceanu, *Dragul Meu Turnător*, 47.

73. Gilles Deleuze, "Postscript on the Societies of Control," *October* 59 (Winter 1992): 5.

74. Antoinette Rouvroy, "The End(s) of Critique: Data Behaviourism Versus Due Process," in *Privacy, Due Process and the Computational Turn: The Philosophy of Law Meets the Philosophy of Technology*, eds. Mireille Hildebrandt and Katja De Vries (London: Routledge, 2013).

75. Deleuze, "Postscript"; Philip Agre, "Surveillance and Capture: Two Models of Privacy," in *The New Media Reader*, eds. Noah Wardrip-Fruin and Nick Montfort (Cambridge: MIT Press, 2003).

76. Agre, "Surveillance and Capture," 740.

77. James Brusseau, "Deleuze's *Postscript on the Societies of Control*: Updated for Big Data and Predictive Analytics," *Theoria* 67, no. 3, issue 164 (September 2020): 11.

78. On the white gaze functioning as "a totalizing surveillance" under the conditions of white supremacy, see Simone Browne, *Dark Matters: On the Surveillance of Blackness* (Durham and London: Duke University Press, 2015), 21. On the roots of big data in chattel slavery, see Yeshimabeit Milner and Amy Traub, *Data Capitalism and Algorithmic Racism* (Data for Black Lives and Demos, 2021), https://www.demos.org/sites/default/files/2021-05/Demos_%20D4BL_Data_Capitalism_Algorithmic_Racism.pdf. For a discussion of accounts of slavery approximating a totalitarian system, see Vaughn Rasberry, *Race and the Totalitarian Century: Geopolitics in the Black Literary Imagination* (Cambridge and London: Harvard University Press, 2016).

79. Cathy O'Neil, *Weapons of Math Destruction: How Big Data Increases Inequality and Threatens Democracy* (New York: Crown Books, 2016), 3, 8.

80. Ibid., 3, 132.

81. Ibid., 150, 162.

82. One example that O'Neil gives in this regard is that of teachers in the United States who corrected their students' responses on standardized tests and

upped the students' scores in order to avoid getting penalized or even losing their jobs (*Weapons of Math Destruction*, 9).

83. Boia, *Strania Istorie*, 112.

84. Neagu Djuvara, *A Brief Illustrated History of Romania*, trans. Cristian Anton (Bucharest: Humanitas, 2014), 339.

85. Jon McKenzie, *Perform or Else: From Discipline to Performance* (London and New York: Routledge, 2001), 5.

86. See, for instance, Ioana Baetica, "Theatre of the Absurd," *New Internationalist* 366, April 2, 2004, http://newint.org/features/2004/04/01/romania/#sthash .8MUcRGyr.dpuf. Here, the author offers an account of some of the ways in which Romanian youth might get by in post-communist Romania and its "theatre of the absurd." Some of the survival strategies Baetica mentions involve tricking the state (or, "the system") in some way or another; finding "consolation in a brand new mode of alienation comparable perhaps to that of drugs in America: the computer game"; or simply leaving the country.

87. Vilém Flusser, "Our Program," in *Post-History*, trans. Rodrigo Maltez Novaes, ed. Siegfried Zielinski (Minneapolis: Univocal Publishing, 2013), 23, 26. In fact, for Flusser, "we must learn to accept the absurd" and learn to play "an absurd game" with programs if freedom is to be attained (26). In light of this, the kind of dissimulation used as a survival strategy in communist Romania may perhaps be seen as a way to play an absurd game with an absurd program.

88. For examples of the kinds of TV programming that were available in the 1970s and 80s (in Romanian), see Alin Ion, "Ce Vedeau Românii la Postul Public de Televiziune în Anii '70–'80," *Adevărul*, September 6, 2018, https://adevarul.ro/stiri -locale/targu-jiu/ce-vedeau-romanii-la-postul-public-de-televiziune-1888913.html.

89. Bogdan Ghiu, "The Subalternative (the Film-Politics)," *IDEA artă + societate* 38, 2011, http://idea.ro/revista/en/article/XOkYJhIAACMAgMmS/the-subal ternative-the-film-politics.

90. From the DVD cover of *The Autobiography of Nicolae Ceaușescu*, Andrei Ujică (dir.), 2010.

91. All of the scenes described here are taken from *The Autobiography of Nicolae Ceaușescu*. The translations from Romanian are sometimes my own and sometimes from the English subtitles.

92. Douglas Holt, *How Brands Become Icons: The Principles of Cultural Branding* (Boston: Harvard Business School Press, 2004), 7, 6.

93. Ghiu, "The Subalternative"; italics in original.

94. Ibid.

95. I use "developing countries" here as that was the terminology in use in Ceaușescu's time—a terminology that is evidently tied to the ideology of progress.

96. Oprea, "Development Discourse in Romania," 121–122.

97. Ovidiu Țichindeleanu, "The Author of the Autobiography of Nicolae Ceaușescu," trans. Alex Moldovan, *IDEA artă + societate* 38, 2011, http://idea.ro

/revista/en/article/XOkX8BIAACIAgMii/the-author-of-the-autobiography-of-ni
colae-ceausescu.

98. Ibid.

99. Walter Benjamin, "Theses on the Philosophy of History," *Illuminations*, ed.
Hannah Arendt, trans. Harry Zohn (New York: Shocken Books, 1969), 262.

100. Țichindeleanu, "The Author."

101. Walter Mayr, Christian Neef, and Jan Puhl, "How Poland and Hungary
Led the Way in 1989," *Spiegel Online*, October 30, 2009, http://www.spiegel.de/in
ternational/spiegel/winds-of-change-from-the-east-how-poland-and-hungary
-led-the-way-in-1989-a-657805-6.html. As this article points out, at this meeting, "[t]he cracks in the Warsaw Pact were unmistakable," with evident tensions between the reformers (which included the leaders of Poland, Hungary,
and the Soviet Union) and the conservatives (the leaders of Romania and East
Germany).

102. Transcribed from Ujică's film *The Autobiography of Nicolae Ceaușescu*.

103. David Graeber, *Debt: The First 5,000 Years* (Brooklyn and London: Melville
House, 2011), 361, 367.

104. Ibid., 361.

105. Ibid., 375–376.

106. Ibid., 379; italics in original.

107. Ibid., 363; italics in original.

108. Ibid., 364.

109. François Chesnais, *Finance Capital Today: Corporations and Banks in the
Lasting Global Slump* (Leiden and Boston: Brill, 2016), 51, 53.

110. Ban, "Sovereign Debt," 757.

111. Ibid., 758. For a detailed account, see Ban's full article.

112. Ibid., 746.

113. Ibid., 760.

114. Cornel Ban, *Dependență și Dezvoltare: Economia Politică a Capitalismului
Românesc*, trans. Ciprian Șiulea (Cluj-Napoca: TACT, 2014), 75. Under neoliberal
president Traian Băsescu and in order to meet conditions imposed by the IMF,
Romania experienced its share of austerity measures. See, for instance: Leigh
Phillips, "Romania Sees Biggest Protest Since 1989 over Austerity Measures," *eu-
observer*, May 20, 2010, https://euobserver.com/eu-political/30111.

115. Ban, "Sovereign Debt," 746.

116. Ibid., 765, 743.

117. Alain Badiou, *The Century*, trans. Alberto Toscano (Cambridge and
Malden: Polity Press, 2007), 48, 51.

118. This is in fact Pirandello's stage direction, which Badiou cites in *The Century*, 51.

119. Cited in Rozalinda Borcilă, "INVAZIE (22 Decembrie 1989)," in *Revoluția
Română Televizată: Contribuții la Istoria Culturală a Mediilor*, eds. Konrad

Petrovszky and Ovidiu Țichindeleanu (Cluj: IDEA Design & Print, 2009), 7–23.

120. Andaluna Borcilă, in conversation with Ovidiu Țichindeleanu and Konrad Petrovszky, "Debutul Televizual al Postcomunismului," in *Revoluția Română Televizată*, 196.

121. Colin Powell, *My American Journey* (New York: Random House, 1995), 413.

122. Victoria Graham, "URGENT: General Assembly Condemns Panama Invasion 75–20," *AP News*, December 29, 1989, https://apnews.com/article/f968dc18cc 41ccc76a33b43baf4018b4; A. Borcilă, "Debutul," 196.

123. Greg Grandin, "How Our 1989 Invasion of Panama Explains the Current US Foreign Policy Mess," *Mother Jones*, December 23, 2014, http://www.motherjones .com/politics/2014/12/our-forgotten-invasion-panama-key-understanding-us -foreign-policy-today.

124. Ibid.

125. For instance, Ian Bremmer, "The New Cold War Could Soon Heat Up," *Foreign Affairs*, May 5, 2022, https://www.foreignaffairs.com/articles/russia-fsu/2022 -05-05/new-cold-war-could-soon-heat; Editorial Board, "With Russia's Invasion, a New Cold War Arrives," *Wall Street Journal*, February 22, 2022, https://www .wsj.com/articles/cold-war-ii-arrives-vladimir-putin-russia-ukraine-sanctions-us -biden-europe-11645571764.

126. A. Borcilă, "Debutul," 196.

127. The Romanian Revolution started in the city of Timişoara on December 15, 1989, and culminated in the trial and execution of the dictatorial couple on December 25, 1989.

128. Țichindeleanu, "The Author."

129. Ujică in Andrei Ujică in conversation with Milo Rau, "1000 Stunden Ceausescu," in Milo Rau, *Die Letzten Tage der Ceausescus* (Berlin: Verbrecher Verlag Berlin, 2010), 59.

130. Martin Heidegger, *Being and Time*, trans. John Macquarrie and Edward Robinson (New York: Harper & Row, 2008), 103.

131. Ibid.

132. Martin Heidegger, "The Age of the World Picture," in *The Question Concerning Technology and Other Essays*, trans. William Lovitt (New York: Harper & Row, 1977).

133. Jean Baudrillard, "Fatal Strategies," in *Selected Writings,* 2nd edition, ed. Mark Poster (Stanford: Stanford University Press, 2001), 190.

134. Andrei Codrescu, *The Hole in the Flag: A Romanian Exile's Story of Return and Revolution* (New York: William Morrow, 1991), 18, 219.

135. All of the scenes described here are from Harun Farocki and Andrei Ujică (dirs.), *Videograms of a Revolution*, 2006.

136. Mary Ann Doane, "Information, Crisis, Catastrophe," in *New Media, Old Media*, eds. Wendy Hui Kyong Chun and Thomas Keenan (New York and London: Routledge, 2005), 251.

137. Vilém Flusser, "Puterea Imaginii," in *Revoluția Română Televizată*, eds. Konrad Petrovszky and Ovidiu Țichindeleanu (Cluj: IDEA Design & Print, 2009), 143.

138. The quotation is in German in Rau's *Die Letzten Tage der Ceausescus*, 6; the English translation given here is from Søren Kierkegaard, *Repetition: An Essay in Experimental Psychology* by Constantin Constantinus, in *Repetition and Philosophical Crumbs*, trans. M. G. Piety (Oxford: Oxford University Press, 2009), 3.

139. IIPM also refers to this performance with "The Last Hours of Elena and Nicolae Ceaușescu." See http://international-institute.de/en/the-last-days-of-the-ceausescu/.

140. For a discussion of this, in Romanian, see Oana Ghita, "Familia Ceaușescu Pierde Procesul Intentat Teatrului Odeon Privind Folosirea Mărcii 'Ceaușescu,'" *Mediafax.ro*, July 13, 2011, http://www.mediafax.ro/cultura-media/familia-ceausescu-pierde-procesul-intentat-teatrului-odeon-privind-folosirea-marcii-ceausescu-8493848.

141. Milo Rau, "New Realism and the Contemporary World. The Re-Enactments and Tribunals of the International Institute of Political Murder," *Documenta* 34, no. 2 (2016): 126, https://doi.org/10.21825/doc.v34i2.16389.

142. Milo Rau in Rau in conversation with Rolf Bossart, "Jener 25. Dezember 1989," in *Die Letzten Tage der Ceausescus* (Berlin: Verbrecher Verlag Berlin, 2010), 36; my translation from German; Rau, "New Realism," 124.

143. Rau, "Jener 25. Dezember 1989," 35; my translation from German.

144. Milo Rau, "Du Côté de Chez Ceausescus," in *Die Letzten Tage der Ceausescus*, 11.

145. Manfred Schneider, "Tribunalul în Off. Procesul împotriva Ceaușeștilor," in *Revoluția Română Televizată*, eds. Konrad Petrovszky and Ovidiu Țichindeleanu (Cluj: IDEA Design & Print, 2009), 87.

146. Rau, "New Realism," 123.

147. Ibid., 126.

148. Ibid., 122, 128.

149. Rau, "Jener 25. Dezember 1989," 35.

150. Rebecca Schneider, *Performing Remains: Art and War in Times of Theatrical Reenactment* (London and New York: Routledge, 2011), 31.

151. Rau, "New Realism," 126.

152. Milo Rau, *Die Letzten Tage der Ceausescus* (Berlin: Verbrecher Verlag Berlin, 2010).

153. Rau, "New Realism," 126, 128.

154. Samuel Weber, *Theatricality as Medium* (New York: Fordham University Press, 2004), 315; italics in original.

155. Rau, "New Realism," 136.

156. Rau, "Du Côté de Chez Ceausescus," 28.

157. Petrovszky and Țichindeleanu, "Sensuri," 31.

158. I watched the show on YouTube in a video recording posted by a user called "luminaalba"; the quotes are taken from this video (my translation from Romanian). "Lorin Fortuna Invitat la Emisiunea Moderata de Mihai Tatulici, in 1992 la TVR1," published by luminaalba on YouTube on July 1, 2013, https://www.youtube .com/watch?v=ao2REC_OtqY.

159. All of the quotations here are transcribed from the TV show "Lorin Furtuna Invitat"; emphasis added.

160. Ibid.; emphasis added.

161. Vilém Flusser, "Television Image and Political Space in the Light of the Romanian Revolution," April 7, 1990, Kunsthalle Budapest, published on YouTube by Vasily Klenov on May 31, 2011, https://www.youtube.com/watch?v=QFTaY2u4NvI.

162. Ibid.

163. Francis Fukuyama, *The End of History and the Last Man*, 1992, accessed through *Marxists.org*, September 25, 2022, https://www.marxists.org/reference/ subject/philosophy/works/us/fukuyama.htm.

164. Georg Wilhelm Friedrich Hegel, *The Phenomenology of Mind*, trans. J. B. Baillie (New York: Harper Torchbooks, 1967), 805. (*The Phenomenology of Mind* has also been translated as *The Phenomenology of Spirit*.)

165. Heidegger, *Being and Time*, 484; italics in original.

166. Hegel, *The Phenomenology of Mind*, 806.

167. Ibid., 462, 805.

168. Glenn Alexander Magee, *The Hegel Dictionary* (London and New York: Continuum, 2010), 260.

169. Paul Redding, "Georg Wilhelm Friedrich Hegel," *Stanford Encyclopedia of Philosophy*, first published February 13, 1997, substantial revision January 9, 2020, https://plato.stanford.edu/entries/hegel/.

170. Hegel, *The Phenomenology of Mind*, 807. Hegel's *Phenomenology of Mind* is a reenactment at the level of philosophical discourse of the teleological history of the self-realization of Spirit. Besides Hegel's book-long reenactment of the history of the development of Spirit towards self-realization, there is another reenactment of this history to be performed by Spirit itself at the moment of attaining Absolute Knowledge, discussed at the very end of the *Phenomenology*. More precisely, this history is to be recalled/recollected, which will result in "History [being] (intellectually) comprehended" (*begriffen*, grasped as concept): in other words, it will result in the attainment of the "Absolute Notion/Concept" through the union of "History" and "Science" (Hegel, *The Phenomenology of Mind*, 808). In a certain manner of reading Hegel, at this point of universal recognition, history comes to an end.

171. Heidegger, *Being and Time*, 484.

172. Ibid., 480. As the translators of my edition of Heidegger's *Being and Time* note (Macquarrie and Robinson, 499nxviii), the phrase "the non-sensuous sensuous" does not appear in the section of Hegel's work where Heidegger credits it to

be. In that section, Hegel writes instead that "Time is the totally abstract, sensuous" (my translation from German).

173. Georg Wilhelm Friedrich Hegel, *Hegel's Philosophy of Nature: Part Two of the* Encyclopaedia of the Philosophical Sciences (1830), trans. A. V. Miller (Oxford: Oxford University Press, 1970), 35; italics in original.

174. *Oxford English Dictionary Online*, s.v. "chronology, n." (Oxford University Press, 2022).

175. R. Harvey, *Philadelphus* (1593), 15; cited in *OED Online*, "chronology, n."

176. Magee, *The Hegel Dictionary*, 220; italics in original.

177. Alfred Sohn-Rethel, *Intellectual and Manual Labor: A Critique of Epistemology* (London and Basingstoke: Macmillan, 1978), 48.

178. Raymond Williams, *Television: Technology and Cultural Form*, ed. Ederyn Williams (London and New York: Routledge, 2003), 88.

179. Heidegger, *Being and Time*, 485.

180. Ibid.

181. Flusser, "Television Image and Political Space."

182. During the last years of the communist regime in Romania, television broadcasting was restricted to two hours per day. Radio Free Europe had a significant presence in many Romanians' daily lives, but it was officially banned in the country. By contrast, in 2014, there were 750 channels with non-stop programming in Romania; "Istoria Televiziunii în România: De la Două Ore de Program pe Zi la 750 de Canale cu Program Non-Stop," *Digi24*, December 29, 2014, https://www.digi24.ro/special/campanii-digi24/1989-anul-care-a-schimbat-lumea/istoria-televiziunii-in-romania-de-la-doua-ore-de-program-pe-zi-la-750-de-canale-cu-program-non-stop-340597.

183. Petrovszky and Țichindeleanu, "Sensuri," 44.

184. I borrow the phrase "planned flow" from Raymond Williams's analysis from *Television*, 71–111.

185. Doane, "Information, Crisis, Catastrophe," 255.

186. Buck-Morss, *Dreamworld and Catastrophe*, ix.

187. National Bank of Romania, "First Polymer Banknote in Europe and the Northern Hemisphere," accessed May 15, 2022, https://www.bnr.ro/First-polymer-banknote-in-Europe-and-in-the-Northern-hemisphere-18835-Mobile.aspx; Ping Wang, "The Future Is Plastic," *International Monetary Fund* 53, no. 2, June 2016, https://www.imf.org/external/pubs/ft/fandd/2016/06/currency.htm.

Chapter 3

1. "Metaphysical subtleties" is taken from Karl Marx's analysis of the fetishism of the capitalist commodity from Karl Marx, *Capital: A Critique of Political Economy, Volume 1*, trans. Ben Fowkes (Harmondsworth: Penguin Books, 1976), 163.

2. Razvan Exarhu, "Sacoja si Pojeta," *Evz.ro*, August 30, 2008, http://www.evz.ro/senatul-evz-sacoja-si-pojeta-818673.html; my translation from Romanian.

3. Ursula K. Le Guin, "The Carrier Bag Theory of Fiction," 1986, accessed

through *The Anarchist Library.org,* September 25, 2022, https://theanarchistlibrary
.org/library/ursula-k-le-guin-the-carrier-bag-theory-of-fiction.

4. Elena Ceaușescu, "Polimerizarea Stereospecifică a Izoprenului" (PhD dissertation, 1983), https://doi.org/10.1016/C2013-0-03695-X.

5. Ramin Bahrani (dir.), *Plastic Bag,* 2009. The film can be viewed on YouTube, published by Dr. Bashi Publisher on January 2, 2014, https://www.youtube.com/watch?v=stqyjxRmW30.

6. All the quotes in this paragraph are from Bahrani's *Plastic Bag.*

7. Suzan-Lori Parks, "From Elements of Style," in *The America Play, and Other Works* (New York: Theatre Communications Group, 1995), 15.

8. René Descartes, *Meditations on First Philosophy,* in *Descartes: Selected Philosophical Writings,* trans. John Cottingham, Robert Stoothoff, and Dugald Murdoch (Cambridge and New York: Cambridge University Press, 1998), 116 (AT VII 80).

9. Ibid.

10. V. E. Yarsley and E. G. Couzens, *Plastics* (Harmondsworth: Allen Lane, Penguin Books, 1941), 19.

11. Ibid.

12. Ibid.

13. Ellis cited in ibid., 10; modified. This sense of plastic and plasticity is linked to the etymological root of the word, *"plassein,"* which means that which "may be moulded, belonging to moulding or modeling, in Hellenistic Greek also gifted in sculpture" (*OED Online*).

14. Yarsley and Couzens, *Plastics,* 35.

15. Cited in Jeffrey Meikle, *American Plastic: A Cultural History* (New Brunswick: Rutgers University Press, 1995), 126.

16. Yarsley and Couzens, *Plastics,* 31.

17. Ibid., 35.

18. David M. Kiefer, "DuPont Strikes Pay Dirt at Purity Hall," *Today's Chemist at Work,* April 2001, http://pubs.acs.org/subscribe/archive/tcaw/10/i04/html/TCAW04chemch.html.

19. DuPont, "About Us," accessed June 19, 2022, https://www.dupont.com/about.html.

20. Charles M. A. Stine cited in Meikle, *American Plastic,* 128.

21. The phrase "project of pure inquiry" is borrowed from Bernard Williams's *Descartes: The Project of Pure Enquiry* (London and New York: Routledge, 2005).

22. Yarsley and Couzens, *Plastics,* 35.

23. Ibid., 36.

24. Friedrich Kittler, "Fiktion und Simulation," in *Philosophien der neuen Technologie,* ed. Ars Electronica (Berlin: Merve Verlag, 1989), 64.

25. *Merriam-Webster,* s.v. "synthetic," accessed June 11, 2022, https://www.merriam-webster.com/dictionary/synthetic.

26. Yarsley and Couzens, *Plastics,* 117.

27. Jean Otis Reinecke, "Design Dates Your Product," *Modern Plastics* 15 (October 1937): 123.

28. Heather Davis, "Life & Death in the Anthropocene: A Short History of Plastic," in *Art in the Anthropocene: Encounters Among Aesthetics, Politics, Environments and Epistemologies*, eds. Heather Davis and Etienne Turpin (London: Open Humanities Press, 2015), 351.

29. Heather Davis, *Plastic Matter* (Durham and London: Duke University Press, 2022), 5.

30. Amanda Boetzkes and Andrew Pendakis, "Visions of Eternity: Plastic and the Ontology of Oil," *e-flux*, issue 47 (September 2013), https://www.e-flux.com/journal/47/60052/visions-of-eternity-plastic-and-the-ontology-of-oil/; Alfred Sohn-Rethel, *Intellectual and Manual Labor: A Critique of Epistemology* (London and Basingstoke: Macmillan, 1978), 48–49.

31. Davis, "Life & Death," 352.

32. Charles Q. Choi, "Invisible Plastic Trash Poses Newfound Threat to Sea Life," *Live Science*, November 2, 2007, http://www.livescience.com/1992-invisible-plastic-trash-poses-newfound-threat-sea-life.html.

33. Daniel Zalko, Carine Jacques, Hélène Duplan, Sandrine Bruel, and Elisabeth Perdu, "Viable Skin Efficiently Absorbs and Metabolizes Bisphenol A," *Chemosphere* 82, no. 3 (January 2011): 424–430.

34. National Institute of Environmental Health Sciences, "Bisphenol A (BPA)," accessed June 3, 2022, https://www.niehs.nih.gov/health/topics/agents/sya-bpa/.

35. Davis, "Life & Death," 348.

36. Mr. McGuire, played by Walter Brooke, in *The Graduate*, Mike Nichols (dir.), 1967; John Barcus, "I Have Seen the Future, and It Is 3D Printing," *Forbes*, February 17, 2020, https://www.forbes.com/sites/oracle/2020/02/17/i-have-seen-the-future-and-it-is-3d-printing/?sh=16ec13db38fe.

37. Roland Barthes, "Plastic," *Mythologies*, trans. Annette Lavers (New York: Hill and Wang, 1972), 99.

38. Sohn-Rethel, *Intellectual and Manual Labor*, 53; italics in original.

39. Ibid., 58.

40. Ping Wang, "The Future Is Plastic," *International Monetary Fund* 53, no. 2, June 2016, https://www.imf.org/external/pubs/ft/fandd/2016/06/currency.htm.

41. Meikle, *American Plastic*, 7.

42. U.S. House of Representatives, "Hearings Before the Subcommittee on Consumer Affairs of the Committee on Banking, Finance, and Urban Affairs," in *The Consumer Credit Protection Act Amendments of 1977*, Hearings 20, 22, 23, and 26, September 1977 (Washington, DC: GPO, 1977); cited in Josh Lauer, "Plastic Surveillance: Payment Cards and the History of Transactional Data, 1888 to Present," *Big Data & Society* 7, no. 1 (January–June 2020): 11.

43. Meikle, *American Plastic*, 190.

44. Ioana B. Jucan, "Remain x Remain(s)," in Ioana B. Jucan, Jussi Parikka, and

Rebecca Schneider, *Remain* (Minneapolis and London: University of Minnesota Press; Lüneburg: Meson Press, 2018), ix–xx.

45. Bernard London, "Ending the Depression Through Planned Obsolescence," 1932, accessed through Wikimedia, July 26, 2022, https://upload.wikimedia.org /wikipedia/commons/2/27/London_%281932%29_Ending_the_depression_ through_planned_obsolescence.pdf.

46. Garnet Hertz and Jussi Parikka, "Appendix: Zombie Media: Circuit Bending Media Archaeology into an Art Method," in Jussi Parikka, *A Geology of Media* (Minneapolis: University of Minnesota Press, 2015), 142.

47. Jucan, "Remain x Remain(s)," xiii; Santiago Castro-Gómez, *Zero-Point Hubris: Science, Race, and Enlightenment in Eighteenth-Century Latin America*, trans. George Ciccariello-Maher and Don T. Deere (Lanham: Rowman & Littlefield, 2021), 12; Davis, *Plastic Matter*, 5.

48. Victoria Pitts-Taylor, "The Plastic Brain: Neoliberalism and the Neuronal Self," *Health* 14, no. 6 (November 2010): 635–652.

49. I take the notion of "the experience economy" from B. Joseph Pine II and James H. Gilmore, *The Experience Economy: Work Is Theatre and Every Business a Stage* (Boston: Harvard Business School Press, 1999).

50. "The World's Most Valuable Resource Is No Longer Oil, but Data," *The Economist*, May 6, 2017, https://www.economist.com/leaders/2017/05/06/the -worlds-most-valuable-resource-is-no-longer-oil-but-data.

51. Lauer, "Plastic Surveillance," 2, 3, 12, 9; Shoshana Zuboff, *The Age of Surveillance Capitalism: The Fight for a Human Future at the New Frontier of Power* (New York: Public Affairs, 2019).

52. Boetzkes and Pendakis, "Visions of Eternity."

53. Meikle, *American Plastic*, 67.

54. "Plastics in 1940," *Fortune Magazine* 22 (October 1940): 93. The *Synthetica* map can be viewed at https://www.fulltable.com/vts/f/fortune/xa/57.jpg.

55. Ibid.

56. Meikle, *American Plastic*, 67.

57. Martin Heidegger, "The Age of the World Picture," in *The Question Concerning Technology and Other Essays*, trans. William Lovitt (New York: Harper & Row, 1977).

58. Ibid., 130.

59. Martin Heidegger, "The Question Concerning Technology," in *The Question Concerning Technology and Other Essays*, 5.

60. Martin Heidegger, "Science and Reflection," in *The Question Concerning Technology and Other Essays*, 168, 170; Heidegger, "The Question Concerning Technology," 17.

61. Heidegger, "The Age of the World Picture," 142.

62. Phil Lord and Christopher Miller (dirs.), *The Lego Movie*, 2014.

63. Ibid.

64. "Lego®," *Visit Nordic*, accessed June 19, 2022, https://www.visitnordic.com/en/attraction/lego.

65. "The LEGO® Brand Values," *Lego.com*, accessed June 19, 2022, https://www.lego.com/en-us/aboutus/lego-group/the-lego-brand.

66. Ian Bogost, *Alien Phenomenology, or What It's Like to Be a Thing* (Minneapolis and London: University of Minnesota Press, 2012), 126, 28; italics in original.

67. Ibid., 25.

68. Ibid., 25, 26.

69. Descartes embraced a corpuscularian, mechanistic theory of matter. Roughly, this theory held that matter is divisible into unbreakable units that function according to mechanical patterns.

70. I borrow this phrasing from Thomas Nagel, *The View from Nowhere* (New York and Oxford: Oxford University Press, 1989).

71. Bogost, *Alien Phenomenology*, 23.

72. For an overview of speculative realism as well as of his own object-oriented ontology, see Graham Harman, *Speculative Realism: An Introduction* (Cambridge and Medford: Polity, 2018). For different perspectives within new materialism(s), see Diana Coole and Samantha Frost, eds., *New Materialisms: Ontology, Agency, and Politics* (Durham: Duke University Press, 2010) and Rick Dolphijn and Iris van der Tuin, *New Materialism: Interviews & Cartographies* (Ann Arbor: Open Humanities Press, 2012).

73. For a critique of OOO from feminist perspectives, see Katherine Behar, ed., *Object-Oriented Feminism*, and especially Behar's introduction to it (Minneapolis and London: University of Minnesota Press, 2016). In his essay "The Poverty of Philosophy: Realism and Post-Fordism," Alexander Galloway highlights connections between speculative realism and post-Fordist capitalism (*Critical Inquiry* 39, no. 2 [2012]). Kimberly DeFazio shows that new materialist theories evacuate historical and social processes in an article titled "The Spectral Ontology and Miraculous Materialism," *The Red Critique*, Winter–Spring 2014, http://redcritique.org/WinterSpring2014/spectralontologyandmiraculousmaterialism.htm. Pushing the critique further, Julie Torrant argues that "It Is Time to Give Up Liberal, Bourgeois Theories, Including New Materialist Feminism, and Take Up Historical Materialist Feminism for the 21st Century" (in an essay by this title), *The Red Critique*, Winter–Spring 2014, http://www.redcritique.org/WinterSpring2014/historicalmaterialistfeminismforthe21stcentury.htm. For an engagement with and critique of new materialisms in relation to performance (studies), see Rebecca Schneider, "New Materialisms and Performance Studies," *TDR: The Drama Review* 59, no. 4 (Winter 2015): 7–17.

74. Bogost, *Alien Phenomenology*, 9.

75. Ibid.

76. Adrian Mackenzie, *Cutting Code: Software and Sociality* (New York: Peter Lang, 2006), 2.

77. Bogost, *Alien Phenomenology*, 9.

78. Ibid.

79. "Elephants in Tourism," *Elephant Voices*, accessed July 25, 2022, captured on the Internet Archive Wayback Machine on April 2, 2014, https://web.archive .org/web/20140402192410/https://www.elephantvoices.org/elephants-in-captivity -7/-in-tourism.html.

80. Bogost, *Alien Phenomenology*, 11.

81. Ibid., 19; emphasis added.

82. Bogost admits that *"all things equally exist, yet they do not exist equally"* (*Alien Phenomenology*, 11; italics in original). Levi Bryant explains this statement by way of the following example:

> Both the sun and my coffee mug *equally* exist, but it is not the case that they *exist equally*. In terms of its range of effects, the sun has a far more extensive impact on other objects than my coffee mug. (In "Flat Ontology," *Larval Subjects*, February 24, 2010, https://larvalsubjects.wordpress.com/2010/02/ 24/flat-ontology-2/; italics in original)

The kind of inequality that Bryant points out in this example—residing in the degree to which things relate to and impact other things—is obvious but not very illuminating. Such an account of inequality fails to take into consideration the ways in which massive inequalities are (and have historically been) often violently produced and sustained through social systems of domination and exclusion.

83. Olga Goriunova, "The Digital Subject: People as Data as Persons," *Theory, Culture & Society* 36, no. 6 (2019): 142.

84. Levi R. Bryant, *The Democracy of Objects* (London: Open Humanities Press, 2011), 32; quoted also in Bogost, *Alien Phenomenology*, 12.

85. Timothy Morton, *Hyperobjects: Philosophy and Ecology After the End of the World* (Minneapolis and London: University of Minnesota Press, 2013), 1, 6; Timothy Morton, *The Ecological Thought* (Cambridge and London: Harvard University Press, 2010), 17.

86. Morton, *Hyperobjects*, 92; italics in original.

87. I cite these words from Ursula K. Heise's review of Morton's *Hyperobjects*, where she offers an astute critique of this book. "Ursula K. Heise Reviews Timothy Morton's *Hyperobjects*" [Review], *Critical Inquiry* 41, no. 2 (June 4, 2014), http:// criticalinquiry.uchicago.edu/ursula_k._heise_reviews_timothy_morton.

88. Morton, *Hyperobjects*, 201.

89. Heise, "Ursula K. Heise Reviews Timothy Morton's *Hyperobjects*."

90. Morton, *Hyperobjects*, 100; see also Bryant, *The Democracy of Objects*, 32.

91. Ibid., 105; italics in original.

92. Bogost, *Alien Phenomenology*, 21; italics in original.

93. Vilém Flusser, "Time Reconsidered," Vilém Flusser Archiv: Manuscript No. 2797 [Encounters "Computer Culture," Villeneuve, July 12, 1983], 1.

94. Jean-Luc Nancy, *The Sense of the World*, trans. Jeffrey S. Librett (Minneapolis and London: University of Minnesota Press, 1997), 8.

95. Ibid., 156.

96. Pinar Yoldas, "An Ecosystem of Excess" Aksioma lecture, *Aksioma.org*, published on Vimeo on February 15, 2014, https://vimeo.com/86789460.

97. Bernhard Waldenfels, *Phenomenology of the Alien: Basic Concepts*, trans. Tanja Stähler and Alexander Kozin (Evanston: Northwestern University Press, 2011), 74; also cited in Bogost, *Alien Phenomenology*, 34.

98. Bogost, *Alien Phenomenology*, 34.

99. Ibid., 65.

100. Ibid.

101. Rob Nixon, *Slow Violence and the Environmentalism of the Poor* (Cambridge and London: Harvard University Press, 2013).

102. National Human Genome Research Institute, "Synthetic Biology," last updated August 14, 2019, accessed July 25, 2022, https://www.genome.gov/about -genomics/policy-issues/Synthetic-Biology.

103. Pinar Yoldas, "What Is Speculative Biology?" *Medium.com*, February 8, 2016, https://medium.com/@pinaryoldas/what-is-speculative-biology -c35a57de6990#.diphfay8e.

104. Ibid.

105. Michael Inwood, *A Hegel Dictionary* (Oxford and Malden: Blackwell, 1992), 271.

106. Ibid., 271, 272.

107. Pinar Yoldas in conversation with the author, May 2016.

108. Pinar Yoldas, "An Ecosystem of Excess: Exhibition Documentation," 2014, https://vimeo.com/103016513.

109. Pinar Yoldas, "An Ecosystem of Excess," in *Art in the Anthropocene: Encounters Among Aesthetics, Politics, Environments and Epistemologies*, eds. Heather Davis and Etienne Turpin (London: Open Humanities Press, 2015), 362.

110. The Plastisphere bacteria can be viewed in an image featured in Erik R. Zettler, Tracy J. Mincer, and Linda A. Amaral-Zettler, "Life in the 'Plastisphere': Microbial Communities on Plastic Marine Debris," *Environmental Science & Technology* 57, no. 13 (2013): 7137–7146, accessed through http://pubs.acs.org/doi/ abs/10.1021/es401288x.

111. Pinar Yoldas, "An Ecosystem of Excess," accessed October 15, 2022, https: //www.pinaryoldas.info/WORK/Ecosystem-of-Excess-2014; the different specimens can be viewed at this link. See also Yoldas, "An Ecosystem of Excess: Exhibition Documentation."

112. Yoldas, "An Ecosystem of Excess," in *Art of the Anthropocene*, 365, 366, 367.

113. See Zettler et al., "'Life in the 'Plastisphere,'" 7140.

114. According to J. L. Austin, a performative utterance becomes "hollow or void" if produced in the theatre; J. L. Austin, *How to Do Things with Words* (London: Oxford University Press, 1962), 22.

115. Ralph Cudworth, *The True Intellectual System of the Universe* (Andover: Gould & Newman, 1837), 244.

116. Keith Allen, "Cudworth on Mind, Body, and Plastic Nature," *Philosophy Compass* 8, no. 4 (2013): 342.

117. Cudworth, *The True Intellectual System*, 226.

118. Ibid., 213.

119. Margaret Cavendish, "The Blazing World," in *The Blazing World and Other Writings*, ed. Kate Lilley (London: Penguin Books, 2004), 170; Margaret Cavendish, *Observations upon Experimental Philosophy*, ed. Eileen O'Neill (Cambridge: Cambridge University Press, 2001), 48.

120. Cavendish, *Observations*, 219.

121. Ibid., 82.

122. Ibid., 113; see also 30.

123. Ibid., 182.

124. Chris Jordan, *Plastic Bags* (2007), in *Running the Numbers: An American Self-Portrait* (2006–current), http://www.chrisjordan.com/gallery/rtn/#plastic -bags. The image can be viewed at this link.

125. Chris Jordan, *Return of the Dinosaurs* (2011), in *Running the Numbers II: Portraits of Global Mass Culture* (2009–current), http://www.chrisjordan.com/ gallery/rtn2/#t-rex. The image can be viewed at this link.

126. Chris Jordan, "TEDxRainier—Chris Jordan—Midway Journey," *TEDx-Rainier*, published on YouTube on January 8, 2012, https://www.youtube.com/ watch?v=MjKocvbm2oM.

127. Chris Jordan in Nick Lavars, "Interview: Environmental Artist Chris Jordan talks sustainability," *New Atlas*, February 19, 2014, https://newatlas.com/ environmental-artwork-phones-protest-consumerism-e-waste/30860/.

128. I learned about the way in which the plastic bags were obtained in a conversation that I had with Jordan in March 2017.

129. Chris Jordan, *Venus* (2011), in *Running the Numbers II: Portraits of Global Mass Culture*, http://www.chrisjordan.com/gallery/rtn2/#venus.

130. *An American Dream of Venus* from *Fortune Magazine*'s "Plastics in 1940" can be viewed at https://www.fulltable.com/vts/f/fortune/az/plastics/SH376.jpg; quotation modified.

131. Ibid.

132. Ibid.

133. Ibid.

134. Jeanette Kohl, "Intra-Venus," in *Venus as Muse: From Lucretius to Michel Serres*, eds. Hanjo Berressem, Günter Blamberger, and Sebastian Goth (Leiden: Brill Rodopi, 2015), 81.

135. Chris Jordan in conversation with the author, March 2017.

136. Ibid.

137. Jones's remark concerns an exhibition titled *Botticelli Reimagined*; Jonathan Jones, "Botticelli Reimagined Review—Venus in the Gutter, More Beau-

tiful Than Ever," *The Guardian*, March 2, 2016, https://www.theguardian.com/artanddesign/2016/mar/02/botticelli-reimagined-review-vanda-venus.

138. Eugene Thacker, *In the Dust of This Planet: Horror of Philosophy, Volume 1* (Winchester and Washington: Zero Books, 2011), 8.

139. Cavendish, *Observations*, 182.

140. Chris Jordan in conversation with the author, March 2017.

141. Chris Jordan in Daniel Miller, "What Is Not Seen: An Interview with Chris Jordan," *Sarasota Visual Art*, May 23, 2012, https://sarasotavisualart.com/2012/05/seen-interview-chris-jordan/.

142. Maurizio Lazzarato, "Immaterial Labor," in *Radical Thought in Italy: A Potential Politics*, eds. Paolo Virno and Michael Hardt (Minneapolis: University of Minnesota Press, 1996).

143. This is what Chris Jordan would tell U.S. corporate people and what he practices in the workshops he leads in high schools and other places, he told me in a conversation, March 2017.

144. Jean-Luc Nancy, *The Creation of the World or Globalization*, trans. François Raffoul and David Pettigrew (Albany: SUNY Press, 2007), 42; italics in original.

145. Alejandro Durán, "Statement," accessed October 15, 2022, https://alejandroduran.com/statement. The images can be viewed at https://alejandroduran.com/photoseries.

146. Ibid.

147. See https://alejandroduran.com/photoseries.

148. Durán cited in Anna Gragert, "Riveting Trash-Based Sculptures Mirror Significant Environmental Issues," *My Modern Met*, April 20, 2015, https://mymodernmet.com/trash-based-photo-series-mirrors-environment-issues/.

149. Alejandro Durán, "International Flotsam," accessed June 15, 2022, https://alejandroduran.com/international-flotsam.

150. David Kidner cited in Brooke Jarvis, "The Messengers," *Pacific Standard*, September 8, 2015, https://psmag.com/the-messengers-888070eeod67#.zgd8jekp6.

151. National Ocean Service, "What Are Microplastics?" accessed August 1, 2022, https://oceanservice.noaa.gov/facts/microplastics.html#:~:text=Plastic%20debris%20can%20come%20in,as%20some%20cleansers%20and%20toothpastes.

152. Chris Jordan, "Midway: Message from the Gyre," *LensCulture*, accessed October 16, 2022, https://www.lensculture.com/articles/chris-jordan-midway-message-from-the-gyre. The story of Midway recounted here is based on a conversation I had with Chris Jordan in March 2017, unless otherwise indicated.

153. U.S. Government Accountability Office, "GAO: Midway Atoll's History and Habitat," published on YouTube on June 2, 2016, https://www.youtube.com/watch?v=v8nXHXPrUGg.

154. Ibid.

155. For more information about the Papahānaumokuākea Marine National Monument and its name, see Papahānaumokuākea Marine National Monument,

"About Papahānaumokuākea," accessed June 19, 2022, http://www.papahanaumo kuakea.gov/new-about/.

156. Oliver Milman, "US to Strafe Crucial Nesting Area for 3M Birds with Poison to Eradicate Mice," *The Guardian*, May 24, 2019, https://www.theguardian .com/us-news/2019/may/24/midway-atoll-birds-albatross-terns-mice.

157. Chris Jordan in conversation with the author, March 2017.

158. Carl Safina, "Wings of the Albatross," *National Geographic Magazine*, December 2007, captured on the Internet Archive Wayback Machine on March 26, 2008, https://web.archive.org/web/20151015165818/http://ngm.nationalgeographic .com/2007/12/albatross/safina-text/1.

159. Chris Jordan (dir.), *Albatross*, 2017, https://www.albatrossthefilm.com/ watch-albatross.

160. Jarvis, "The Messengers."

161. Chris Jordan, "The Story of *ALBATROSS*," accessed October 16, 2022, https://www.albatrossthefilm.com/ourstory.

162. The film can be watched at https://www.albatrossthefilm.com/watch-alba tross and the images from *Midway: Message from the Gyre* can be viewed at http:/ /www.chrisjordan.com/gallery/midway/#CF000313%2018X24.

163. Jordan, "The Story of *ALBATROSS*."

164. Kim TallBear, "Standing With and Speaking as Faith: A Feminist-Indigenous Approach to Inquiry," *Journal of Research Practice* 10, no. 2 (2014), http://jrp .icaap.org/index.php/jrp/article/view/405/371.

165. Jordan (dir.), *Albatross*.

166. I take the detail of the red whistle from artist Pam Longobardi's account of her work on Lesvos, in "Lesvos: Heartbreak and Joy in Equal Measure," *Drifters Project*, July 8, 2016, https://driftersproject.net/lesvos-heartbreak-and-joy-in -equal-measure/.

167. "Operational Data Portal: Mediterranean Situation," *UNHCR* (United Nations High Commissioner for Refugees), accessed June 19, 2022, https://data2 .unhcr.org/en/situations/mediterranean.

168. Denise Ferreira Da Silva, "The 'Refugee Crisis' and the Current Predicament of the Liberal State," *L'Internationale*, March 9, 2017, captured on the Internet Archive Wayback Machine on August 3, 2017, https://web.archive.org/web /20170803144433/http://www.internationaleonline.org:80/research/politics_of_ life_and_death/88_the_refugee_crisis_and_the_current_predicament_of_the_ liberal_state.

169. Natasha Frost, "President Trump, Moria Migrants, Beirut Explosion: Your Thursday Briefing," *New York Times*, September 9, 2020, https://www.nytimes. com/2020/09/09/briefing/trump-moria-beirut.html; Eva Cossé cited in Patrick Kingsley, "Fire Destroys Most of Europe's Largest Refugee Camp, on Greek Island of Lesbos," *New York Times*, September 9, 2020, https://www.nytimes.com/2020/09 /09/world/europe/fire-refugee-camp-lesbos-moria.html?campaign_id=51&emc

=edit_MBE_p_20200910&instance_id=22055&nl=morning-briefing&regi_id=
94295572&section=topNews&segment_id=37739&te=1&user_id=14142eb5d6cb51
def1d8a20e3c653e95.

170. James Martin, "A 360 View of Lesvos's Refugee Life Jacket Graveyard,"
CNET, October 11, 2016, https://www.cnet.com/news/greece-refugee-crisis-lesvos
-life-jacket-graveyard-360-view/.

171. "Safe Passage Bags Workshop," *Lesvos Solidarity*, accessed June 10, 2022,
https://www.lesvossolidarity.org/en/what-we-do/safe-passage-bags.

172. A video of *Sans Gravity* is available through the Hemispheric Institute's
Digital Video Library at https://hemisphericinstitute.org/en/hidvl-collections/
item/1294-nao-sans-gravity.html. The dates of the performance are taken from
Nao Bustamante's website: http://naobustamante.com/archive/sans-gravity/.

173. Argelys Samuel Oriach, "Breaking the Circle of the Plantation: Violence,
Affect and the Ephemeral in Junot Díaz's Afro-Caribbean Literary Imagination"
(honors thesis, Wesleyan University, 2015), 4, https://digitalcollections.wesleyan
.edu/object/ir-73.

174. I borrow the quoted words from Christina Sharpe, *In the Wake: On Blackness and Being* (Durham: Duke University Press, 2016), 20, 53.

175. Jose Esteban Muñoz, "The Vulnerability Artist: Nao Bustamante and the
Sad Beauty of Reparation," *Women and Performance: A Journal of Feminist Theory*
16, no. 2 (July 2006): 194.

176. Ibid.

177. Nao Bustamante, "The Personal Evolution of the Performance Object,"
in *Perform, Repeat, Record: Live Arts in History*, eds. Amelia Jones and Adrian
Heathfield (Bristol and Chicago: Intellect, 2012), 298.

178. I borrow these words from Donna Haraway, "A Cyborg Manifesto: Science,
Technology, and Socialist-Feminism in the Late Twentieth Century," in *Simians,
Cyborgs, and Women: The Reinvention of Nature* (New York and Oxford: Rout-
ledge, 1991), 149.

179. The notion of "material objection" is inspired from Fred Moten's *In the
Break: The Aesthetics of the Black Radical Tradition* (Minneapolis and London:
University of Minnesota Press, 2003).

180. *Sans Gravity*, https://hemisphericinstitute.org/en/hidvl-collections/item/
1294-nao-sans-gravity.html.

181. Muñoz, "The Vulnerability Artist," 196.

Chapter 4

1. Ganaele Langlois, Joanna Redden, and Greg Elmer, "Introduction: Compro-
mised Data—From Social Media to Big Data," in *Compromised Data: From Social
Media to Big Data*, eds. Ganaele Langlois, Joanna Redden, and Greg Elmer (New
York and London: Bloomsbury, 2015), 2.

2. On the digital divide, see, for instance: Cheng Li, "Worsening Global Dig-

ital Divide as the US and China Continue Zero-Sum Competitions," *Brookings*, October 11, 2021, https://www.brookings.edu/blog/order-from-chaos/2021/10/11 /worsening-global-digital-divide-as-the-us-and-china-continue-zero-sum-com petitions/.

3. Randy Martin, *Financialization of Daily Life* (Philadelphia: Temple University Press, 2002).

4. American Artist, "About," accessed June 3, 2022, https://americanartist.us/ about.

5. Ian Sample, "What Is the Internet? 13 Key Questions Answered," *The Guardian*, October 22, 2018, https://www.theguardian.com/technology/2018/oct/22/ what-is-the-internet-13-key-questions-answered; Samuel Weber, *Theatricality as Medium* (New York: Fordham University Press, 2004), 99. Jonathan Beller similarly states that the digital computer "becomes the primary medium of social exchange"; Jonathan Beller, *The World Computer: Derivative Conditions of Racial Capitalism* (Durham and London: Duke University Press, 2021), 19.

6. See, for instance: "15.1 Data Versus Information," in *Exploring Business* (University of Minnesota, 2010), https://open.lib.umn.edu/exploringbusiness/chapter /15-1-data-versus-information/; TechTarget Contributor, "Definition: Information," *TechTarget*, accessed June 3, 2022, https://www.techtarget.com/searchdata management/definition/information.

7. Connor Brooke, "What Is the Difference Between Data and Information," last updated August 6, 2014, accessed July 25, 2022, https://www.business2community .com/strategy/difference-data-information-0967136.

8. Beller, *The World Computer*, 24, 16, 37; italics in original.

9. Ibid., 23.

10. Alfred Sohn-Rethel, *Intellectual and Manual Labor: A Critique of Epistemology* (London and Basingstoke: Macmillan, 1978), 119–122, 173–175.

11. Claude E. Shannon, "The Mathematical Theory of Communication," in Claude E. Shannon and Warren Weaver, *The Mathematical Theory of Communication* (Urbana: University of Illinois Press, 1964), 31; italics in original, emphasis added.

12. On effectiveness (the logic of what works best) as the key driver in engineering (as opposed to "science" for Lin), see Jimmy Lin, "On Building Better Mousetraps and Understanding the Human Condition: Reflections on Big Data in the Social Sciences," in *Annals of the American Academy of Political and Social Science* 659, no. 1 (May 2015): 33–47. However, I disagree with Lin's insistence on there being a "dichotomy between science and engineering"; the logic of (dis)simulation blurs the lines between the two.

13. Claire Wardle and Hossein Derakhshan, *Information Disorder: Toward an Interdisciplinary Framework for Research and Policy Making* (Strasbourg, France: Council of Europe, September 27, 2017), https://rm.coe.int/information-disorder -report-version-august-2018/16808c9c77.

14. Evgeny Morozov (@evegenymorozov), "The political economy of post-truth," Twitter, December 31, 2016, https://twitter.com/evgenymorozov/status/815130875574841344.

15. Bill Gates in Jorge Gasca, "Content Is King—Original Bill Gates Essay & How It Applies Today," *Three Steps Business*, accessed June 19, 2022, https://threestepsbusiness.com/content-is-king-bill-gates/.

16. Guy Debord, *Society of the Spectacle* (Detroit: Black & Red, 1983), theses 6, 49.

17. Josh Lauer, "Plastic Surveillance: Payment Cards and the History of Transactional Data, 1888 to Present," *Big Data & Society* 7, no. 1, January–June 2020, 12.

18. The notion of an "enduring ephemeral" is borrowed from Wendy Hui Kyong Chun, "The Enduring Ephemeral, or the Future Is a Memory," *Critical Inquiry* 35, no. 1 (Autumn 2008): 148–171.

19. Mary Ann Doane, "Information, Crisis, Catastrophe," in *New Media, Old Media*, eds. Wendy Hui Kyong Chun and Thomas Keenan (New York and London: Routledge, 2005), 251; italics in original.

20. Herbert A. Simon, "Designing Organizations for an Information Rich World," in *Computers, Communications, and the Public Interest*, ed. Martin Greenberger (Baltimore: Johns Hopkins Press, 1971), 40.

21. Tim Wu, *The Attention Merchants: The Epic Scramble to Get Inside Our Heads* (New York: Vintage Books, 2016), 282.

22. Jonah Peretti, "Notes on Contagious Media," in *Structures of Participation in Digital Culture*, ed. Joe Karaganis (New York: Social Science Research Council, 2007), 159.

23. Ibid.

24. *Black People Love Us!*, accessed June 3, 2022, http://blackpeopleloveus.com/index.html.

25. Ibid.

26. Cedric Robinson, *Black Marxism: The Making of the Black Radical Tradition* (Chapel Hill: University of North Carolina Press, 2000); Beller, *The World Computer*, 10.

27. Safiya Umoja Noble, "Teaching Trayvon: Race, Media, and the Politics of Spectacle," *The Black Scholar* 44, no. 1 (Spring 2014): 12–29.

28. See Robert Mejia, Kay Beckermann, and Curtis Sullivan, "White Lies: A Racial History of the (Post)Truth," *Communication and Critical/Cultural Studies* 15, no. 2 (2018): 109–126.

29. Lola Ogunnaike, "NOTICED; Black–White Harmony: Are You Kidding Me?" *New York Times*, November 17, 2002, https://www.nytimes.com/2002/11/17/style/noticed-black-white-harmony-are-you-kidding-me.html.

30. Weber, *Theatricality as Medium*, 315; italics in original.

31. In Ogunnaike, "NOTICED."

32. Poe's law as articulated by danah boyd, "What Hath We Wrought?," *SXSW*

EDU, 2018, https://www.sxswedu.com/news/2018/watch-danah-boyd-keynote-what-hath-we-wrought-video/.

33. As a reminder, in Phillips and Milner's definition, "deep memetic frames" refer to socially shared and maintained "paradigms through which we viscerally experience everyday life," anchored in emotions; Whitney Phillips and Ryan M. Milner, *You Are Here: A Field Guide for Navigating Polarized Speech, Conspiracy Theories, and our Polluted Media Landscape* (Cambridge and London: MIT Press, 2021), 20.

34. "Entertainment," *Wikipedia,* accessed June 4, 2022, https://en.wikipedia.org/wiki/Entertainment.

35. Miles Beckett cited in Elena Cresci, "Lonelygirl15: How One Mysterious Vlogger Changed the Internet," *The Guardian,* June 16, 2016, https://www.theguardian.com/technology/2016/jun/16/lonelygirl15-bree-video-blog-youtube; emphasis added.

36. Richard Rushfield and Claire Hoffman, "Mystery Fuels Huge Popularity of Web's Lonelygirl15," *Los Angeles Times,* September 8, 2006, https://www.latimes.com/entertainment/la-et-lonelygirl15-story.html.

37. See Jane Feuer, "The Concept of Live Television: Ontology as Ideology," in *Regarding Television: Critical Approaches,* ed. E. Ann Kaplan (Washington, DC: University Press of America, 1983), 12–22; Doane, "Information, Crisis, Catastrophe"; Alla Gadassik, "At a Loss for Words: Televisual Liveness and Corporeal Interruption," *Journal of Dramatic Theory and Criticism* 24, no. 2 (Spring 2010): 117–134.

38. Cresci, "Lonelygirl15."

39. Ibid.

40. Ibid.

41. Ibid.

42. J. L. Austin, *How to Do Things with Words* (London: Oxford University Press, 1962), 5.

43. Ibid., 6, 4.

44. Beckett cited in Cresci, "Lonelygirl15."

45. See, for instance, Tommaso Venturini, "From Fake to Junk News, the Data Politics of Online Virality," in *Data Politics: Worlds, Subjects, Rights,* eds. Didier Bigo, Engin Isin, and Evelyn Ruppert (London: Routledge, 2019).

46. Alexandra Juhasz, Xiomara Liana Rodriguez, and Craig Dietrich, "#80, Outlast Virality," April 6, 2017, in *#100hardtruths,* https://scalar.usc.edu/nehvectors/100hardtruths-fakenews/80-outlast-virality.

47. Joshua Gillin, "The More Outrageous the Better: How Clickbait Ads Make Money for Fake News Sites," *PolitiFact,* October 4, 2017, https://www.politifact.com/article/2017/oct/04/more-outrageous-better-how-clickbait-ads-make-mone/.

48. House of Commons Digital, Culture, Media and Sports Committee, "Disinformation and 'Fake News': Final Report," Eighth Report of Session 2017–19, Feb-

ruary 14, 2019, 11–12, https://publications.parliament.uk/pa/cm201719/cmselect/cmcumeds/1791/1791.pdf.

49. See, for instance, Brendan Nyhan and Jason Reifler, "When Corrections Fail: The Persistence of Political Misperceptions," *Political Behavior*, 32, no. 2 (2010): 303–330.

50. Jacques Derrida, "Signature Event Context," in *Limited Inc* (Evanston: Northwestern University Press, 1977), 13.

51. Venturini, "From Fake to Junk News," 126.

52. Ibid., 123.

53. Ibid., 126.

54. This expression is borrowed from Chun, "The Enduring Ephemeral."

55. Craig Silverman, *Lies, Damn Lies, and Viral Content* (Tow Center for Digital Journalism, February 2015), 51, https://www.rcmediafreedom.eu/Publications/Reports/Lies-Damn-Lies-and-Viral-Content.

56. Ibid., 53, 55.

57. Christopher Seneca, "How to Break Out of Your Social Media Echo Chamber," *Wired*, September 17, 2020, https://www.wired.com/story/facebook-twitter-echo-chamber-confirmation-bias/.

58. Kevin Roose, "The Making of a YouTube Radical," *New York Times*, June 8, 2019, https://www.nytimes.com/interactive/2019/06/08/technology/youtube-radical.html.

59. Frances Haugen appearing on *60 Minutes*, "Facebook Whistleblower Frances Haugen: The 60 Minutes Interview," published on YouTube on October 3, 2021, https://www.youtube.com/watch?v=_Lx5VmAdZSI.

60. Wendy Hui Kyong Chun, "Critical Data Studies or How to Desegregate Networks," Institute of the Humanities and Global Cultures, published on YouTube on July 31, 2018, https://www.youtube.com/watch?v=Qhp8oUXTvaQ.

61. Wendy Hui Kyong Chun and Jorge Cotte, "Reimagining Networks: An Interview with Wendy Hui Kyong Chun," *The New Inquiry*, May 12, 2020, https://thenewinquiry.com/reimagining-networks/.

62. Jennifer Golbeck, "Your Social Media 'Likes' Expose More Than You Think," *TedxMidAtlantic*, 2013, https://www.ted.com/talks/jennifer_golbeck_the_curly_fry_conundrum_why_social_media_likes_say_more_than_you_might_think/transcript?language=en#t-326069.

63. Derrida, "Signature Event Context," 13, 14, 17.

64. Phillips and Milner, *You Are Here*, 20.

65. "r/TheRedPill," Reddit, accessed June 19, 2022, https://www.reddit.com/r/TheRedPill/.

66. boyd, "What Hath We Wrought?"

67. Abigail Brooks, "Popping the Red Pill: Inside a Digital Alternate Reality," *CNN Business*, November 10, 2017, https://money.cnn.com/2017/11/10/technology/culture/divided-we-code-red-pill/index.html.

68. Rebecca Lewis, *Alternative Influence: Broadcasting the Reactionary Right on YouTube* (Data & Society Research Institute, 2018), 35, https://datasociety.net/wp-content/uploads/2018/09/DS_Alternative_Influence.pdf.

69. Blonde in the Belly of the Beast, "My Red Pill Journey," published on YouTube on August 12, 2017, https://www.youtube.com/watch?v=e8E3VjkSDqo&t=7s.

70. Ibid.

71. Lewis, *Alternative Influence*, 28.

72. Blonde, "My Red Pill Journey."

73. Ibid.

74. Lewis, *Alternative Influence*, 27.

75. Blonde, "My Red Pill Journey."

76. Ibid.

77. Wendy Hui Kyong Chun, "Taking the Reparative Pill: Cyberspace, Machine Learning and the Closure of the Real," *Discourse* 45, no. 1 (forthcoming).

78. Blonde in the Belly of the Beast, "The Desperate Left: Data & Society Study," published on YouTube on September 21, 2018, https://www.youtube.com/watch?v=PUd2RBEk9do&list=PLg8m50Yi1CvIynrL8jZVa_4s-LbhtaEYnp&index=13&t=0s.

79. Chun, "Taking the Reparative Pill" (forthcoming). The quotation ("the new home of the Mind") is from John Perry Barlow, "A Declaration of the Independence of Cyberspace," *Electronic Frontier Foundation*, 1996, https://www.eff.org/cyberspace-independence.

80. Chun, "Taking the Reparative Pill" (forthcoming).

81. Blonde, "My Red Pill Journey."

82. See also Lewis, *Alternative Influence*, 30–34.

83. Roose, "The Making of a YouTube Radical."

84. Ibid.

85. Lewis, *Alternative Influence*, 35.

86. See Brooks, "Popping the Red Pill."

87. Mark Coniglio and Matthew Ragan, with host Andrew Scriver, "Digital Rehearsal and Remote Performance Spaces," *LevelUp with ToasterLab*, January 19, 2021, https://www.levelup.designers.ca/drarps.

88. Steve Dixon with contributions by Barry Smith, *Digital Performance: A History of New Media in Theatre, Dance, Performance Art, and Installation* (Cambridge and London: MIT Press, 2007), 3; italics in original.

89. Kate Bergstrom, "Beyond Wandering: Critical Engagement in a World-Widening Web," *HowlRound*, January 11, 2021, https://howlround.com/beyond-wandering.

90. Jared Mezzocchi in Barbara Fuchs and Jared Mezzocchi, "Reverse-Engineering Zoom with Isadora: Site-Specific Performance for the Internet," *HowlRound*, January 4, 2021, https://howlround.com/reverse-engineering-zoom-isadora.

91. The performance team consisted of Patrick Elizalde, Andra Jurj, Marcela Mancino, Fabiola Petri (performers); Tong Wu, Nuntinee Tansrisakul, and Yuguang Zhang (digital design and development); Marcela Mancino (theatrical design); Roopa Vasudevan (bot design); Roopa Vasudevan and Anthony Burton (bot concept); Adriana Bârză-Cârstea (choreography); Peter Bussigel (sound design); Madeline Greenberg (production manager); Melody Devries (dramaturgy); Wendy Hui Kyong Chun, Alex Juhasz, and the Beyond Verification Team associated with the Digital Democracies Institute at Simon Fraser University (performance consultants).

92. At the time of the performance, what is now the Brown Arts Institute at Brown University was called the Brown Arts Initiative.

93. The design platform ohyay can be accessed at https://ohyay.co/. According to a note on the website (as of January 25, 2023), "[c]hanges are happening at ohyay. You can expect to use the platform as is through March 1, 2023."

94. Jon McKenzie, *Perform or Else: From Discipline to Performance* (London and New York: Routledge, 2001), 137, 19–20.

95. Ibid., 22, 18.

96. Ella Koeze and Nathaniel Popper, "The Pandemic Changed the Way We Internet," *New York Times*, April 7, 2020, https://www.nytimes.com/interactive/2020/04/07/technology/coronavirus-internet-use.html.

97. Philip Auslander, "Digital Liveness: A Historico-Philosophical Perspective," *Performing Arts Journal* 102 (2012): 5.

98. Jeremy N. Bailenson, "Nonverbal Overload: A Theoretical Argument for the Causes of Zoom Fatigue," *Technology, Mind, and Behavior* 2, no. 1 (February 23, 2021), https://tmb.apaopen.org/pub/nonverbal-overload/release/2.

99. Ibid.

100. Carolin Gerlitz and Anne Helmond, "The Like Economy: Social Buttons and the Data-Intensive Web," *New Media and Society* 15, no. 8 (2013): 1348–1365.

101. Jessica Klein, "The Darkly Soothing Compulsion of 'Doomscrolling,'" *BBC*, March 3, 2021, https://www.bbc.com/worklife/article/20210226-the-darkly-soothing-compulsion-of-doomscrolling; Oxford Languages, "2020: Words of an Unprecedented Year," accessed April 28, 2022, https://pages.oup.com/ol/word-of-the-year-2020.

102. Auslander, "Digital Liveness," 6.

103. Sol P. Hart, Sedona Chinn, and Stuart Soroka, "Politicization and Polarization in COVID-19 News Coverage," *Science Communication* 42, no. 5 (October 2020): 679, https://www.ncbi.nlm.nih.gov/pmc/articles/PMC7447862/.

104. Craig Silverman, "The Information Apocalypse Is Already Here, and Reality Is Losing," *BuzzFeed News*, May 22, 2020, https://www.buzzfeednews.com/article/craigsilverman/coronavirus-information-apocalypse. On the supposed information apocalypse produced by deepfakes, see, for instance, Nina Schick, *Deepfakes: The Coming Infocalypse* (New York and Boston: Twelve/Hachette Book

Group, 2020). Claire Wardle has offered a compelling argument for why deepfakes in fact do *not* signal an information apocalypse in "Deepfakes: Is the Video Even Real?," *New York Times,* August 14, 2019, https://www.nytimes.com/video/opin ion/100000006635241/deepfakes-adele-disinformation.html.

105. Silverman, "The Information Apocalypse."

106. Ibid.

107. Ganaele Langlois, "Faking It Until It's Real," in Alexandra Juhasz, Ganaele Langlois, and Nishant Shah, *Really Fake* (Minneapolis and London: University of Minnesota Press; Lüneburg: Meson Press, 2021), 5.

108. For video essays including an expanded trailer for *Left and Right,* as well as insights into the creation process of the bots and the digital design of the performance, see Ioana B. Jucan, Roopa Vasudevan, Anthony Glyn Burton, Tong Wu, and Yuguang Zhang, "Performing 'Left and Right,'" *Theatre Journal* 73, no. 3 (September 2021), https://jhuptheatre.org/theatre-journal/online-content/issue/volume-73-issue-3-september-2021/performing-left-and-right.

109. Melody Devries, Ioana Jucan, and Alexandra Juhasz, "Authenticity, Performativity, and Performance," paper circulated at the "Beyond Disinformation: Authenticity and Trust in the Online World" workshop organized by the Social Science Research Council, 2020.

110. Melody Devries, "Archetypes and Homophilic Avatars: New Approaches to Studying Far-Right Facebook Practice," *Canadian Journal of Communication* 47, no. 1 (2022): 156.

111. Brian Resnick, "Cambridge Analytica's 'Psychographic Microtargeting': What's Bullshit and What's Legit," *Vox,* March 26, 2018, https://www.vox.com/science-and-health/2018/3/23/17152564/cambridge-analytica-psychographic-mi crotargeting-what.

112. Devries, "Archetypes and Homophilic Avatars," 168, 160.

113. See Devries, "Archetypes and Homophilic Avatars."

114. Langlois, "Faking it," 5; Silverman, "The Information Apocalypse."

115. The notion of "information disorders" is from Wardle and Derakhshan, *Information Disorder.* The definition of theatricality is from Weber, *Theatricality as Medium*, 315; italics in original.

116. Patrick Elizalde, Andra Jurj, Marcela Mancino, Fabiola Petri, Ioana Jucan, and Melody Devries, *Left and Right, Or Being Who/Where You Are* (unpublished script, 2021).

117. The notion of the "lecture machine" is taken from McKenzie, *Perform or Else*, 20–21.

118. Stephen Hawkins, Daniel Yudkin, Miriam Juan-Torres, and Tim Dixon, *Hidden Tribes: A Study of America's Polarized Landscape* (New York: More in Common, 2018), https://hiddentribes.us/media/qfpekz4g/hidden_tribes_report .pdf. We used the findings of the *Hidden Tribes* study with permission from More in Common, the organization that produced it, but this organization was not a

partner of *Left and Right,* and the performance does not represent the views of More in Common.

119. Hawkins et al., *Hidden Tribes,* 27.

120. Hawkins et al., *Hidden Tribes.*

121. The quiz is available at https://hiddentribes.us/quiz/.

122. To interact with the bots, check out http://bots.left-and-right.art/. To see the bots narrating their mode of functioning, watch Roopa Vasudevan's video essay "Just Bots," in Jucan et al., "Performing 'Left and Right,'" https://www.you tube.com/watch?v=e7dY4g9nQ_Y.

123. Anthony G. Burton, "Discourse and Feedback: What Bots Talk About," in Jucan et al., "Performing 'Left and Right,'" https://www.youtube.com/watch?v=YP1kB_nVY7A. For a detailed description of how the bots were constructed, see Burton's video essay.

124. Ibid.

125. Ibid.

126. The definition of "liveness" in terms of responsiveness to the audience's input is drawn from Margaret Morse, *Virtualities: Television, Media Art, and Cyberculture* (Bloomington: Indiana University Press, 1998), 15; Auslander, "Digital Liveness," 6.

127. Brenda Laurel, *Computers as Theatre* (Reading: Addison-Wesley, 1991), 116.

128. Anonymous, personal correspondence, 2021.

129. McKenzie, *Perform or Else,* 19.

130. Ibid., 177.

131. Ibid., 215.

132. Hawkins et al., *Hidden Tribes,* 71.

133. Tong Wu and Yuguang Zhang, "Mediated Bodies on Digital Stages," in Jucan et al., "Performing 'Left and Right,'" https://www.youtube.com/watch?v=T5pvomYxqJc.

134. Ibid., 10.

135. Wendy Hui Kyong Chun, "Big Data as Drama," *ELH* 83, no. 2 (Summer 2016): 363, 368.

136. Auslander, "Digital Liveness," 5.

137. Zhang in Wu and Zhang, "Mediated Bodies on Digital Stages."

138. Ibid.

139. Wu in Wu and Zhang, "Mediated Bodies on Digital Stages."

140. McKenzie, *Perform or Else,* 262, 267.

141. Thomas Vits, "The Crucial Role of Networks and Edge Cloud for Truly Immersive XR Experiences," *The Academy of International Extended Reality (AIXR),* July 9, 2021, https://aixr.org/insights/the-crucial-role-of-networks-and-edge-cloud-for-truly-immersive-xr-experiences/.

142. Ibid.

143. Kerry Maxwell, "BuzzWord: Augmented Reality," *Macmillan Dictionary,*

accessed October 2021, https://www.macmillandictionary.com/buzzword/entries/augmented-reality.html.

144. Mark Zuckerberg in Casey Newton, "Mark in the Metaverse," *The Verge,* July 22, 2021, https://www.theverge.com/22588022/mark-zuckerberg-facebook-ceo-metaverse-interview.

145. Schneider in Rebecca Schneider and Lucia Ruprecht, "In our Hands: An Ethics of Gestural Response-ability," *Performance Philosophy* 3, no.1 (2017): 112, https://doi.org/10.21476/PP.2017.31161.

146. Sarah Sharma, *In the Meantime: Temporality and Cultural Politics* (Durham and London: Duke University Press, 2014), 9.

147. Ibid., 7, 4.

148. Ibid., 8.

149. Jacques Derrida, *Writing and Difference*, trans. Alan Bass (Chicago: University of Chicago Press, 1978), 212.

150. In a recent panel discussion, Mark Coniglio emphasized this very sense of liveness. See Ragan and Coniglio, "Digital Rehearsal and Remote Performance Spaces."

151. McKenzie, *Perform or Else*, 195, 249.

152. Venturini, "From Fake to Junk News," 137.

153. American Artist, exhibition description, *Dignity Images: Bayview-Hunters Point* (installation view, Museum of African Diaspora, San Francisco), 2019, https://americanartist.us/works/dignity-images-bvhp.

154. Tina Campt, "Black Visuality and the Practice of Refusal," *Women & Performance* 29, no. 1 (February 25, 2019), https://www.womenandperformance.org/ampersand/29-1/campt.

155. American Artist, "About."

156. American Artist, "A Declaration of the Dignity Image," *The New Inquiry*, September 13, 2016, https://thenewinquiry.com/a-declaration-of-the-dignity-image/. American Artist's works revolving around the dignity image include: two solo exhibitions, one at the Blackwood Gallery, University of Toronto Mississauga (2021) and the other, titled *Dignity Images: Bayview-Hunters Point*, at the Museum of African Diaspora, San Francisco (2019); *Dignity Images: Harlem* (2017); *Prosthetic Knowledge of the Dignity Image,* an installation at the SLEEPCENTER in New York City (2016); and *A Refusal,* an online performance (2015–2016).

157. American Artist, exhibition description, *Dignity Images: Bayview-Hunters Point*; Artist, "A Declaration of the Dignity Image."

158. See Simone Browne, *Dark Matters: On the Surveillance of Blackness* (Durham and London: Duke University Press, 2015), 17.

159. Ibid., 9.

160. American Artist, "American Artist: Dignity Images—Bayview-Hunters Point," Museum of African Diaspora, published on YouTube on May 6, 2019, https://www.youtube.com/watch?v=I3iu7m-KqR8.

161. The framing text for the exhibition can be read at https://americanartist.us /works/dignity-images-bvhp.

162. Artist, "A Declaration of the Dignity Image."

163. Ibid.; Campt, "Black Visuality and the Practice of Refusal."

164. Shoshana Zuboff, *The Age of Surveillance Capitalism: The Fight for a Human Future at the New Frontier of Power* (New York: Public Affairs, 2019).

165. See Lilian G. Mengesha and Lakshmi Padmanabhan, "Introduction: Performing Refusal/Refusing to Perform," *Women & Performance* 29, no. 1 (February 26, 2019), https://www.womenandperformance.org/bonus-articles-1/29-1/intro.

166. The title of this performance pays homage to an article by Laura Portwood-Stacer on "Care Work and the Stakes of Social Media Refusal," *New Criticals*, March 18, 2014, http://www.newcriticals.com/care-work-and-the-stakes-of-social -media-refusal/print; American Artist, *A Refusal*, accessed June 15, 2022, https:// americanartist.us/works/a-refusal.

167. American Artist, in an e-mail to their mother, *A Refusal* (2015–2016), accessed June 15, 2022, https://americanartist.us/works/a-refusal.

168. American Artist, "New Glory Blue," *Medium*, September 1, 2015, https:// medium.com/@artpresident/new-glory-blue-c030ec9f6025.

169. Ibid.

170. Ibid.

171. Ibid.

172. Rob Arthur, "We Analyzed More Than 1 Million Comments on 4Chan," *Vice*, July 10, 2019, https://www.vice.com/en/article/d3nbzy/we-analyzed-more -than-1-million-comments-on-4chan-hate-speech-there-has-spiked-by-40-since -2015; Vice News Tonight Special Report, "How 8chan Became the Worst Place on the Internet," published on YouTube on September 5, 2019, https://www.youtube .com/watch?v=Kerg2rrIdAU.

173. Drusilla Moorhouse and Emerson Malone, "Here's Why BuzzFeed News Is Calling QAnon a 'Collective Delusion' from Now On," *BuzzFeed News*, September 4, 2020, https://www.buzzfeednews.com/article/drumoorhouse/qanon-mass -collective-delusion-buzzfeed-news-copy-desk.

174. The notion of "deep memetic frames" is borrowed from Phillips and Milner, *You Are Here*, 19.

175. Ethan Zuckerman, "QAnon and the Emergence of the Unreal," *Journal of Design and Science* 6 (July 15, 2019), https://doi.org/10.21428/7808da6b.6b8a82b9 .

176. EJ Dickson, "The Attempted Coup at the Capitol Proves This Is the United States of QAnon," *Rolling Stone*, January 6, 2021, https://www.rollingstone.com /culture/culture-news/united-states-of-qanon-capitol-insurrection-riot-conspira cy-theory-1110622/.

177. The video can be viewed at https://www.youtube.com/watch?v=FeU8Au RHLoA.

178. The Vigilant Networker, "American Artist Refusal EXPOSED!!! Satanic

Conspiracy DO NOT FOLLOW!!! THE VIGILANT NETWORKER 2016," published on YouTube on January 25, 2016, https://www.youtube.com/watch?v=FeU8 AuRHLoA.

179. Phillips and Milner, *You Are Here,* 18.

180. See, for instance, Paul Thomas, "How QAnon Uses Satanic Rhetoric to Set Up a Narrative of 'Good vs. Evil,'" *The Conversation,* October 20, 2020, https://theconversation.com/how-qanon-uses-satanic-rhetoric-to-set-up-a-narrative-of -good-vs-evil-146281; Chapter 1, "The Devil's In the Deep Frames" in Phillips and Milner, *You Are Here;* Alex Greenberger, "Marina Abramović Satanism Controversy Explained," *ARTnews,* April 16, 2020, https://www.artnews.com/art-news/ news/marina-abramovic-satanism-controversy-explained-1202684150/.

181. Artist, e-mail to their mother, *A Refusal* (2015–2016), accessed June 15, 2022, https://americanartist.us/works/a-refusal.

182. Nick Couldry and Ulises A. Mejias, *The Costs of Connection: How Data Is Colonizing Human Life and Appropriating It for Capitalism* (Stanford: Stanford University Press, 2019), 84.

183. The quotation is taken from the description of Hassan Khan's *The Keys to the Kingdom* in the Palacio de Cristal at the time of the exhibition (2019).

184. Weber, *Theatricality as Medium,* 315; italics in original.

185. "Hassan Khan: The Keys to the Kingdom," online lecture (July 9, 2020) blurb, accessed June 19, 2022, https://staedelschule.de/en/calendar/hassan-khan -the-keys-to-the-kingdom.

186. Ibid.

187. Hassan Khan, "Hassan Khan: The Keys to the Kingdom," lecture presented at Städelschule, July 9, 2020, https://vimeo.com/515668710.

188. In fact, in 2015, Trump retweeted an image of himself as Pepe; Libby Nelson, "Why the Anti-Defamation League Just Put the Pepe the Frog Meme on Its Hate Symbols List," *Vox,* September 28, 2016, https://www.vox.com/2016/9/21/ 12893656/pepe-frog-donald-trump.

189. See Ryan M. Milner's analysis of the logics of memes in *The World Made Meme: Public Conversations and Participatory Media* (Cambridge and London: MIT Press, 2016).

190. Adam Clarkson and Alex Taylor, "Ding Ding! Crazy Frog to Make a Comeback in December," *BBC News,* November 17, 2021, https://www.bbc.com/news/en tertainment-arts-59296288.

191. Khan, "Hassan Khan: The Keys to the Kingdom," lecture presented at Städelschule.

192. "Hassan Khan: The Keys to the Kingdom," online lecture (July 9, 2020) blurb.

193. Khan, "Hassan Khan: The Keys to the Kingdom," lecture presented at Städelschule.

194. Ibid.

195. Hassan Khan, *The Keys to the Kingdom,* artist statement in exhibition program, exhibition in Parque del Retiro, Palacio de Cristal, Madrid, October 18, 2019–March 1, 2020; in capital letters in original. Khan also reads this statement in his lecture presented at Städelschule, "Hassan Khan: The Keys to the Kingdom."

196. Khan, "Hassan Khan: The Keys to the Kingdom," lecture presented at Städelschule

197. Christina Sharpe, *In the Wake: On Blackness and Being* (Durham: Duke University Press, 2016), 20, 53.

Epilogue

1. Ioana B. Jucan, *Resistance (Happening),* in *Cosmology of Worlds Apart* (New York: O Balthazar Press, 2017), 142–143.

2. Ibid., 163–164.

3. Helen Wright and Silver Tambur, "The Baltic Way—The Longest Unbroken Human Chain in History," *Estonian World,* August 23, 2021, https://estonianworld .com/life/estonia-commemorates-30-years-since-the-baltic-way-the-longest -unbroken-human-chain-in-history/.

4. Ibid.

5. Jucan, *Resistance (Happening),* 151. This idea of a general world strike is drawn from an essay by Alexandru Polgár, "Restul Comunist," in *Genealogii ale Postcomunismului,* eds. Adrian T. Sîrbu and Alexandru Polgár (Cluj: Idea Design & Print, 2009), 42; also published in *IDEA: Artă și Societate* 29, 2008, http://www .idea.ro/revista/ro/article/XIgcdBAAACQAwZha/restul-comunist.

6. This idea draws from Judith Butler, building on Raymond Williams's call to find ways to practice forms of critique "which [do] not assume the habit (or right or duty) of judgment," in "What Is Critique? An Essay on Foucault's Virtue," *Transversal Texts,* May 2001, https://transversal.at/transversal/0806/butler/en.

7. Jucan, *Resistance (Happening),* 142. This is adapted from the texts that Romanian actors Fabiola Petri (who played Roza) and Maria Soilică (who played R, Roza's double) wrote in response to an improvisation prompt during the rehearsals of *Resistance (Happening).* The prompt was to articulate Roza's life philosophy.

8. For more information about this initiative, see (in Romanian) Andra Marinescu, "Militarii NATO au Schimbat Teatrul de Operațiuni cu Teatrul de la Sibiu," *Tribuna,* June 13, 2017, https://www.tribuna.ro/stiri/eveniment/militarii-nato-au -schimbat-teatrul-de-operatiuni-cu-teatrul-de-la-sibiu-126773.html.

9. I refer here specifically to Russia's police-backed propaganda machine.

10. See, for instance, Ian Bremmer, "The New Cold War Could Soon Heat Up," *Foreign Affairs,* May 5, 2022, https://www.foreignaffairs.com/articles/russia -fsu/2022-05-05/new-cold-war-could-soon-heat; Editorial Board, "With Russia's Invasion, a New Cold War Arrives," *Wall Street Journal,* February 22, 2022, https://www.wsj.com/articles/cold-war-ii-arrives-vladimir-putin-russia-ukraine -sanctions-us-biden-europe-11645571764.

11. Vishwas Satgar, "The US, Russia and Ukraine: Thinking Beyond the New Cold War and World War 3," *Socialist Project,* March 28, 2022, https://socialistpro ject.ca/2022/03/us-russia-ukraine-thinking-beyond-new-cold-war-ww3/.

12. Denise Ferreira Da Silva, "The 'Refugee Crisis' and the Current Predicament of the Liberal State," *L'Internationale,* March 9, 2017, captured on the Internet Archive Wayback Machine on August 3, 2017, https://web.archive.org/web /20170803144433/http://www.internationaleonline.org:80/research/politics_of_ life_and_death/88_the_refugee_crisis_and_the_current_predicament_of_the_ liberal_state.

13. Adrienne Rich, "Notes toward a Politics of Location," in *Blood, Bread, and Poetry* (New York and London: W. W. Norton, 1986), 220.

14. See, for instance, Philip S. S. Howard, Bryan Chan Yen Johnson, and Kevin Ah-Sen, "Ukraine Refugee Crisis Exposes Racism and Contradictions in the Definition of Human," *The Conversation,* March 21, 2022, https://theconversation.com /ukraine-refugee-crisis-exposes-racism-and-contradictions-in-the-definition-of -human-179150; Laurel Wamsley, "Race, Culture and Politics Underpin How—or If—Refugees Are Welcomed in Europe," *NPR,* March 3, 2022, https://www.npr .org/2022/03/03/1084201542/ukraine-refugees-racism.

15. Ferreira Da Silva, "The 'Refugee Crisis'"; Denise Ferreira Da Silva, "Nobodies: Law, Raciality and Violence," *Griffith Law Review* 18, no. 2 (August 2009): 212–236.

16. Rich, "Notes toward a Politics of Location," 213.

17. Satgar, "The US, Russia and Ukraine."

18. Rich, "Notes toward a Politics of Location," 223–224, 225; italics in original.

INDEX

abstraction: AI systems and, 49; capitalism and, 3, 35–36, 183; Cartesian metaphysics and, 3, 35, 183; computation and, 37, 46–47; data and, 46, 49; "I" and, 4; internet and, 3, 26, 200; malicious deceiver scenario and, 183; mathematics and, 35–36; modernity and, 46; news and, 235; plastics and, 26, 143, 145–46; race and, 185; software and, 52; synthetic and, 3, 20, 106, 143; television and, 3, 26, 133; theatre and, 29; thinking machines and, 49. *See also* (dis)simulation; sameness

aestheticization, 66, 155–56, 167–68

Agre, Philip, 84–85, 108

AI systems: abstraction and, 49; auto-history and, 93; automation and, 37; biases in, 43, 49; deepfakes and, 66; embodiment and, 49; gender and, 48–49; race and, 49; reinforcement learning and, 195; Romania and, 103

Albatross (film), 173–76

Alecu, Marian, 98–99

algorithms: algorithmic theatre, 45, 53–61, 67–89, 204; auralization and, 53; big data and, 7, 43; capitalism and, 63–64, 87; deep memetic frames and, 187, 191; deepfakes and, 66; deviousness and, 63, 64, 71; disrupting of, 219; (dis)simulation and, 52; echo chambers and, 107; fallibility and, 64; homophily and, 191; infelicities and, 63–64; internet and, 188; mathematics and, 109; performativity and, 63–64, 187, 191; as ruling the world, 7, 41; social media and, 190–91; software and, 52, 53, 63; subjectivity and, 68, 85; theatricality and, 45, 53–61, 69, 80, 82–83, 88, 204; thinking machines and, 44, 47–48, 52; voiding and, 47–49. *See also* big data; computation; software; thinking machines

alien phenomenology, 158–60

Alien Phenomenology (Bogost), 153

and, 188–89, 196–215; malicious
deceivers and, 3–6; performative
thinking, 20–23, 28, 148, 150–51,
183; plastics and, 143–44, 162; post-
Fordism and, 84–85; post-truth
and, 23, 184; radical doubt and, 22,
28; red-pilling and, 194; refusal
practice against, 215–16; Romania
and, 110–12; social media and, 215;
software and, 61–67; television and,
120–22; theatricality as counter to,
4, 157, 162–63, 203, 207–9, 221–24;
thinking machines and, 48, 66–67;
truth's relation to, 22–23; voiding
and, 23–24, 26, 122, 144, 215; world
picture and, 26, 149–51. *See also*
(dis)simulation; voiding
petrodollar, 118–19
Phenomenology of Mind (Hegel),
275n170
Phillips, Whitney, 13, 191
picture of the world. *See* world picture
A Piece of Work (2013): abstraction
in, 60, 83, 85; algorithms in, 57,
59–61, 69–70, 74, 76, 79; audience
responses to, 70–74; BAM rendition
of, 57, 59, 74, 83, 88; big data and, 7,
59; capitalism and, 84–85, 88; code
visible in, 69–70; debut of, 57; development of, 74; digital machines in,
72–74; fallibility in, 75–76; Hamlet's soliloquy in, 72–73; intended
audience of, 72–74; language in,
84–86; Markov chains in, 61, 74, 76;
memory in, 77–80; OtB rendition
of, 57, 70, 72, 74; overview of, 57–58;
set of, 58, 58f; subjectivity in, 83–86;
temporality in, 88–89; theatricality
of, 76, 78, 81, 85, 88–89
Pine, B. Joseph, 51
Pitts-Taylor, Victoria, 147–48
The Plandemic (film), 199

Plastic Bag (film), 140
Plastic Bags (2017), 164
plastics: as abolishing hierarchy of
substances, 145; abstraction and, 26,
143, 145–46; aestheticization and,
167–68; big data and, 8, 148; capitalism and, 3, 5–6, 144–49, 151, 172;
Cartesian metaphysics and, 3, 141–
49, 172, 182; colonialism and, 170–
71; consumerism and, 8, 139, 170–71;
credit cards, 118, 146, 148; defining
characteristics of, 141–44; development of, 141–43; disposability of,
145–48, 163; (dis)simulation and, 3,
8, 139, 143, 148–49, 172; ecological
destruction resulting from, 148, 155,
168; fake news and, 190; hyperobjects and, 155, 157–58; internet and,
148, 182, 184; malicious deceivers
and, 3, 8, 139, 141, 148–49, 172, 182;
metaphysical subtleties of, 141–49,
166; microplastics, 144, 157, 162, 171;
Midway island and, 171–77; modernity and, 8; overview of, 139–41;
performativity and, 143, 162; Plastic
Bag, 139–40, 177–80; Romania and,
139–40; sameness and, 144, 150, 165;
subjectivity and, 147, 149, 169; *Synthetica* and, 149–63, 166; television
and, 151; theatricality and, 160–71;
voiding and, 144, 167; world picture
and, 149–63
Plastics (Yarsley and Couzens), 141–42
Pocheron, Bruno, 74
post-truth: capitalism and, 182, 184,
186; computer simulation hypothesis and, 11; definition of, 3, 23; (dis)
simulation and, 3, 11, 129, 131, 184;
fake news and, 189, 199; genealogy
of, 11; "I" and, 23; internet and, 8,
182, 184, 186, 220; malicious deceivers and, 3, 11, 182; performativity

Romania (*cont.*)
    totalitarianism in, 105–10; transition from communism to capitalism in, 2, 4–5, 7, 92–93, 97–98, 104, 119–20, 134–36; voiding in, 107–8, 110, 113, 122, 124, 128; West's relation to, 7, 100, 134–35. *See also* Ceaușescu, Nicolae
Roose, Kevin, 195
Rouvroy, Antoinette, 108, 248n53
Running the Numbers (2006-current), 164, 168
Running the Numbers II (2009-current), 164–65, 165–66f

Safina, Carl, 172
sameness, 3, 7, 22, 38, 124, 127, 135, 144, 150, 165, 183, 196
Sans Gravity (1993–2003), 178–79
Savičić, Gordan, 52
Schellekens, Elisabeth, 68–69
Scheman, Naomi, 4
Schneider, Rebecca, 79, 81, 88, 126–27
Securitate (secret police), 94, 105–7, 109–10, 112, 119, 130
the self. *See* "I"; subjectivity
self-history. *See* auto-history
the senses, 2, 13–19, 25
Shannon, Claude, 183
Sharma, Sarah, 213
Shepherd, Scott, 57, 59, 74, 80, 83
Silverman, Craig, 190, 199
simulation. *See* computer simulation hypothesis; (dis)simulation; performativity
Slavin, Kevin, 52
social media, 5, 129, 187–88, 190–91, 198–99, 207, 215, 217, 220. *See also* internet
The Society of the Spectacle (Debord), 25
software, 3, 6–7, 26, 49, 50, 52–53, 61–

67, 69, 71, 79–80, 86–97. *See also* AI systems; algorithms
Sohn-Rethel, Alfred: abstraction and, 35–37, 252n145, 261n117; capitalism and, 35–37; commodity exchange and, 35–36, 133, 145–46; mathematics and, 36; mind/body divide and, 36–37; plastics and, 146; postulate of automatism and, 35, 37–38, 84, 183; time and space and, 133
Souvarine, Boris, 102
the spectacle, 26, 41, 184, 186
speculative realism, 153, 155–56
Speed and Politics (Virilio), 87
Stein, Gertrude, 88
Steyerl, Hito, 65
subjectivity: algorithms and, 68, 85; art and, 68; automation and, 84; capitalism and, 84–85, 147, 169; communication and, 84–86; language and, 84–86; neoliberal subjectivity, 84–85, 147–48, 169; plastics and, 147, 149, 169; post-Fordist model of, 84–86; theatre and, 77, 82–83; voiding and, 92
surveillance, 7, 16, 65, 93–94, 105–12, 148, 215–16, 218
the synthetic: abstraction and, 3, 20, 26, 106; definition of, 3, 19–20, 106; (dis) simulation and, 6, 20, 23, 43, 48, 106, 190; fakeness and, 120, 188; internet and, 26, 188, 190; malicious deceivers and, 3, 7, 11, 26, 94; mathematics and, 19–20, 24; modernity and, 25, 100; post-truth and, 23; Romania and, 103, 106, 120; software and, 64–66; synthetic data, 103; synthetic media, 64, 66; television and, 26; thinking machines and, 48; world picture and, 19–20, 24–25, 48
Synthetica, 149–63, 166
Szendy, Peter, 22

··· **Sensing Media**
Aesthetics, Philosophy,
and Cultures of Media
EDITED BY WENDY HUI KYONG CHUN
AND SHANE DENSON

What does it mean to think, feel, and sense with and through media? In this cross-disciplinary series we present books and authors exploring this and related questions: How do media technologies, broadly defined, transform artistic practices and aesthetic sensibilities? How are practices, encounters, and affects entangled with the deep infrastructures and visible surfaces of the media environment? How do we "make sense"—cognitively, perceptually, and culturally—of media?

We are especially interested in contributions that open our understanding of media aesthetics beyond the narrow confines of Western art and aesthetic values. We seek works that reestablish the environmental connections between art and technology as well as between the aesthetic, the sensible, and the philosophical. We invite alternative epistemologies and phenomenologies of media rooted in the practices and subjectivities of Black, Indigenous, queer, trans, and other communities that have been unjustly marginalized in these discussions. Ultimately, we aim to sense the many possible worlds that media disclose.

—

Vilém Flusser, *Communicology: Mutations in Human Relations?*, edited by Rodrigo Maltez Novaes, foreword by N. Katherine Hayles

Mark Amerika, *My Life as an Artificial Creative Intelligence*